A PILOT'S SURVIVAL MANUAL

Paul H. Nesbitt, Ph.D.
Alonzo W. Pond
William H. Allen

VAN NOSTRAND REINHOLD COMPANY
New York   Cincinnati   Toronto   London   Melbourne

Published in 1978 by Van Nostrand Reinhold Company
A division of Litton Educational Publishing, Inc.
135 West 50th Street, New York, NY 10020, U.S.A.

Van Nostrand Reinhold Limited
1410 Birchmount Road
Scarborough, Ontario M1P 2E7, Canada

Van Nostrand Reinhold Australia Pty. Ltd.
17 Queen Street
Mitcham, Victoria 3132, Australia

Van Nostrand Reinhold Company Limited
Molly Millars Lane
Wokingham, Berkshire, England

16 15 14 13 12 11 10 9 8 7 6 5 4 3 2 1

Preface

This book has only one purpose—to aid and insure your survival after emergency aircraft landings regardless of geographic location. The information it contains is based on actual individual and group survival experiences and on the recommendations of explorers and travelers, representing many years of experience in the desolate and isolated areas of the world. The value of this book in terms of its intended purpose can be compared to the value you place upon your own life.

This book will tell you what to do, how to do it, and when to do it—whether your survival problem is in the arctic, the desert, or the tropics, or on land, on sea, or on ice. It recognizes your immediate and probable future problems and attempts to help you solve them. It describes the proper use of survival equipment and the means of recognizing and utilizing the natural resources at hand. This information, combined with your own ingenuity, plus the all-important will to live, are absolutely necessary to survival and rescue.

The book opens with a discussion of the stresses that affect individuals in a survival situation—cold, heat, solar radiation, shock, motion sickness, injuries, and similar contributing factors. This is followed by an analysis of the problems, procedures, and techniques of basic land and water survival, involving such items as immediate action, camping and woodcraft, how to travel through various terrains, what kind of clothing to wear, how to signal, what food to eat, how to obtain water, and other related topics. The ensuing chapters cover the special requirements for successful survival in the arctic and subarctic, in the desert, in the tropics, and at sea.

Contents

Introduction

The urge to survive is basic in both humans and animals. It underlies all of man's relations and adjustments to the society and culture in which he lives. Survival, more appropriately labeled "struggle for existence," has many forms—biological, economic and social. We speak of survival against disease, survival against business competitors, survival against communism, and even survival against the weather.

The development of the airplane and its wide use as a medium of transportation is responsible for the emergence of a new type of survival which we call "emergency survival." Emergency survival is the ability to live through unusual conditions of deprivation, emotional shock, and hardship for an indefinite period of time. Such conditions are commonly brought about by forced landing of aircraft at sea or in sparsely populated and remote jungle, desert, and arctic land areas.

Today all parts of the world are linked through a network of national and international airlines. Between the military air bases as well as commercial air terminals of America, Europe, and Asia there are hourly passenger flights, cargo flights, military missions and training operations. These flights cross the arctic and even the North Pole, as well as the tropics, all of the continents, the oceans and seas, the deserts, the Near East and the Far East. When one considers the vastness of these operations and the variety of terrain they encompass, one can realize the dangers faced by the passengers and crew of an aircraft forced to crash-land or bail out under such a wide range of environmental conditions.

Many such environments present survival problems not met elsewhere in the world. Constant study, experimentation, and testing are required to adapt men, machines, and matériel to its demands. Yet however successfully the environmental rigors are conquered or by-passed, in-flight emergencies are bound to occur in which basic survival becomes the paramount issue.

Practically everyone who flies regularly over terrain of the type mentioned is exposed to such emergencies. You, the reader, may frequently be a passenger or a crew member on long flights over

1

oceans, deserts, or jungles. Everyone who flies should learn to expect the unexpected.

The conditions obtaining in a survival situation often depend upon the factors that preceded it. Not all survival experiences result from a crash landing. Crack-ups in forced landings, bail-outs, running out of fuel, or even isolation from a ground party can also bring about the problem of survival.

An unexpected crash usually results in the demolition of the aircraft and severe injury or death to many of the crew and passengers. A crash landing or a ditching near shore means a hazardous yet controllable operation in which the aircraft is damaged but the crew is relatively intact. A forced landing due to engine troub'? or fuel shortage would indicate that the aircraft and its crew were intact, but that the aircraft was at least temporarily inoperative. Individuals or groups involved in a ground operation, such as the installation or operation of a weather station or some form of exploration, might easily become separated from the rest of the party and find themselves suddenly faced with a definite survival problem. Bailout from a disabled aircraft over land or ocean also presents a problem in individual or group survival.

When faced with a survival situation, you should remember several facts. First, the obstacles to be overcome are not so much physical as mental. Except for ocean landings, the terrain you find yourself in has in all probability been covered by others, and some people may even make it their home. With varying degrees of effort, these people have adjusted to the demands of terrain, climate and environment. Your problem is merely that, because you didn't expect to land there, you are not prepared to live there. Chances are that you *never* expect to have a crash landing in a jungle or to bail out over the ocean; regardless of your flight preparations, you will probably remain unconvinced that "it can happen to you."

But emergencies do happen, as the records show. Accordingly, before collecting survival facts and information on how to live off the land, it is important first to understand the psychological obstacles that must be overcome. These obstacles all have in common that very normal human emotion called *fear*—fear of the unknown, fear of discomfort, fear of people, and fear of one's own weaknesses. We fear the terrain and the climate because they are new and strange. Fear of the environment leads us to fear the discomforts we may suffer and the strange people we may meet.

Moreover, even though we overcome these fears to some extent, a lack of confidence in our own fortitude and ability may seriously weaken our will to survive.

Though all these fears are natural, they are wholly unnecessary. There are ways of alleviating the needless extra burden of these implanted fears. Fear of the unknown is lessened by proper training and by knowledge of the geography, topography, and climate of the areas covered by the flight course for each trip or mission.

The information in this book will eliminate much of the fear of discomfort. The book tells how to find natural shelter and how to give medical aid. Most important, it demonstrates that rest can be more valuable than speed. Whether you are struggling through jungle undergrowth, fighting the battle of a dwindling water supply in the desert, or making your way across arctic ice, you will be more successful and comfortable if you proceed by careful planning instead of a blind and exhausting dash. The intelligent discipline and organization with which the individual or group approaches the problem determines the success of any survival procedure. The establishment of an unhurried routine will bring about the calm and confidence without which considered decisions are impossible—and in a survival situation every decision is vital.

Fear of the natives, like fear of the terrain, can be relieved by previous knowledge combined with common sense. There is little to fear and everything to gain from open-handed contact with the natives of whatever friendly or neutral country in which you may find yourself. By respecting their customs and using common decency, you will have little trouble from natives, and possibly obtain much assistance. One survivor in the South Pacific during World War II taught the natives how to make hunting bows and quickly won his way to their hearts and to safety.

The tools for survival are furnished by the commercial airlines, by the Air Force, by the individual, and by the natural environment. The training for survival will stem from this book and your own ingenuity. But tools and training are not enough; none is effective without the will to survive. In fact, the records show that will alone has been the only factor in many survival case histories. While these histories are not held up as ideal examples of how to survive, they do show that strong, stubborn will power can conquer many obstacles.

One man, stranded without food or water on a vast stretch of Arizona desert for eight days, traveled 150 miles while exposed to

daytime temperatures as high as 120° F. The lack of water caused him to lose 25 per cent of his weight (a 10 per cent loss is often fatal) through dehydration. He had crawled the last eight miles completely naked. Doctors found his blood had become so thickened that the lacerations he suffered did not bleed until he had taken considerable water into his system. He had done nothing right, had no knowledge of survival techniques. But he wanted to survive, and did—through nothing but will power and the grace of God.

You will encounter other stories of equally harrowing experiences in this book. Don't mistake them for advice. They merely show what some individuals have done without experience, planning, or training. By adding your equipment and survival knowledge to this *will to survive,* you can survive with a lot less discomfort and bodily injury should the emergency arise.

An analysis of some 4,000 aircraft survival experiences shows clearly that successful survival depends on numerous requirements, some of which must be met or satisfied long before a man climbs into his aircraft. The successful survivor must (a) be mentally prepared for the fact that he will go down, (b) be in good physical condition, (c) have survival equipment attached to his parachute harness or accessible in the aircraft, (d) be proficient in the use of the survival equipment, (e) be dressed for ground conditions, (f) be thoroughly familiar with bailout, ditching, and crash landing procedures, (g) know how to guide the parachute and how to get out of the harness after landing, and (h) know how to procure food, water and shelter in areas of environmental extremes. The essential techniques of survival are mastered only through constant drill and indoctrination under actual or simulated emergency survival conditions.

1

Survival Stresses

Before discussing the stresses that affect individuals in a survival situation we should define what we mean by survival. The Air Force Dictionary defines survival as: "1. The primitive act or state of continuing to live, esp. by the preservation of one's life against any immediate peril, such as drowning, starvation, dehydration, oxygen deficiency, heat, cold, low atmospheric pressure, bacteria, or radioactivity, as in 'survival was my main concern as I faced the jungle.' 2. The discipline that a person must observe in order to protect, or to give himself a good chance to protect, his life against such peril, as in 'survival is taught to all members of the crew.' "

Survival has also been defined much more briefly as "staying alive."

SURVIVAL PHASES

Survival begins with the aircraft emergency and continues until the survivor or survivors have been rescued. Analysis of several hundred aircraft crashes and emergency parachute jumps show that a survival incident is divided into three phases, as outlined below.

Phase 1 we call *lifesaving*. In air emergencies, this means getting out of a burning aircraft on the ground or getting into a life raft from a sinking aircraft at sea.

Phase 2 in most incidents is *signaling,* which should begin as soon as the lifesaving phase is completed.

Phase 3 is *shelter and subsistence.* In this phase a man is concerned with keeping himself alive and reasonably healthy while awaiting rescue.

Obviously, Phase 2, *signaling,* should be continued throughout Phase 3. In some environments, such as that of extreme cold, the survivor will first have to find shelter before he can be concerned with signaling. If signals were properly used in all incidents, very few survivors would be faced with prolonged shelter and subsistence problems.

5

The stresses a survivor may have to face are cold, heat, solar radiation, hunger, food poisoning, shock, motion sickness, gas poisoning, animal hazards, injuries, lack of sanitation, and insufficient oxygen. Each stress listed has been faced by one or more survivors in the incidents studied. In some instances the stresses were too great for the survivor and death resulted. In others, the stress was combatted successfully without injury to the survivor or else was not severe enough to be harmful.

TYPES AND DEGREES OF STRESS

Let us consider the degree of stress that may occur in a typical survival situation and the tolerance of individuals to the stress as determined by experiment or by actual survival experience. We will consciously ignore the likelihood of rescue, although speed of rescue is obviously the most important factor in survival. For example, in the summer of 1956 several Air Force pilots bailed out into the Mojave Desert or Death Valley without survival kits. Some were injured and could not walk. In all instances temperatures were over 100° F and no water was available. All the men survived because rescue, either by passing car or by an Air Force rescue unit, was prompt. If these men had been in the Sahara instead of the Mojave, many would have died from the effects of heat and dehydration before rescue units could have reached them.

Cold. Cold is a killer. Many individuals who have survived aircraft accidents or ditchings have succumbed to the effects of cold before they could be rescued. Individual tolerance to cold varies greatly. Some men have survived immersion in water barely above the freezing point for 14 hours, while others have died within a few minutes of entering water of the same temperature. Some men have lived through many hours or even days of exposure to subzero temperatures, while others in the same situation have died within a very few hours, presumably from the effects of the cold. Shock, which affects all survivors to some degree, undoubtedly lowers survival time.

Dry Cold. Consider the case of a man or woman resting or doing very light work in relatively still air. Figure 1 gives a series of curves showing expected tolerance to dry cold for a healthy man dressed in various types of dry military clothing. The curves show tolerance time as a function of air temperature. Air movement is assumed to be 200 feet per minute (slightly more than 2 miles per hour).

In Fig. 1-1 a body temperature decrement of one degree Centigrade has been used as the tolerance limit. Obviously a man can stand a much greater heat loss than this for limited periods, but if he continues to lose heat steadily to the environment, obviously death is inevitable. Curve *A*, which represents tolerance limits for a man dressed in light coveralls such as an aircraft mechanic wears, gives an exposure time of only 20 to 30 minutes for a temperature of −5° C and an indefinite period of maintaining body temperature at 20° C. Curve *B* shows the limits for a man

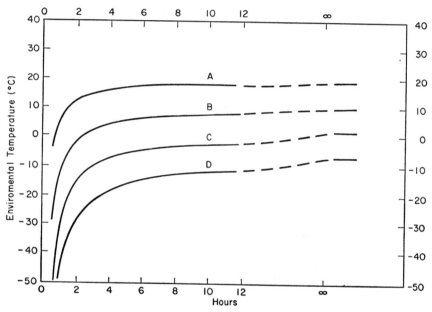

Fig. 1.1. Time Tolerance in Hours—Dry Cold Exposure.

wearing long wool underwear, the same coveralls, and a jacket. He can endure half an hour or more at −30° C before his temperature will fall 1 degree C, and can endure a temperature of 10° C indefinitely. In curve *C* the tolerance limits are for a man wearing wool underwear, wool trousers, wool shirt, and a jacket. He can endure 30 or 40 minutes at −50° C before his temperature falls and can remain comfortable indefinitely at 2 or 3° C. In curve *D* the man has added an extra layer of outer clothing, down-filled or quilted. With this extra clothing he can endure a few minutes

8

more of the −50° C temperature and remain comfortable indefinitely at −8° C.

There is no *definite* fatal exposure time for a man exposed to dry cold. None of the physiologists writing on cold tolerance commit themselves on this point, primarily because the individual, by working or exercising, can generate heat for an indeterminate period to replace the heat he is losing to the atmosphere.

Note that these curves are for a man wearing *dry clothing*. If his clothing is wet, either by rain, melting snow, or sweat, its insulation is much less and his tolerance time decreases.

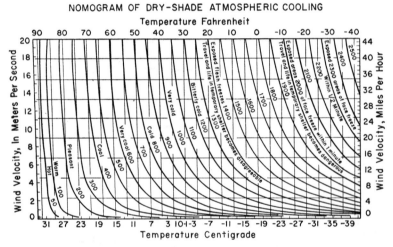

Fig. 1.2. Windchill Nomogram.

Windchill. For the same man dressed in dry clothing at the same environmental temperature, the presence of a high wind increases heat loss tremendously. The military, especially the Army, use the "windchill index" to describe the heat loss and environmental stress on a man exposed to a combination of low temperature and wind. Figure 1-2 is the famous windchill diagram developed by Dr. Paul Siple of South Pole fame. Windchill is related directly to air temperature and wind velocity. The windchill factor is a number giving the rate of cooling in kilogram-calories per square meter per hour of an unclad inactive body exposed to specific temperatures and wind velocities. Although expressed as a precise number, the windchill factor is not fully precise in its application to actual environments, and hence should be used only to compare conditions and approximate the order of magnitude of the environmental stress.

Note that the curves in the diagram have such labels as "exposed flesh freezes, travel and life in a temporary shelter becomes disagreeable," "bitterly cold," and the like. These descriptions have proved valid in field tests.

TABLE 1-1

CONDITIONS AT WHICH EXPOSED FLESH FREEZES

Wind Velocity, MPH	Temperatures, °F
43	20
26	15
18	10
14	5
13	−0
9	−5
7	−10
6	−15
5	−20
4	−25
3	−30
2	−40

Note also that many different combinations of air temperature and wind velocity can give the same windchill factor. For example, the dangerous 1400 windchill factor, where exposed flesh freezes, can be expected in the combination of conditions shown in Table 1-1.

Although the windchill diagram omits many important factors —for example solar radiation—it is recommended first because it is easy to use, requiring only temperature and wind velocity and second because it has proved useful in forecasting cold stress in actual operations.

Cold Water. Up to now we have been discussing the effects of only dry cold. A person immersed in cold water will lose body heat more rapidly than under even the most severe natural conditions of dry cold. The relation of survival time to water temperature is not a simple one. The type of clothing worn, the activity or lack of activity of the survivor while in the water, and the body temperature of the survivor on entering the water all affect survival time.

The outstanding record of survival in cold water is reported in a British study which states "A corpulent man of 29, clad in an indoor rig and an overcoat, remained swimming in the Bering Sea in July for 9 to 14 hours." The sea temperature was 30° F. In contrast with this, there are numerous records of people dying from a loss of body heat in 30 minutes in water of 30° F. There are also several incidents reported of persons falling into cold water who have died within 5 to 10 minutes. In these cases, since the person would not have lost enough body heat to kill him, it must be assumed that death was due to shock. Two fairly recent incidents involving Air Force personnel give an indication of effective survival time in cold water for men not wearing exposure suits.

In one well-documented case, an F-86D pilot who bailed out into Lake Michigan in March lost consciousness after approximately 25 minutes in water at an estimated 33° F temperature. He was picked up by a surface craft after approximately 1 hour in the water. He suffered no lasting ill effects from his experience.

In a second case an F-89 radar observer who bailed out in 40° F water was unable to climb into a sling lowered by a rescue helicopter after having been approximately 1 hour and 30 minutes in the water. He was in the water for a total of 1 hour and 45 minutes before being hauled aboard the helicopter, but suffered no permanent ill effects.

Figure 1-3 shows expected survival time for men immersed in the sea. This map, based on a U.S. Hydrographic Office report, gives the sea conditions in February, which are the most severe. In Area A, the majority of men will not survive more than three-quarters of an hour. In Area B the expected survival time is approximately 1½ hours; Area C, 3 hours; Area D, 6 hours, and Area E, 12 hours. In the warmer water areas, survival time depends mainly on the extent of fatigue. Reports from survivors show that the survival times shown on this chart are a bit pessimistic, but not extremely so.

What can a survivor do to protect himself against cold? First, pilots, crew and passengers should be dressed in clothing that will partially protect them against cold environmental conditions. Second, the aircraft can carry additional clothing, shelter, and heat-producing devices in the survival kits. (The Army Air Force used this precaution in World War II but found that

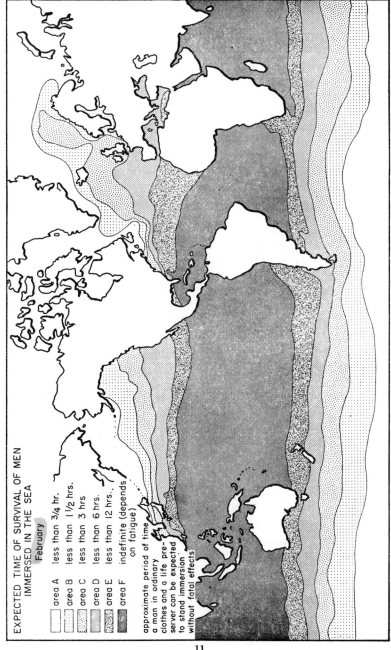

Fig. 1.3. Expected Time of Survival of Men Immersed in the Sea.

carrying such equipment usually decreased the useful load of the aircraft—an important consideration in wartime.) Third, the aircraft itself can be used as a shelter, in which case stoves or other heating devices will have to be carried. Few aircraft are well enough insulated to be used for shelters in really cold climates. The fourth alternative, therefore, is to construct shelters from natural materials, or from emergency equipment. The 20-man raft has been used as an arctic shelter, and effective shelters can be made from snow blocks. In some areas survivors have dug snow caves.

For protection against cold water we have only two alternatives: first, the survivor can wear an exposure suit; second, he can get out of the water or, preferably, he can avoid getting in by going directly from the ditched aircraft to the raft.

Wet Cold. We have discussed the effects of dry cold and of immersion in water. What happens to a man in wet clothing on land? The answer is that he loses body heat very rapidly, especially when a wind is blowing. Many survivors in the tropics and in life rafts on warm water report being awakened or kept from sleeping by cold when their clothing had been wet by rain or by sea water. Continuous exposure to wet cold conditions with air temperatures a few degrees above freezing can cause tissue damage as in "immersion foot."

Hands and Feet. Extremities require special protection from both dry cold and wet cold. In very cold conditions it is impossible to provide gloves with enough insulation to protect the hands of a man at rest. The only alternative is to get your hands inside your clothing. Survivors of ditching and water bailouts into cold water report that they have lost effective use of their hands within 5 minutes. One man reported that he had to pull the lanyard on his raft with his teeth because he couldn't close his hands after 5-6 minutes in cold water. Chilled feet do not create quite the same problem as cold hands because we do not use our feet to work with. Although the military has numerous types of shoes for different cold environments, survivors of aircraft in arctic regions report that frostbitten feet is one of the most common injuries.

Although we do not usually think of the head as an "extremity," one can lose a great deal of body heat by radiation from an uncovered head. Hoods or large stocking caps will cut down this form of heat loss.

Heat. Environmental heat does not kill as readily as cold. Moreover, relatively few persons exposed to excessive heat are killed by heat alone; in most of the reported deaths in hot conditions, heat was merely a contributing factor to *dehydration,* discussed in more detail later. However, men have died from an excessive heat load, even when drinking water was available. Figure 1-4 shows conditions of temperature and vapor pressure

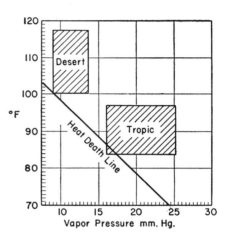

Fig. 1.4. Correlation of Heat Illnesses with Heat-Death Line. The entire area above the Heat-Death Line indicates combinations of temperature and vapor pressure which can impose a fatal heat load on the human body. At 75° F on the heat-death line the relative humidity is 99%; at 100° F the relative humidity is 19%.

involved in heat deaths in military training camps during the summer of 1943. Note that the graph shows vapor pressure to be as significant as heat. In terms of relative humidity, the heat death line is at 99 per cent at 75° F and 19 per cent at 100° F.

The graph is based on a study of 265 cases of heat illness occurring under conditions to which several thousand men were exposed. The heat death line indicates the danger limit for healthy young men working at average activity in the sun for several hours during the hottest part of the day. These conditions can be found within most of the temperate areas of the world during the summer and in the tropics the year round. The rectangles labeled "desert" and "tropic" show the ranges of environmental conditions in desert and tropic areas where heat deaths have occurred.

Obviously, the best way to avoid heat illness is to provide the survivor with shelter from the sun and with ample drinking water.

Solar Radiation. Exposure to the direct or (in some cases) reflected rays of the sun—can cause sunburn or eye injury and can contribute to sunstroke or heat prostration. Sunburn alone is seldom if ever fatal, although several survivors' accounts mention extreme misery caused by sunburn. Some survivors in life rafts report that they became sunburned from reflected light, even with the raft canopies shading them from the direct rays of the sun. Snow blindness has been reported both in snow-covered regions and on the desert, where it is also known as "sun blindness."

Thirst. Perhaps the greatest hazard from exposure to the sun is dehydration. In hot climates body temperature is maintained by evaporation of sweat from the skin—a very efficient process, but one requiring the constant replenishing of body water.

Table 1-2 shows days of expected survival at various environ-

TABLE 1-2

EXPECTED DAYS OF SURVIVAL AT VARIOUS ENVIRONMENTAL TEMPERATURES AND WITH VARYING AMOUNTS OF AVAILABLE WATER

	Max. daily in shade temperature, °F	Available water per man, U.S. quarts					
		0	1	2	4	10	20
NO WALKING	120	2	2	2	2.5	3	4.5
	110	3	3	3.5	4	5	7
	100	5	5.5	6	7	9.5	13.5
	90	7	8	9	10.5	15	23
	80	9	10	11	13	19	29
	70	10	11	12	14	20.5	32
	60	10	11	12	14	21	32
	50	10	11	12	14.5	21	32
WALKING AT NIGHT AND RESTING THEREAFTER	120	1	2	2	2.5	3	
	110	2	2	2.5	3	3.5	
	100	3	3.5	3.5	4.5	5.5	
	90	5	5.5	5.5	6.5	8	
	80	7	7.5	8	9.5	11.5	
	70	7.5	8	9	10.5	13.5	
	60	8	8.5	9	11	14	
	50	8	8.5	9	11	14	

From Adolph and Associates, *Physiology of Man*, Interscience Publishers, New York, 1947.

mental temperatures and with varying amounts of water available. Note that the days of expected survival decrease with increased temperatures and also decrease with increased activity. The table covers only the two conditions (1) resting in the shade and (2) resting during the daytime and moving about at night. If a man without water attempts to work during the heat of the day or is exposed to direct rays of the sun—especially at the higher air temperatures—his survival time decreases to a matter of hours instead of days.

Note also that at the higher temperatures a small increase in water supply gives very little increase in expected survival time. For example: at 110° F a man with two quarts of water can expect only a half day more of survival than a man with no water at all. A man with four quarts of water can expect only one day more of survival than a man with no water at all. Table 1-2 applies also to survivors afloat on a life raft.

Drinking water is necessary for survival regardless of air temperature. Although a man can survive at temperatures between 50° and 70° F for eight to ten days with no water, he cannot, while doing even light work, maintain water balance with less than approximately two quarts a day. The U.S. Army, in experiments in Alaska, found that one of the big factors in poor performance of troops in the arctic was inadequate water intake. Because of low temperatures, men did not feel the need for water even when performing fairly hard work, and consequently became—and remained—partially dehydrated. Partial dehydration is insidious in its effects. A man can dehydrate 5 per cent or more of his body weight without becoming incapacitated, but his efficiency decreases tremendously, without his being aware either of the fact or of the cause. The only remedy for dehydration is water.

Hunger. Hunger is not a serious problem in most survival incidents where rescue can be expected in a few days. The great majority of survivors in aircraft accidents since World War II have been rescued within 48 hours of the time of the crash. Very few survivors seem to be hungry for the first day or so after the crash. Some report that they were extremely weak when rescued, even though they had missed only one or two meals. Crash survivors can be considered to be in a mild state of shock, which in itself may be the weakening factor. Whatever the cause, this weakness of the survivors does hamper rescue efforts.

Although the great majority of survivors are rescued before

hunger becomes a problem, some groups have been stranded long enough to require foraging for food. Survival manuals, including the present work, devote much space to describing plants that might possibly be used for food, but the simplest rule for a survivor attempting to live off the land is to eat only fruits and plants with which he is familiar. This subject is covered in greater detail on pages 54-63, 239-47, and 265-67. (See also Food in the Index.)

Food Poisoning. Very few animals are poisonous to eat. Some toads and salamanders have poison glands in their skin which are very difficult to get rid of, even by skinning. The livers of the polar bear and the arctic seal are often poisonous because of an excess of Vitamin A. But in general, anything that creeps, crawls, or walks is a potential meal, depending, of course, on the survivor's degree of hunger.

Fish are quite a different problem, however. Since World War II there has been a tremendous increase in reports of fish poisoning in the Pacific. Toxic species of fish have been found in the Pacific Ocean from the Galapagos Islands to the Philippine Islands and Okinawa, and from Midway to the Society Islands. In some island groups, 75 per cent of the fish caught on the reefs were poisonous. Some species which are edible in one area—for example, the red snapper—are extremely poisonous in another. Survivors should avoid all reef fish in the Pacific.

In general, fish in the open Pacific and throughout the Atlantic, except for puffers and related species, are safe to eat. In the North Pacific, and to a lesser extent the North Atlantic, the black mussel and other shellfish on exposed coasts are often poisonous. This is caused by an accumulation of poisonous dinoflagellates in the meat of the shellfish.

Shock. Almost all survivors are affected by shock. Here, we are using the term "shock" in the layman's sense, not as a medical term. But it is a fact that a great many survivors exhibit marked apathy, and are unable to follow even simple instructions, even though they have no specific injury to account for this condition.

A corollary problem to shock is the irrational behavior of many survivors. Southern California newspapers frequently carry accounts of men who have been found wandering in the desert and seemingly do not even recognize their rescuers. The usual story is that the man's car broke down when he was on a hunting or prospecting trip; he decided to walk to the nearest spring or habitation; he became confused; and then he panicked. These people seem not to know what they are doing once they realize they are lost or in trouble, yet their impulse seems to be to do *something*. The same behavior is exhibited by some survivors after aircraft accidents; many deaths are traceable to this cause. At best, irrational behavior can cause great inconvenience to the members of the group who remain rational.

The only cure for apathy and irrational behavior is training. A man well trained in emergency procedures will usually be guided by them even if he is dazed.

Motion Sickness. Motion sickness is debilitating and sometimes disabling to many survivors. While seasickness is seldom fatal in itself, there is no doubt that it contributes to many deaths. From the rescuer's standpoint, seasickness is a serious complication because it often makes the survivor in the raft completely helpless and unable to assist in his own rescue, thus increasing the difficulty of rescue.

Gas Poisoning. (a) *Carbon Monoxide.* The only gas identified as causing fatalities in a survival situation is carbon monoxide. Carbon monoxide, a product of incomplete combustion of carbon, is mildly toxic at concentrations as low as 100 parts per million and is extremely dangerous, for even short exposures, at concentrations of 4,000 parts per million. Carbon monoxide poisoning is quite common in the arctic and other cold-weather areas where gasoline or kerosene stoves are used in confined space.

Carbon monoxide poisoning can be prevented by adequate ventilation and by adjusting stoves and burners for more complete combustion.

(b) *Carbon Dioxide.* No records of survival incidents show deaths from carbon dioxide poisoning, but it is undoubtedly dangerous wherever large groups of people are confined in a relatively small space, such as a 20-man raft being used as a cold-weather shelter. As with carbon monoxide, poisoning can be prevented by adequate ventilation.

Carbon dioxide will increase the respiration rate in concentrations as small as 1 per cent. If the concentration is in excess of approximately 10 per cent, breathing becomes difficult.

(c) *Gasoline.* Survivors have reported skin irritations from contact with liquid gasoline and other fuels after a crash or ditching. They have also reported nausea and vomiting from swallowing fuel floating on the water, and from inhaling gasoline fumes. Gasoline vapor presents an additional hazard in that it rapidly forms an explosive mixture in air. In cold weather gasoline on bare flesh will increase the probability of frostbite because of the cooling effect of rapid evaporation.

Animal Hazards. A discussion of animal hazards is complicated by the fact that relatively few survivors have ever actually been harmed or killed by animals, yet the hazards are definitely present in a survival situation.

(a) *Man.* Actually, the most dangerous animal is man—particularly in wartime. In times of peace we can assume that the great majority of even primitive tribes are friendly, but we also know that there are hostile tribes in the Amazon Basin of South America, in Equatorial Africa, and in Southeast Asia.

(b) *Bears.* Among mammals other than man, the bears have the worst reputation. Bears actually are a world-wide hazard. Even the lightly regarded black bear of the United States has mauled and killed people. The brown bear and grizzly of Alaska are guilty of unprovoked attacks on humans, and the polar bear, especially in the eastern arctic, is more than likely to approach any individual or group that he sights. Usually, the only way to get rid of an inquisitive polar bear is to shoot him.

(c) *Big Cats.* The big cats of the tropical areas are also a definite hazard. In India tigers and leopards kill a great many people every year. It should be assumed that these animals would also be dangerous to survivors in these areas.

(d) *Snakes.* Snakes are a minor hazard, but a real one. In the Western Hemisphere poisonous snakes are present from Canada to Argentina. Africa has poisonous snakes from the Mediterranean to the Cape. In Asia snakebites kill thousands of people every year. Most of the deaths recorded are in India and are probably due more to population density and lack of shoes than to any special viciousness on the part of the snakes.

There is no sure cure for snakebite unless the proper antivenin is administered immediately after the bite. Not all bites by poisonous snakes are fatal, even if left untreated, because the snake does not always inject a lethal dose of venom; therefore almost any treatment can appear to be successful against some snakebites.

(e) *Insects.* Biting insects are extremely annoying pests in the arctic and subarctic in the summer months as soon as the temperature gets above 40° F, and in the tropic areas throughout the year. In swampy areas of temperate regions the insect density approaches that of the arctic. There are no reports of survivors being killed by isolated insect bites alone, but insects have made many survivors extremely miserable. Men have, however, died from the effects of insect stings when attacked by large swarms of stinging insects. In the tropics and some temperate regions, insects are vectors of diseases such as malaria and yellow fever which do prove fatal to survivors.

Insect pests can be combatted either by protective clothing or netting, or by use of suitable repellents.

(f) *Animal Hazards at Sea.* At sea sharks and other ferocious fish are definitely a hazard to the lives of survivors. However few shark attacks have occurred outside the area between 40° N. and 40° S. latitude. This may be due to the greater concentration of sharks in warm-water areas, or to the fact that few humans go swimming in cold water. Barracuda have also been reported as attacking survivors, as have numerous smaller, unidentified fish.

In addition to fish that attack humans floating in the sea, there are many other venomous marine organisms such as jellyfish, sea urchins, sponges, Portuguese Men-of-War, and others that poison by contact. In coral reefs the coral itself contains stinging organisms, and many others are found in the shallow waters of the reef.

Sanitation. When large groups of people are gathered together —or even small groups in confined quarters—the problem of disposal of human waste presents both a sanitary and a psychological problem. Survivors' accounts list the presence of human waste in the immediate living area or life raft as contributing to nausea, seasickness, and general discomfort. On survival exercises the Air Force has found that the paper disposal bags usually carried by commercial airliners make satisfactory emergency latrines. However, survivors will simply have to face the fact that life rafts do not have lavatories.

Injuries. Care of the injured after an aircraft accident presents the relatively unscathed survivors with many problems. Treatment of major injuries may be beyond the capabilities of the group, while treatment of minor injuries may be so time-consuming as to hinder efforts toward survival and rescue of the group as a whole.

The succeeding chapters give more data on the problems discussed briefly above and give advice on how to meet these problems—or, preferably, how to avoid them.

2

Emergency Procedures

The first few minutes following a crash or landing after bailout are crucial. Taking the wrong action or not taking the necessary action may mean the difference between life or death. Because few people can think clearly during an unexpected emergency the alert pilot or passenger has an emergency plan, such as the one given below, ready for use at all times. When the emergency does occur, this plan can be put into action without the need for devising one step at a time. Before going on a cross-country flight, the pilot or passenger should review these procedures to have them fresh in mind.

The first thing the occupants of a plane should do after a crash is to get themselves and their emergency gear out of the aircraft as fast as possible. Stay a safe distance away until the engines have cooled and the spilled gas has evaporated. Failure to follow this simple rule may cost you your life.

Second, check injuries. The uninjured or ambulatory should give first aid and make the injured as comfortable as possible. When removing casualties from the airplane, be particularly careful not to aggravate their injuries, especially fractures and back injuries.

Third, protect survivors from exposure to wind and rain. Find natural shelter or construct temporary shelter from any materials available. Except in very hot weather you will need a fire. Get one started as soon as possible.

Fourth, if you have an emergency radio transmitter or if the aircraft radio is in working condition, get it operating as soon as possible and transmit at regular intervals until help arrives. In any case get all signals out and ready for immediate use.

Fifth, relax. Take a long drink of water or (in cold weather) a hot drink. If your medical kit includes "pep pills" such as benzedrine, take a dose now. Then sit back and rest until you feel you are over the shock of the crash. Put off any long-range planning or extensive work until later.

After you have rested—which may take from an hour to half

a day, depending on your reaction to the crash—plan your next move. Your first problem is whether to stay at the scene of the crash (or bailout) and wait for rescue, or to travel in search of aid. Except for tropical rain forest areas, the best plan is to stay where you are unless you know where help is and are confident that you can reach it before searchers will find you. However, if you have bailed out and your crashed plane is within easy walking distance, go to it and make your permanent camp there. A plane is more easily seen from the air than an individual or group.

If you decide to wait for rescue, construct signals immediately that can be seen from the air. Use the ICAO Ground-Air Emergency Code which is in world-wide use (see Fig. 2-4). If you decide to walk away from the crash site, leave a note giving your destination and route for ground searchers and construct Signal Number 7 of the Ground-Air Emergency Code.

While waiting for rescue, organize your camp. Decide who will be in charge and let him run the show. Everyone should be assigned a specific duty. Pool all food and equipment and issue it on a share-and-share-alike basis. If your temporary shelter is not adequate, build a better one. Collect fuel, and stockpile at least one day's supply. Look for a water source, and for animal and plant food. After your camp is organized sit back, wait, and conserve your energy but keep your signals handy and be sure you can get them into action in a hurry. Take life easy. Don't run risks that might result in injury. You will be easier to rescue if you are in good health and all in one piece.

The search planes and ground search parties are relying on you to signal them. Do your best, and once you are sighted follow instructions given by your rescuers. Don't collapse when the rescue party arrives—they can use all the help you can give. Remember, whether or not you have been designated group leader, *in your own rescue you are the key man.*

FIRST AID

First aid following an aircraft accident is no different from first aid after any other accident except that you will be limited to use of the medications you are carrying on your person or in your aircraft. No first aid kit can carry all the items that might possibly be needed, but if the kit is to be of use it should contain at least a compress to stop bleeding, bandages, a disinfectant for scratches and wounds, ointment for burns, and an ample supply of APC (aspirin-phenaticin-caffein) pills.

Many military fliers also carry "pep pills" (usually benzedrine), an antibiotic to combat infection, and a drug to stop diarrhea (a common ailment in survival incidents). Check with your family physician to find what drugs you can carry that will serve these purposes.

Although tourniquets are often needed they can usually be improvised, so that there is no need to carry one in a medical kit.

The most likely injuries will be cuts, fractures, concussions, internal injuries, burns, and shock. Keep injured men off their feet, preferably lying flat, and keep them warm. Watch carefully for symptoms of shock.

Pack a first aid manual in your survival kit. The best manual for your purpose is the First Aid Guide of the U.S. Forest Service, available from the Superintendent of Documents, U.S. Government Printing Office, Washington 25, D.C., for 20 cents.

Treat injuries in the order of their danger to the victim, as follows: (a) serious bleeding, (b) stoppage of breath, (c) shock, and (d) other injuries. In other words, take immediate action to keep the patient alive and breathing and put off the repair work until the patient is out of immediate danger.

BLEEDING

Stop bleeding by the fastest means possible. Pressure directly on the wound by a sterile pad, tightly held by a bandage or by hand will stop all but the most serious bleeding. If you don't have a sterile pad, jam a wad of any available cloth into the wound and apply pressure. You can fight infection later—the important thing is to stop the loss of blood. If the bleeding does not stop after the pad is applied, use pressure by hand on pressure points shown in Fig 2-1 or apply a tourniquet between the wound and the heart. Use a tourniquet only as a last resort. Raising the bleeding limb will aid in stopping bleeding. Loosen the tourniquet every 20 or 30 minutes to see if the bleeding has stopped or lessened enough to be handled by a pressure bandage.

STOPPAGE OF BREATH

If breathing has stopped, apply artificial respiration at once. The approved methods of artificial respiration are shown in Fig. 2-2. Continue artificial respiration until the victim begins to breath for himself, a physician pronounces him dead, or he appears to be dead beyond any doubt. When the victim is revived, keep him as quiet as

BLEEDING IN SCALP ABOVE THE EAR. Light pressure in front of the middle ear.

BLEEDING ON OUTSIDE OR INSIDE OF HEAD. Moderate pressure on neck about 3" below ear and 3" above collarbone — push artery against spine.

BLEEDING IN THE CHEEK. Very light pressure in notch on under edge of jaw ⅔ back from tip of chin.

BLEEDING IN THE LOWER ARM. Strong pressure on inside of arm halfway between shoulder and elbow.

BLEEDING IN THE ARM. Firm pressure behind the middle of collarbone — push artery against first rib.

BLEEDING ABOVE THE KNEE. Strong pressure in groin with heel of hand — push artery against pelvic bone.

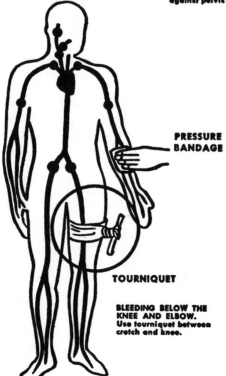

PRESSURE BANDAGE

TOURNIQUET

BLEEDING BELOW THE KNEE AND ELBOW. Use tourniquet between crotch and knee.

Fig. 2.1. Pressure Points.

possible until he is breathing regularly. Keep him from becoming chilled and treat him for shock. Because respiratory and other disturbances may develop as an aftermath, a doctor's care is necessary during the recovery period.

SHOCK

The commonest injury in an aircraft accident is shock. Symptoms of shock are rapid breathing, pallid cold skin, sweating, weak pulse, and confused actions. Anyone acting irrationally after an accident is probably suffering from mild shock. Treat shock by laying the patient down flat with feet raised, and keep him warm but not overheated. If he is conscious give him warm drinks. Persons in mild shock may wander away from the scene of the accident if they are not watched. Treat such persons as if they were injured and keep close watch on them or you may have to waste valuable time searching for them.

FRACTURES

Fractures present a special problem in that the act of removing the victim from the scene of the crash may cause additional injury. Handle injured men with care if a fracture is even suspected.

Don't remove clothing from a fractured limb unless it must be taken off to treat a wound, in which case cut the clothing away from the wound.

If help is close by don't splint. Leave that to the experts. If splinting is necessary make splints long enough to immobilize the joints above and below the fracture. Pad splints with soft materials.

CHEST WOUNDS

Open chest wounds through which air can be heard sucking as the patient breathes, should be covered tightly with a large dressing. Apply the pad at the moment of maximum inhalation and secure it in place by tight bandaging. Fractured ribs should be treated in a similar manner. Have the patient exhale, then wrap long bandages or strips of cloth tightly around the chest. Soaking the bandage in water will result in a tighter and better bandage.

BURNS

Cover burned areas with burn ointment, apply a gauze pack or cover with heavy aluminium foil molded to the shape of the

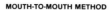

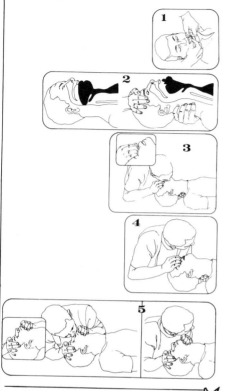

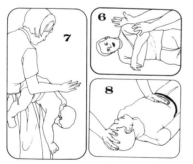

MOUTH-TO-MOUTH METHOD

1. If foreign matter is visible in the mouth, wipe it out quickly with your fingers, wrapped in a cloth, if possible.

2. Tilt the victim's head backward so that his chin is pointing upward. This is accomplished by placing one hand under the victim's neck and lifting, while the other hand is placed on his forehead and pressing. This procedure should provide an open airway by moving the tongue away from the back of the throat.

3. Maintain the backward head-tilt position and, to prevent leakage of air, pinch the victim's nostrils with the fingers of the hand that is pressing on the forehead.

   Open your mouth wide; take a deep breath; and seal your mouth tightly around the victim's mouth with a wide-open circle and blow into his mouth. If the airway is clear, only moderate resistance to the blowing effort is felt.

   If you are not getting air exchange, check to see if there is a foreign body in the back of the mouth obstructing the air passages. Reposition the head and resume the blowing effort.

4. Watch the victim's chest, and when you see it rise, stop inflation, raise your mouth, turn your head to the side, and listen for exhalation. Watch the chest to see that it falls.

   When his exhalation is finished, repeat the blowing cycle. Volume is important. You should start at a high rate and then provide at least one breath every 5 seconds (or 12 per minute).

   When mouth-to-mouth and/or mouth-to-nose resuscitation is administered to small children or infants, the backward head-tilt should not be as extensive as that for adults or large children.

   The mouth and nose of the infant or small child should be sealed by your mouth. Blow into the mouth and/or nose every 3 seconds (or 20 breaths per minute) with less pressure and volume than for adults, the amount determined by the size of the child.

   If vomiting occurs, quickly turn the victim on his side, wipe out the mouth, and then reposition him.

MOUTH-TO-NOSE METHOD

5. For the mouth-to-nose method, maintain the backward head-tilt position by placing the heel of the hand on the forehead. Use the other hand to close the mouth. Blow into the victim's nose. On the exhalation phase, open the victim's mouth to allow air to escape.

RELATED INFORMATION

6. If a foreign body is prohibiting ventilation, as a last resort, turn the victim on his side and administer sharp blows between the shoulder blades to jar the material free.

7. A child may be suspended momentarily by the ankles or turned upside down over one arm and given two or three sharp pats between the shoulder blades. Clear the mouth again, reposition, and repeat the blowing effort.

8. Air may be blown into the victim's stomach, particularly when the air passage is obstructed or the inflation pressure is excessive. Although inflation of the stomach is not dangerous, it may make lung ventilation more difficult and increase the likelihood of vomiting. When the victim's stomach is bulging, always turn the victim's head to one side and be prepared to clear his mouth before pressing your hand briefly over the stomach. This will force air out of the stomach but may cause vomiting.

   When a victim is revived, keep him as quiet as possible until he is breathing regularly. Keep him from becoming chilled and otherwise treat him for shock. Continue artificial respiration until the victim begins to breathe for himself or a physician pronounces him dead or he appears to be dead beyond any doubt.

   Because respiratory and other disturbances may develop as an aftermath, a doctor's care is necessary during the recovery period.

Fig. 2.2. Artificial Respiration.

affected area and bandage firmly. Keep the burned part at rest. Splint if necessary to stop movement. When burn ointment or aluminium foil is not available leave the burn alone. Don't try to clean or wash.

INFECTION

Do what you can to keep all wounds clean. Cut away clothing from wounds. Never touch a wound with a finger or anything but a sterile bandage unless you must do so to stop bleeding. Apply disinfectants according to the instructions on the package.

VENOMOUS BITES AND STINGS

The treatment of venomous bites and stings, especially snakebite, is the subject of much controversy. Most firstaid manuals advise (a) using a rather loose tourniquet to stop the flow of lymph from the poisoned area, (b) slashing the fang or sting punctures, (c) applying suction to the punctures, (d) as the swollen area around the bite enlarges, making additional shallow incisions and applying suction to these incisions. In addition to these firstaid measures the use of antivenin is advocated as soon as possible.

Another method, called the L-C method by its originator Dr. Herbert L. Stahnke, Director of the Poisonous Animals Research Laboratory, Arizona State College, is now gaining favor, although many authorities oppose it. This method uses a very tight ligature (L), preferably of a thin string such as a shoelace, to restrict the spread of the poison in the body, followed by application of cold (C) to the affected part. This method has been used successfully on several types of snakebites, Gila Monster bites, and scorpion stings. Stahnke claims that the L-C method not only halts the toxic action of snake venom but also stops the tissue-destroying action of the enzymes in the venom.

Obviously, ice packs will not be available in a survival situation, yet there may be means of producing ice. Carbon dioxide and carbon tetrachloride, both used in fire extinguishers, and Freon, used in aerosol bombs, can be used to make ice packs. Make a pad three or four inches square of two or three layers of any cloth. Saturate this with water. Then spray the pad with the gas until the water is frozen. Place the pad on the site of the bite or sting and keep the water frozen by occasional light spraying without removing it. The pad should be kept on for two

hours for a scorpion sting, and from 12 hours to four to six days for rattlesnake bites. The supply of gas in a fire extinguisher can keep a pad frozen only a few hours at most, but this may be long enough to get the victim to a spot where more ice is available.

SIGNALING

The proper use of signals may end your survival incident alm before it begins. A lone man, a group of men, or even an airpla not always easy to see from the air even when visibility is good the *proper signals* can make you effectively bigger and easier to

Your crash locator beacon, which will be activated automa in case of a crash, is your primary aid in increasing your visib searchers. Since the establishment of the requirement that all carry a crash locator beacon, more than 100 crashed aircr year have been located through beacon signals.

For a visual marker of your position use smoke by day a flame by night. To make black smoke add rubber, such a floor mat or electrical insulation, engine oil, or oily rags smoke add green leaves, moss or a bit of water. Black smo best on a murky day, white smoke best on a clear day.

If you have a radar reflector, erect it immediately. blanket" with an aluminized surface sold by most st backpacking and camping equipment is a fairly e reflector. These "survival blankets" come in several si enough to be carried in a jacket pocket.

The signal mirror is second only to the radio a Air Rescue Service pilots report that the flash f aimed signal mirror cannot be mistaken or ign several types of signal mirrors. The type usually surplus stores is aimed as shown in Fig. 2-3. N small window of reflective material. Signaling

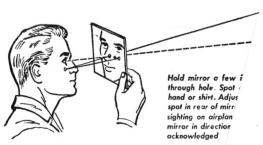

Hold mirror a few i
through hole. Spot
hand or shirt. Adjus
spot in rear of mirr
sighting on airplan
mirror in direction
acknowledged

Fig. 2-3. How to Use Sign

dow the user can direct the beam at the target by aiming the "bright spot" he sees through the window directly over the target. All signal mirrors have directions for use printed on the back.

Improvised mirrors have saved lives, too. An RAF pilot down in the Red Sea without even a life jacket used the lid of a ration tin to signal a rescue aircraft. Any shiny surface can serve as a signal mirror. If using metal, punch a hole in the center and sight as shown in Fig. 2-3.

On hazy days the flash of a signal mirror is visible from the air before the signaler can see the aircraft; accordingly, flash the mirror at the sound of an aircraft even if you can't see it. Also sweep the horizon with the signal beam at frequent intervals even if there is no sound of aircraft.

At night, signal with a flashlight, or if your airplane landing lights are intact and you can get power by running an engine, remove the lights and extend them for signaling. However, *don't drain the battery*—save it for the radio.

Make yourself as conspicuous as possible. Spread out parachutes. Take off engine cowlings and line them up on the ground or on top of the wings. Clean the inside surfaces so they will act as reflectors. Lay orange-colored "Mae Wests" in a pattern on the ground. They are highly visible. Arrange your ground signals in geometric patterns, preferably in one of the International Ground-Air Emergency Signals shown in Fig. 2-4. As previously noted, these signals are in world-wide use. Do everything you can to disturb the natural look of the ground and provide a visual stimulus for the searchers. Cut, trample, or burn giant markers in grass and scrub.

On water or snow, fluorescein sea marker dye is the best bet. A little bit goes a long way and it has a distinctive appearance. Be careful to spread it *down-wind* of your camp, because otherwise the fine powder will penetrate clothing, food, or anything else it touches.

Keep flares, smoke grenades, fusees or other pyrotechnic signals close at hand but keep them dry. Use them only when a plane is in sight. Try to save one smoke signal for firing when the rescue helicopter approaches. The pilot would like to know the wind before he tries to "sit down."

In general the best course for the survivor of an airplane crash is to make himself as comfortable as possible near the scene of the crash, prepare his signals and wait for rescue. Don't leave the scene of the crash unless (a) you know your position and know

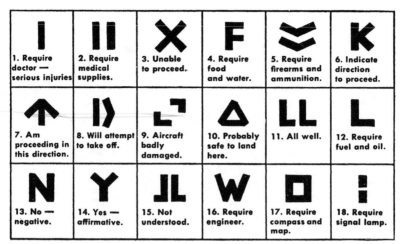

I	**II**	**X**	**F**	**≋**	**K**
1. Require doctor — serious injuries	2. Require medical supplies.	3. Unable to proceed.	4. Require food and water.	5. Require firearms and ammunition.	6. Indicate direction to proceed.
↑	**I)**	**⌐」**	**△**	**LL**	**L**
7. Am proceeding in this direction.	8. Will attempt to take off.	9. Aircraft badly damaged.	10. Probably safe to land here.	11. All well.	12. Require fuel and oil.
N	**Y**	**⊥⊥**	**W**	**□**	**⋮**
13. No — negative.	14. Yes — affirmative.	15. Not understood.	16. Require engineer.	17. Require compass and map.	18. Require signal lamp.

Our receiver is operating.

Use drop message.

All OK, do not wait.

Affirmative (yes).

Negative (no).

Need mechanical help or parts — long delay.

Pick us up aircraft abandoned.

Do not attempt to land here.

Can proceed shortly, wait if practicable.

Need medical assistance URGENTLY.

Land here (point in direction of landing).

Fig. 2.4. ICAO Signals—Body Signals.

29

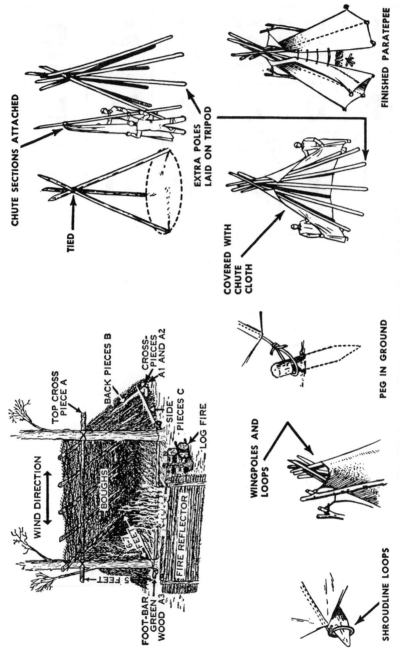

CHUTE SECTIONS ATTACHED

TIED

EXTRA POLES LAID ON TRIPOD

FINISHED PARATEPEE

COVERED WITH CHUTE CLOTH

PEG IN GROUND

WINGPOLES AND LOOPS

SHROUDLINE LOOPS

TOP CROSS PIECE A

BACK PIECES B

CROSS-PIECES A1 AND A2

SIDE-PIECES C

LOG FIRE

WIND DIRECTION

BOUGHS

6 FEET

5 FEET

FOOT-BAR GREEN WOOD A3

FIRE REFLECTOR

Fig. 2.5. Lean-to of Evergreen Boughs and the Paratepee.

30

that you can reach help with the equipment available, or (b) you are certain that no search will be made and you are equipped to travel.

The advantages of staying at the scene of the crash are:

1. Any organized search will be relying largely on signals from the crash locator beacon. The airplane and your stationary signals are easier to spot from the air than a man or men traveling. Also there is a good chance that someone will have seen you go down and will be along to investigate.

2. The airplane provides you with material for shelter, fire, and signaling—more material than you can pack on your back.

3. Travel is more hazardous than camping, especially in rugged country.

Remember that very few survivors have died of starvation or exposure when they stayed at the scene of the crash, but that a great many have died while trying to walk to safety. In far too many cases the aircraft has been sighted within a day or two of the crash while the wandering survivors were not located in time to save their lives.

If you take all those things into account and still decide it is better to walk than to wait, do as previously directed—leave a note and construct Signal Number 7 of the Ground-Air Emergency Code.

SHELTER

In any area you can improvise shelter from parts of your airplane or your emergency equipment, especially your parachute, or from natural materials. Figures 2-5 through 2-7 show many types of shelters. The kind you make will depend on the materials available and on whether you need protection from heat, cold, rain, sun, or insects.

Pick the location of your camp carefully and stay as close to the airplane as possible, but try to be near fuel and water. Water supply is probably the most important factor in selecting a camp site. Pick a location protected from the wind but away from the dangers of rock falls, avalanches, or floods. In other words, use your common sense.

FIRE-MAKING

In almost any survival situation you will need a fire—if not for warmth, at least for cooking and signaling. Like any other task, fire-building is easier if you know what you are trying to do. To get a fire going you have to heat the fuel to its kindling point. To keep it going you have to provide it with fuel and oxygen. For safety's sake you have to keep the fire within bounds.

First, prepare a fireplace. Clear away all burnable material (leaves, moss, twigs, forest litter) so that you won't start a forest or grass fire. If the ground is dry, scrape down to bare dirt or rock. If the ground is wet or if you must build the fire on snow,

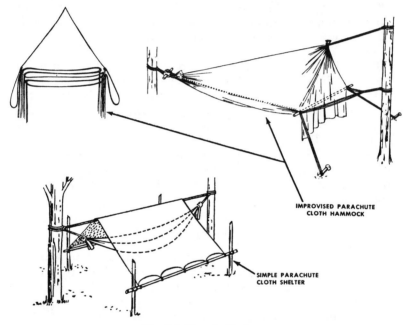

IMPROVISED PARACHUTE
CLOTH HAMMOCK

SIMPLE PARACHUTE
CLOTH SHELTER

Fig. 2.6. Tropic Shelters.

build a platform of logs or stones. Cooking fires should be walled in by logs or stones, both to concentrate the heat and to provide a platform for cooking utensils. For maximum heating effect, build the fire against a rock or a wall of logs which will reflect the heat into your shelter. The reflector will also protect the fire from the wind (Fig. 2-5a).

Second, gather kindling and fuel. Very few natural fuels can be started burning directly from a match. Kindling is needed to get a fire going. Good natural kindling materials are resinous wood, dry wood or bark, twigs, palm leaves, dry grass, dry ferns, and termite nests. If wood is used, split into sticks, and cut long thin shavings. Leave the shavings attached to form "shave sticks." Store kindling in a dry place. Gasoline can be used to start a fire, but remember to use very little, and to pour it on the fuel before you light it. Never pour gasoline directly on a fire even if it is only smoldering.

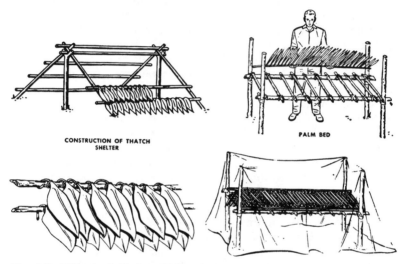

CONSTRUCTION OF THATCH
SHELTER

PALM BED

Fig. 2.7. Thatched Shelter Using A-Frame Construction. Palm fronds or bunches of grass can also be used for thatching. To split a palm frond into halves, nick the tip of the front with your fingernail and pull the two halves apart. Whatever the material used for thatching, arrange it so that the rain will drain downward. Always start the thatching at the lowest point and overlap the upper layers.

For fuel use anything that will burn. Dry dead wood is the easiest to gather and split. It can be broken into usable pieces by pounding with a rock. The interior of fallen tree trunks and branches is often dry even when the outside is wet. Green wood will burn when finely split. Brush, dry grass twisted into bunches, dry animal dung, animal fats, and dry peat from the top of an undercut river bank are all natural fuels. If you can salvage gasoline or oil from your aircraft, your fuel problem is solved even though you have to improvise a stove. No matter what your fuel, get a good supply on hand before starting your fire.

Third, light the fire. Arrange a small amount of kindling in a low pyramid or cone with the individual pieces close enough together so that the flame can lick from one to the next. Leave a small opening in the base of the pyramid for inserting a light. Use a candle for lighting the fire, if you have one, to save your matches. A "shave stick" or a faggot of thin dry twigs tied loosely together can substitute for a candle. Shield the match or lighter from the wind and light the candle and apply it to the lower windward side of the kindling while shielding it from the wind. Lay small pieces of wood or other fuel gently on the kindling, either before or after lighting, but don't crush the kindling. As the small pieces take fire, add larger pieces but keep the fire to a usable size. You won't benefit from a bonfire, and fuel may be hard to get, so don't waste it.

In exceptionally cold weather or in wet weather a *fire starter*— a device that can be ignited without a match and burns with a large and hot flame—will make starting the fire easier. A fusee signal flare can be used as a fire starter.

No one should be caught in a survival situation without matches or a functioning lighter. However, if you find yourself in this unhappy situation you may still be able to get a fire going. The first requisite for "matchless" fire-making is dry tinder. Very dry powdered wood, finely shredded dry bark, fine wood dust produced by insects (often found under the bark of dead trees), threads from cloth, gauze, absorbent cotton, or rope, fine bird feathers or birds' nests are all good tinder if bone dry. If available add a few drops of gasoline or some powder taken from a cartridge just before using. When the tinder has been prepared keep it as dry as possible. Store it in a waterproof container if you have one, otherwise keep it in an inside pocket.

Now that you have tinder you need a spark. The easiest and most reliable way to get a spark is by use of flint and steel. Many waterproof match cases have a bar of flint on the bottom. If you have no flint, find a piece of hard rock from which you can strike sparks. If it scars or breaks when struck with steel, discard it. To start a fire hold the flint over the dry tinder, strike it with the flat of a knife blade or other piece of steel with a downward scraping motion so that the sparks will fall on the tinder. As soon as the tinder begins to smolder, fan or blow it gently into a flame. Add kindling to the blazing tinder or move the blazing timber to a prepared kindling pile. (See Fig. 2-8.)

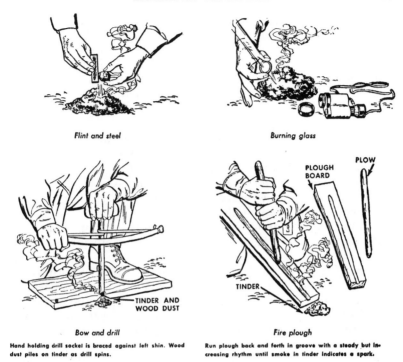

Flint and steel

Burning glass

TINDER AND
WOOD DUST

PLOUGH
BOARD

PLOW

TINDER

Bow and drill

Fire plough

Hand holding drill socket is braced against left shin. Wood
dust piles on tinder as drill spins.

Run plough back and forth in groove with a steady but increasing rhythm until smoke in tinder indicates a spark.

Fig. 2.8. Fire Without Matches.

In bright sunlight a convex lens can be used as a burning glass
to start the tinder burning.

Experienced boy scouts may be able to make fire by friction
(bow and drill or fire drill) but all such methods require practice.
Even those proficient in these techniques can start a fire more
easily with flint and steel.

Faster than flint and steel is an electric spark, which you can
utilize if you are with your airplane and have a live storage battery.

The gas and oil left in your airplane can be used for fuel but
you must improvise a stove. Put one or two inches of sand and
fine gravel in a can or other metal container and add gasoline.
Cut slots near the top of the can to let smoke out when using
the stove for cooking, and punch holes just above the level of the
sand to insure a draft. If you have no metal container dig a shal-

low hole in the ground and fill with sand. Add oil to the gasoline for a longer-burning fire. Be very careful when lighting, as the gasoline may explode and flare up. The best procedure is to stand well back, avert your face, and toss in the match.

Oil alone can be used as a fuel if you can improvise a wick. Make the wick of cloth, rope, string, or anything else that will soak up oil. Fill a container with oil, put one end of the wick in the oil and rest the other on the edge of the container. Oil-soaked paper, rags, or wood are good fuel for a conventional fire.

Don't waste matches. Prepare your fire before you try to light it. Don't use matches for lighting cigarettes, but get a light from your fire. Save your fuel by not building unnecessary fires.

Collect good tinder wherever you find it and keep it dry. When traveling pick up kindling along the trail before you make camp. Keep firewood dry under shelter. Put damp wood near the fire to dry it before use. Save kindling and fuel for your morning fire.

Keep a fire overnight by covering bed of coals first with ashes and then with dry earth. If rain is likely, add a layer of leaves to shed the water. In the morning uncover the coals and add fuel.

If short on matches you can carry fire with you as lighted punk, smoldering coconut husk, or slow-burning coals. Fan the smoldering material into flame when you need a new fire.

Be conservative when building a fire. Keep it small and don't waste fuel. *Put out the fire when you leave.*

FIREARMS

If you carry a gun on your flights for hunting purposes, remember that hunting to obtain food is a more serious matter than hunting for sport. Rules of fair play do not exist for a hungry survivor, and the only ammunition you can count on is what you have taken along in the plane. When using a rifle, follow these rules for best results in collecting a food supply:

(1) Get as close as possible to your target before shooting.

(2) Fire from a steady position, or from prone position when possible. Use a gunrest, such as a log or stone, for the barrel if you can, but put your hand between the barrel and the gunrest to absorb vibration and to prevent your shot from going wild.

(3) Don't fire unless you have a clear shot at a vital spot. The shoulder and chest are the best aiming spots for most medium and large game.

(4) Reload immediately after your first shot while keeping an eye on the game. Reload even if the game appears to have fallen dead. Be ready to shoot again if necessary but don't use ammunition needlessly.

(5) If the game runs away after your first shot, look for blood. If you see blood, wait half an hour or so before following. Wounded game will lie down and stiffen if given time.

(6) With a shotgun, forget about shots on the wing unless you are very good. Get your birds sitting and at close range.

Field maintenance of your guns requires as much attention in a survival situation as on a hunting trip, except that you must make do with the equipment you have. The best maintenance is good care. Don't abuse the weapon in any way.

Keep your gun clean. Cover it or wrap it in cloth when not in use; if it gets dirty, clean it at once. A piece of cloth on a string pulled through the barrel is a handy substitute for a ramrod and cleaning patch. Boiling water poured through the barrel from the breech will perform the function of powder solvent. Remove excess water by pulling a cloth through the barrel; the hot barrel will then dry by itself. Check carefully to be sure that there is no foreign substance in the barrel. Never try to shoot out an obstruction—the barrel will burst and you will probably be seriously wounded.

Never use a pistol, rifle, or shotgun as a club, hammer or pry. No weapon is constructed to take this kind of treatment.

Keep moving parts of your weapon lightly oiled but don't over oil. Excess oil picks up dirt which must be cleaned out.

AXES AND KNIVES

Survival may sometimes depend on the proper use and care of cutting tools. Used properly, an axe is an efficient tool; used improperly or carelessly, it can be a very dangerous instrument. In using an axe, rhythm and aim are more important than brute force—too much power behind a swing spoils the aim and is needlessly tiring. When swung properly the momentum of the axe head provides all the power needed.

As a safety precaution, clear away all obstructions before swinging an axe. Any small obstruction—a branch or vine—can deflect a swinging axe into your foot or leg. Don't use the axe as a pry, as you may easily break the handle this way.

Keep your axe sharp. A little work with a file and whetstone can save a lot of wasted chopping. Use the file every few days and the stone after each using. Push the file away from the blade while keeping the edge wet with water. Put a finer edge on with the whetstone. Move the stone with a circular motion from the middle of the blade to the edge. If you have no file, a stone alone will keep an axe usable.

If you have no whetstone, look for a natural substitute. Any sandstone will sharpen tools, but a clayey sandstone, usually somewhat gray in color, gives better results than a pure quartz sandstone. You can recognize quartz by the fact that it is the only common mineral that will bite into steel. Each grain of quartz will cut a groove.

A machete can be sharpened with only a file, although a whetstone gives a much better edge. Other knives need only the whetstone. Hold the blade at a small angle to the stone and push the blade away from you, alternating the sides of the blade against the stone. Gradually decrease the pressure on the blade to get a keener edge.

CLOTHING

Clothing is your protection against the environment; properly used, it can keep you cool as well as warm, and protect you against sunburn, scratches, and insect pests. Don't discard any clothing even if you see no immediate need for it. Excess clothing can be used as bedding or a shelter cloth, and even for "money" in barter.

Keep clothing and footgear dry whenever possible. In wet weather dry them at night in front of your fire, but don't place shoes too close to the fire or they will stiffen and crack. Repair tears in clothing promptly before they grow larger. Beat loose dirt out of your clothes when they are dry. Dirty clothes lose much of their insulation value.

HEALTH AND HAZARDS

If alone in a survival incident, you will face stresses and environmental conditions foreign to your normal regime. These stresses can sap your energy and make you ill even though you may not catch any disease. If, however, you recognize these stresses and take measures to alleviate them, you can expect to stay in good physical condition until rescued. The most important consideration is to save your strength—or at least to use it wisely. Don't get completely tired out; when doing hard work or walking, rest for ten minutes or so out of every hour. During these rest periods, make a conscious effort to relax—sit or lie down, let your jaw drop, and "sit loose." Fight mental fatigue, too. Make an evaluation of your situation, decide on a course of action, and then follow it. Don't use nervous energy worrying about your decision, but accept the situation and make the best of it. Try to get a normal amount of sleep. If you feel you can't sleep, at least lie down and rest. Wartime experience has shown that, for the devout, prayer is a marvelous aid to relaxation.

Aside from fatigue, the most common ailments among survivors are foot trouble, skin infections, and intestinal upsets. Your feet are obviously important to your eventual rescue; take care of them at the earliest opportunity. If your feet hurt, stop and tend to them—it will save you trouble later on. Inspect your feet at least once a day for red spots or blisters. Use adhesive tape or bandages on your skin where shoes rub. Puncture blisters through the thick skin at the base with a sterilized needle and press out the fluid or run an iodine-soaked thread through the base of the blister to act as a wick. Clean the skin around the blister thoroughly before puncturing, and apply a sterile bandage after puncture.

Your skin is your first line of defense against infection. Use an antiseptic on even the smallest scratch cut, or insect bite. Cuts and scratches are liable to get infected, especially in a tropic environment. Keep your body and clothing clean. Examine yourself carefully for external parasites at least once a day.

Diarrhea and other intestinal upsets are common in survival situations. Part of this may be caused by nervous tension, but much is due to actual infection by harmful bacteria. Purify all the water you drink, either by chemical purification or by boiling for one minute or more. Cook the plants you eat, or wash them in purified water. Wash your hands before you eat and enforce proper sanitation measures. Dump all garbage in a pit or at a distance from camp and set up a definite latrine area away from the camp and water supply. If you get diarrhea and the available medication does not stop it, rest and fast for 24 hours except for drinking water, then eat only liquid foods and avoid sugars and starches. Drink plenty of water and eat several small meals instead of few large ones. You may be constipated but this is nothing to worry about. This situation will correct itself in a few days.

WATER

Water is far more important to survival than food, and in many environments more important than shelter. Start looking for water as soon as you have recovered from the shock of the crash. You can live for weeks without food but you can't survive long without water, especially in a hot environment where your body needs large amounts of water to keep cool through sweating.

A man of average weight needs at least two quarts of water a day to maintain his body water supply. Any lesser intake cuts down his efficiency. In hot weather he will need considerably more. (See Table 1-2, Days of Expected Survival.) Cutting water intake below your body's requirements puts you in a water deficit which you will have to make up sooner or later.

Purify all water before drinking, except rain water collected in clean containers and water taken from plants. Purify either by (1) boiling for at least one minute (the *surest* way of purifying) or by (2) chemical sterilization. Halazone, Globuline, and other commercial chemical sterilizing agents have instructions on the package. A $2\frac{1}{2}$ per cent solution (tincture) of iodine can be used; add 6 drops to a quart of water and let stand for 10 minutes before using. *Note:* Do not use Halazone tablets discarded by the Government. These are out of date. Don't drink seawater or urine. Your body will use more water in excreting the dissolved solids than it will gain.

The most obvious as well as most easily located source of drinking water is surface water such as ponds, lakes and streams. When these are not available you may be able to reach ground water—water that flows underneath the surface. You won't find much by blind digging, but surface clues to ground water supplies often exist (Fig. 2-9). In rocky areas, look for springs and seepages in cracks and caverns. A water source is often indicated by spots of lush vegetation or by dark stains on rock walls. Springs are often found in limestone caverns. Springs and seepages occur at the surface of contact between two lava flows or at the base of vertical "organ pipe" joints. Walls of canyons which cut across sandstone strata often have seepages. If you locate a wet area indicating a seepage, dig a trench to collect the water, although none may be flowing on the surface.

In loose sediments, water is more abundant and easier to find than in rocks. Look for springs along valley floors or along their sloping sides. The flat benches or terraces of land above river

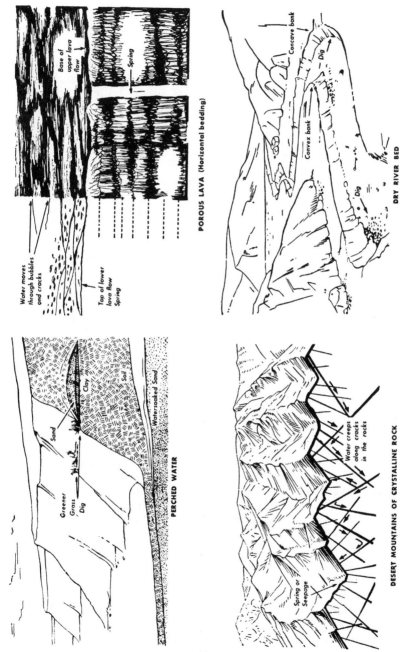

Fig. 2.9. Where to Look for Water.

bottoms often yield springs and seepages even if the river is dry.

Clay deposits do not yield much water even when moist, but many clays contain bands of sand through which water moves freely. Look for wet spots on the face or foot of a clay bluff and dig it out. Along coasts, water collects in the hollows between the dunes and even on the beach itself above the high tide line. Dig if the sand seems moist.

EMERGENCY FOODS

Although most survivors worry more about their food supply than any other item, food (as previously noted) is usually less important than water or shelter. A healthy man can last for several weeks without food even though he may be acutely conscious of the lack.

Since most survivors are picked up within a very few days, there is little to be gained by severe rationing of available food supplies. On the contrary you should try to eat a normal diet for the first day or so while you are establishing a camp and setting out signals. After that you can afford to cut down your intake while you conserve calories by taking things easy. Also, a normal diet for the first day or so will be needed to help counteract the effects of shock which almost always accompany an accident.

After the initial period you may want to start rationing, especially if you anticipate a long wait until rescue. A rule of thumb is to allocate two-thirds of your food stocks to the first half of your estimated time before rescue and the remaining one-third to the last half. If natural foods are plentiful you should keep as much of your rations in reserve as possible. (One U.S. businessman who crashed while on an aerial hunting trip in northern Canada lived for thirty days on a diet of lake trout and blueberries. When rescued he still had almost all of his original stock of rations as insurance against a more extended survival period.)

Individuals or parties sent for help should be given approximately twice the food allotted to the men staying at camp, because the men who are traveling will use about twice as much energy as those remaining at camp.

Drink at least two quarts of water a day, more in hot weather. If you have less than this, restrict your diet to foods with high carbohydrate content, such as sugar and dried fruit. Avoid dry starchy foods and meat as much as possible. If water is no problem, drink more than your normal amount to avoid possibility of even a mild dehydration. If possible eat regularly—don't nibble. Even on limited rations plan to have one good meal daily, preferably hot. Two meals a day are of course even better.

Keep a lookout for wild foods so as to eat off the land whenever possible. Except for berries and fruits, cook all wild foods to make them safer, more digestible, and more palatable. But wild foods are not always available, the supply varying from season to season and from year to year, so don't count too heavily on them when traveling unless you know the resources of the country very well.

Food resources of different environments vary considerably. Probably the best year-round source of survival food is to be found along the seashore between high and low water. Other likely spots are marshes, mud flats, or mangrove swamps; deltas or confluences of rivers; river banks, inland water holes, shores of lakes; margins of forests, natural clearings or abandoned cultivated fields. The poorest locations are dense, continuous forests (especially evergreen forests), high mountains above timberline, and bare ridges.

Animal food will give you more food value for pound than vegetable food. Anything that creeps, crawls, walks, swims, or flies is a possible source of food. Even insects are regarded as choice food by many peoples. Grasshoppers, hairless caterpillars, beetle larvae and pupae, ant eggs and termites are all items of human diet in some countries. Such insects are high in fat. Although you may not have been aware of it, you have undoubtedly eaten insects as contaminants in flour, corn meal, fruits, greens and other stores.

With few exceptions, all animals are edible when freshly killed. Don't eat toads, however, and never risk your life with questionable sea food. Never eat fish with an unpleasant odor or with slimy gills, sunken eyes, flabby flesh or skin. If the flesh remains dented when you press your thumb against it, the fish is probably unsafe to eat. Figure 2-10 shows fish with poisonous flesh; Fig. 2-11 shows poisonous mushrooms.

HUNTING HINTS

The methods you use in hunting should fit your experience and your equipment. The experienced hunter armed with suitable weapons can stalk big game such as deer and solve his food problem with one shot. The novice, unarmed or equipped with unfamiliar weapons, will have to substitute patience and persever-

44

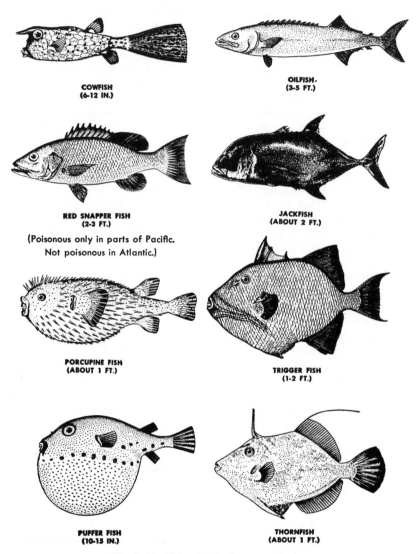

COWFISH
(6–12 IN.)

OILFISH.
(3–5 FT.)

RED SNAPPER FISH
(2–3 FT.)

(Poisonous only in parts of Pacific.
Not poisonous in Atlantic.)

JACKFISH
(ABOUT 2 FT.)

PORCUPINE FISH
(ABOUT 1 FT.)

TRIGGER FISH
(1–2 FT.)

PUFFER FISH
(10–15 IN.)

THORNFISH
(ABOUT 1 FT.)

Fig. 2.10. Fish with Poisonous Flesh.

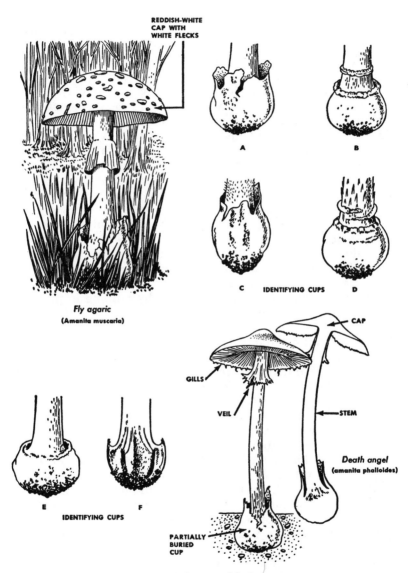

REDDISH-WHITE
CAP WITH
WHITE FLECKS

A

B

C   IDENTIFYING CUPS   D

Fly agaric
(Amanita muscaria)

CAP

GILLS

VEIL

STEM

Death angel
(amanita phalloides)

E   F
IDENTIFYING CUPS

PARTIALLY
BURIED
CUP

Fig. 2.11. Poisonous Mushrooms.

ance for skill if he hopes to live off the land. Both the experienced man and the novice will need a bit of luck.

The best method for a beginner is "still" hunting. Find a place where animals or birds pass or gather, such as a trail, water hole, feeding ground, or roosting area. Hide nearby, downwind so your scent and sound will not be carried to the animals, and wait for the game to come within close range. Remain absolutely motionless unless you see animals which you are sure will not come within range. In this case move upwind toward the game very slowly and quietly. Keep under cover as much as possible. Move only when the animal is feeding or looking away from you. Freeze when he looks your way.

The best time for hunting is early morning or just after sunset. Game is most plentiful and easiest found near water, in forest clearings, in patches of forest or brush in otherwise open land, and in the margins of the forest. Many animals, most of them small but still good eating, live in holes in the ground or in hollow trees. Poke a flexible stick into the hole to find out if it is inhabited. If it is, close off all but one exit and goad the animal into running out. Small animals such as lemmings can sometimes be pulled out of their holes by pushing in a forked flexible stick and rotating it until it entangles the animal's fur or skin.

Fresh-water turtles and frogs are often found on the margins of lakes and streams. Turtles may show a surprising burst of speed in their initial dash for the water but an agile man can usually catch them with his hands even if they reach shallow water—but watch out for mouth and claws. Use two hands to catch a frog; attract its attention with one hand and grab it from behind with the other.

All snakes are edible. Catch snakes by pinning them to the ground with a long forked stick. For safety's sake regard all snakes as poisonous. (Most of them aren't, but why take chances?)

All lizards are edible. In the cool of the morning lizards are slow-moving and can be stalked and clubbed. At any time of the day their habit of lying motionless in the sun makes them good slingshot targets. You can catch them with a baited noose or fishhook.

Salamanders are edible, even in the larval "mud puppy" stage. The axolotl, the larval form of the tiger salamander, is marketed in Mexico. It is reported to taste like eel. Some salamanders have poison glands in their skin. For safety's sake skin all salamanders before eating.

Birds may provide food even for a man without weapons. All bird eggs are edible when fresh, even if they contain embryos. Sea birds and large wading birds, such as egrets, often nest in rookeries. The wading birds usually nest in wooded areas, the sea birds on rocky cliffs or on sand bars. Even single nests of smaller birds may provide enough eggs for a satisfying meal. Eggs can be gathered from the rookeries during the day, the adult birds at night.

Use a flashlight or torch for night hunting of all kinds of game by shining it in the animal's eyes. They will often act as if hypnotized and allow you to get within clubbing distance. Insect eyes are good reflectors so don't be surprised if you see eyes but can't find the rest of the beast.

FISHING

In wilderness areas, except in deserts, fish are probably the most reliable source of food. If you have hook, line, and bait you will not have much trouble getting fish. If you have no equipment, improvise. Line can be obtained by unraveling a parachute shroud line or by twisting threads from cloth or plant fibers. Make hooks from wire or pins and artificial lures from feathers, shiny metal, or brightly colored cloth or plastic. You can usually catch or gather bait at the water's edge. Use worms, shellfish, insects, or particles of any food you have.

In shallow water or in tidal pools fish can sometimes be killed with the back edge of a machete or speared with a sharpened stick. In fresh water the greater depths usually have more fish. The optimum depth depends on many factors, including bottom topography and temperature of different layers of water, so that some experimenting is necessary. In shallow streams the best fishing spots are pools below falls, the foot of rapids, or any deep eddy or sheltered spot to which food would naturally drift. Fish bite best in the early morning or late evening—their natural feeding times. Fishing at night is sometimes good especially if you are using a light to attract the fish.

Shrimp may be lured to the surface of the sea at night by showing a light. Dip them up with a net improvised from parachute cloth. Lobsters and crawfish are bottom feeders in water 10-30 feet deep. Catch them in lobster pots or on a baited hook

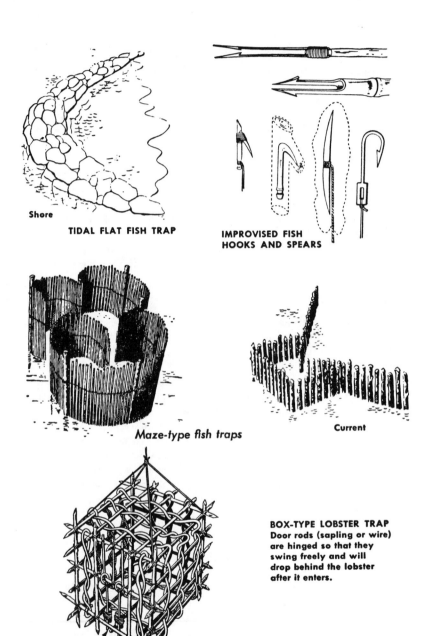

TIDAL FLAT FISH TRAP

IMPROVISED FISH HOOKS AND SPEARS

Shore

Maze-type fish traps

Current

BOX-TYPE LOBSTER TRAP
Door rods (sapling or wire) are hinged so that they swing freely and will drop behind the lobster after it enters.

DOOR

Fig. 2.12. Improvised Fishing Equipment.

When using a hook put a dip net under your catch before you raise it from the water or it will probably let go and fall back into the water. Crabs can be pulled out of shallow water with a dip net or an improvised rake or can be caught in traps baited with any type of meat. Use the heads and offal of your fish for crab bait.

If you think you are in for a long wait before rescue, build a fish trap (Fig. 2-12) to insure a constant food supply. A fish trap is an enclosure with two fencelike walls extending out at an angle from the entrance. In plan, the fish trap resembles a funnel feeding into a box. Fish traps are especially effective in tidal waters, but will catch fish even in fresh water. In lakes and large streams fish tend to feed along the banks in the morning and evening. On the seacoast, fish approach the shore on the incoming tide, schools usually moving parallel with the shore. Select a location for your trap at high tide where natural features can be used to form part of the trap. On rocky shores use natural rock pools; on sandy shores use sand bars and the channels they enclose. The best fishing off sandy beaches is in the lea of an offshore sand bar.

In small shallow streams, build the trap so that the stream is blocked except for a narrow opening into a pen in shallow water. Traps can be made of many materials; usually the most plentiful and lightest material is the best to use (Fig 2-12). On the seashore, rocks and driftwood are usually available. On inland streams and lakes, cut stakes or use brush weighted down with stones. Transfer your catch to an inclosure built in the water and keep them there alive, until you are ready to use them. Fish spoil rapidly; a pen will assure you of a supply of fresh fish.

Nets are more efficient than a hook and line and faster than a fish trap. If you have a seine, attach poles at each end and work it upstream or downstream as fast as possible, moving stones and disturbing the edges and bottom of the stream to frighten fish into the net. Gather the net together quickly so that the fish cannot escape. Place gill nets across the mouths of streams or at right angles to the shore. Mud-bottomed streams can be trampled until roiled and then seined. The mud blinds the fish so that they cannot escape the nets. On narrow streams nets can be used as traps and the fish driven into them. Nets can be improvised with some difficulty from parachute cord or any strong cord. Parachute fabric is not suitable for nets, except dip nets, as water will not pass through the fabric easily.

In fresh waters don't overlook the less mobile forms of edible animal life. Look for crawfish, clams, mussels, and snails under rocks, logs, and overhanging bushes and mud bottoms. River snails, also called periwinkles, are common in U.S. rivers. These snails may be either pointed or globular in form. Boil them and twist the meat out of the shells with a bent pin.

POISONING OF FISH

Catching fish by poisoning them is quite practical if you have the right poison, the most common being the well-known rotenone, the active ingredient in many insecticides. If properly used, one ounce of 12 per cent rotenone (also called derris) will kill every fish for half a mile downstream in a stream 25 feet wide. The limiting factors on using rotenone are (a) temperature of the water and (b) size of the water body in which it is used. Rotenone acts very fast in water 70° F and above but works more slowly in cooler water and is ineffective in water below about 55° F. It is most effective in small streams, ponds, or tidal pools but can be used in back waters of slow moving large rivers or lakes. Fish poisoned by rotenone thrash about as the poison takes effect, then usually float on the surface. Some will sink to the bottom. The poison has no effect on the edibility of the fish.

First mix the rotenone with water to a consistency about that of a milkshake before pouring it into the stream or pool to be poisoned. Follow the poison downstream to pick up the poisoned fish; on small streams build a dam of brush to catch the fish floating downstream. If you carry rotenone in your survival kit keep it in a tightly sealed, opaque container. It loses toxicity when exposed to air or light.

Along the seashore you can make your own fish poison by burning coral or sea shells to make lime. Use the lime to poison fish in small ponds or in tidal pools. Many native groups throughout the world make fish poison from various plants available locally. (Rotenone is extracted from such a fish poison plant.) Locating and using plants requires considerable botanical knowledge and usually some previous experience in preparing the poison; it's much simpler to carry a few ounces of 12 per cent rotenone, obtainable at garden-supply stores, in your survival kit.

SNARES AND DEADFALLS

In an area with much game, snares and traps can provide a survivor's food supply even if he has no firearms. Snares are usually most effective on small game but can be used on animals as large as deer if the size of the snare and its location properly fits the intended victim.

Figures 2-13 and 2-14 show several types of snares and the details of their construction. They are simple to build, requiring no particular skill with tools, but the adjustment of the trigger may be time-consuming and rather nerve-racking to the novice.

Any type of string, flexible cord or wire can be used for snares, but thin copper wire or braided picture wire is usually the choice of experts. Snares of woven wire with a patented self-locking slide, which take up but little space in a survival kit, are commercially available and are recommended for the novice. The expert will prefer to make his own with roll of wire and a pair of pliers.

Set your snares in game trails or frequently used runways which can be recognized by fresh tracks and droppings. In setting the snares, disturb the natural surroundings as little as possible. Where you can, place the snares in narrow places in the trail where the animal will be forced to pass. If there are no natural obstacles that can be used, arrange logs, stones, or brush in such a manner as to force the animal to put his head through the loop of the snare. Set the size of the loop so that the head will pass through easily but the body will not. Set as many snares as you can to increase your chance for a good bag. If you have butchered an animal set snares around the butchering place. Use the entrails and other discards for bait.

Among the various snares illustrated are the "twitch up" and the "drag snare." Both jerk the animal up into the air, giving him less chance to fight free of the snare and also keeping his carcass out of reach of other animals. The twitch up is not recommended for use during cold weather, since the bent sapling may freeze in position and fail to spring up when the trigger is released.

Burrowing animals can be snared with a string noose laid around the entrance to their burrow. Conceal yourself as best you can, keep close watch on the burrow, and jerk the noose tight when the animal puts his head out. The same technique can be used to snare birds by laying the noose on the ground and spreading bait about.

For large game a deadfall is preferable to a snare but its construction requires considerable time and effort and is recommended only where big game is abundant. Build the deadfall in a game trail or at a watering place or salt lick. Use guide poles

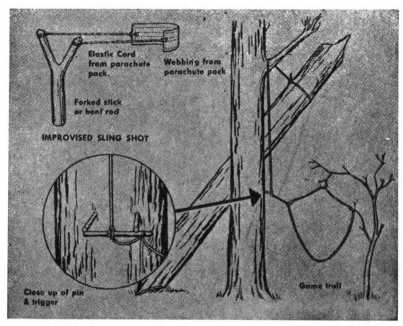

Elastic Cord from parachute pack.

Webbing from parachute pack

Forked stick or bent rod

IMPROVISED SLING SHOT

Close up of pin & trigger

Game trail

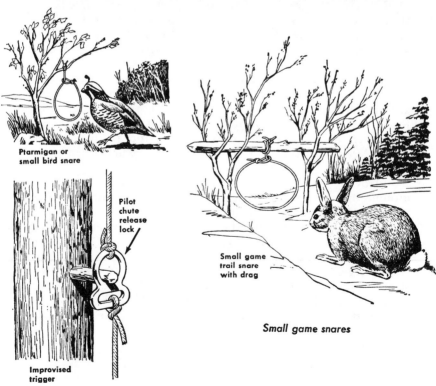

Ptarmigan or small bird snare

Pilot chute release lock

Small game trail snare with drag

Improvised trigger

Small game snares

Fig. 2.13. Snares, Traps, and Deadfalls.

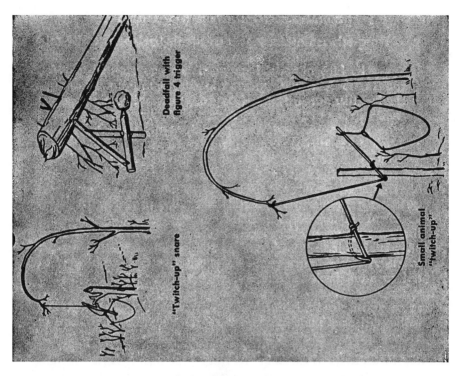

Deadfall with figure 4 trigger

"Twitch-up" snare

Small animal "twitch-up"

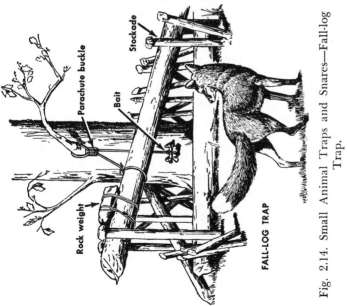

Parachute buckle

Stockade

Bait

Rock weight

FALL-LOG TRAP

Fig. 2.14. Small Animal Traps and Snares—Fall-log Trap.

53

to insure that the log used as a deadfall will hit the right spot, and that the log will fall smoothly. Trigger the deadfall with bait placed so that to get it the animal must expose himself to the deadfall without time to withdraw before it falls, or with a trip line placed across a game trail.

PLANT FOOD

The number of edible wild plants is legion but unfortunately nature does not maintain a constantly stocked larder. Many types of plant food are available only at definite seasons. Even those that are available the year round are widely scattered geographically. The survivor should utilize all the wild plant foods he can find, which, in season, may be sufficient for his needs. But he should not rely on plant food alone in all climates and all seasons, for it simply may not exist. In an area that provides abundant plant food for the permanent resident who can store his harvest, there may be several months each year when very little food can be gathered. Even when food is available the gathering and processing of the food may take more time and energy than the survivor should expend.

Limit your diet to those plants you can positively identify from the illustrations in this book or from your own experience, and to those you see eaten by mammals such as rats, rabbits, squirrels, monkeys, raccoons, and bears. (Birds are not too reliable as indicators. For example, many birds eat mistletoe berries which are poisonous to humans.) Fernald and Kinsay in their *Edible Wild Plants of North America* state that "the number of seriously poisonous plants which might seem tempting to the searcher for salads and potherbs is very limited. They are all readily recognized by the careful observer, and *only the careful observer should ever attempt to use any wild plant for food or to try it on his friends.*"

If you are not sure of your identification of a plant, test it before you eat it in any quantity. First take a mouthful, chew it and hold it in your mouth for a few minutes. If it has a bitter taste or is disagreeable in any other way, spit it out. Obviously a bitter taste is not always an indication of poison—for example, olives and lemons are bitter. But even a nonpoisonous plant with a disagreeable taste can make you ill, so don't take unnecessary chances.

With any plant new to you, even if it is positively identified as edible, eat only a small quantity the first time you try it. If you suffer no ill effects, eat a larger quantity the next day. This procedure will help prevent the disorder known variously as "the GI's," "traveler's tummy," and "the trots," which often affects travelers in strange lands who eat too heartily of unfamiliar foods.

A person who travels a good deal may find it well worth his while to become familiar with edible wild plants. Have someone show you the plants in their natural habitat. Handle each new plant and taste it if possible. By following this procedure you will soon be able to recognize many plants at sight, and, by familiarity with habitats, to spot related species in new areas.

Subsequent chapters in this book list edible and poisonous plants for specific areas. The present chapter discusses only those plants that are widely distributed and are found in several environments.

FERNS

Many ferns are edible, and few if any are poisonous except those that are so bitter as to discourage experiment. Edible kinds occur mainly in forested areas. Some are only a few inches high, while the tree fern of the tropical rain forest may reach one hundred feet in height. The three types of ferns that have edible species are the bracken, the polypody, and the tree fern (Fig. 2-15). The young uncurled fern called "fiddleheads" or "croziers" are a palatable substitute for asparagus. Remove the hairs and scales by rubbing in water, place in fresh water and boil. Some species of bracken have a starchy layer in the root which can be crushed and extracted.

GRASSES

Most of the world lives on grass seeds; wheat, oats, rice, millet, and other cereals are grasses (Fig. 2-16). No grass seed is poisonous, although ergot, a fungus disease of rye and wild grasses, can cause paralysis and death. To avoid ergot poisoning, discard all grain heads having black spurs in place of normal seed grains. Gather the grass seeds by beating the heads of grain with a stick (winnowing) over a collecting cloth. It is generally easier to cut the grass and carry it to a convenient spot for this winnowing, but it can also be performed where the grass is growing. After winnowing, rub the grains to remove husks and spurs.

The grains can be boiled, or heated and parched and then

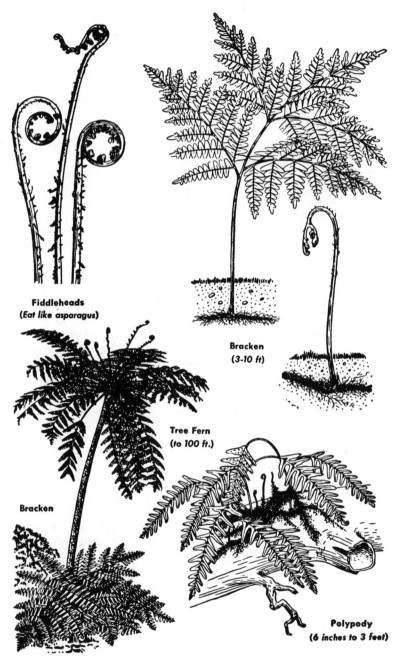

Fiddleheads
(*Eat like asparagus*)

Bracken
(*3-10 ft*)

Tree Fern
(*to 100 ft.*)

Bracken

Polypody
(*6 inches to 3 feet*)

Fig. 2.15. Ferns.

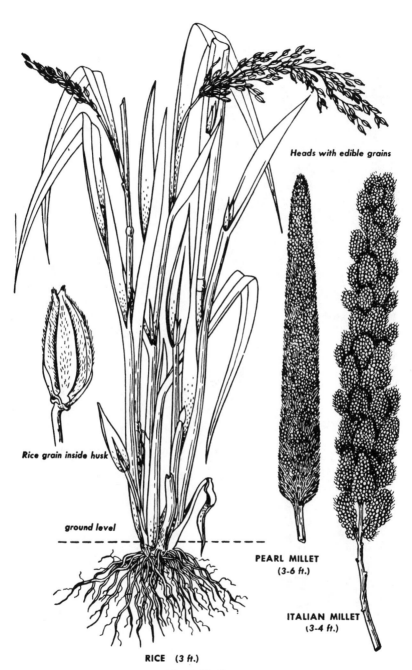

Heads with edible grains

Rice grain inside husk

ground level

RICE   (3 ft.)

PEARL MILLET
(3-6 ft.)

ITALIAN MILLET
(3-4 ft.)

Fig. 2.16. Grasses.

58

Edible
shoots

Edible
shoots

Hollow stem,
use as water vessel

Fig. 2.17 Bamboo.

pounded into a meal. Some grass seeds will pop like popcorn when heated. (*Parching* is cooking by dry heat. The easiest method of parching without burning is to heat the seeds in a container with dry sand. Put the sand in a shallow layer in the heated surface and the seeds on top of the sand.)

BAMBOO

Bamboo, a kind of grass, varies in size from small varieties resembling swamp grass to treelike species over 100 feet tall (Fig. 2-17). It is found in moist tropical and temperate regions. The edible portions of the bamboo are the seeds, and the young shoots which usually appear during and after a rain and which may grow at a rate of over a foot a day. Bamboo does not produce seed every year, but shoots are produced constantly.

To prepare the shoots first remove the tough protective sheaths which are usually covered with reddish, hairlike growths, then boil, changing the water until the bitterness is removed. Be very careful not to eat the red hairs—they can seriously irritate your throat. The seeds can be boiled like rice, or can be pulverized and (with a little water as a binder) formed into cakes.

CATTAIL

Cattail, also called elephant grass (Fig. 2-18), has almost worldwide distribution. It grows in moist areas and along the margins of fresh-water lakes and streams. The core or marrow of the young plant, the pollen, the flower spikes, and the rootstalk are all edible. The rootstalk is most nutritious from autumn to early spring when it is full of stored starch. Prepare by peeling and boiling, or baking. The inner stems of the young plant in early spring can be eaten raw or boiled. The flowering spikes, before the pollen is developed, are edible raw, boiled, as a vegetable or made into a soup. The pollen can be made into a bread and baked or boiled as a porridge.

WATER LILIES

Water lilies (Fig. 2-19) are found on all continents, but are especially plentiful in North and South America, Asia and Africa. Temperate-climate water lilies have large edible rootstalks and the flower floats on the surface of the water. Tropical water lilies have large edible tubers and flowers elevated above the surface of the water. Only one species of water lily, a South African variety, is thought to be poisonous; all others are perfectly safe.

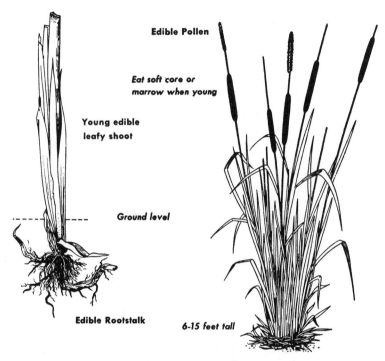

Edible Pollen

Eat soft core or marrow when young

Young edible leafy shoot

Ground level

Edible Rootstalk

6-15 feet tall

Fig. 2.18. Cattail.

The roots are full of starch and most nutritious from autumn to early spring. They often grow in water too deep for wading and must be gathered by diving.

The seeds are available in late summer and fall. The seeds must be taken from the pods—the riper the better—parched for a few minutes, then shelled. Parch the kernels again, causing them to swell, and they are ready to eat. The kernels can also be boiled. The flower buds and the young seed pods can be cooked as a vegetable as can the young stalks and unrolling leaves.

BARK

In spring the inner bark of many trees, especially the pines and other evergreens, is edible and nutritious. The young shoots or growing tips of the evergreens are also edible. Your taste is your guide as to what inner bark to eat, since none is poisonous, although a few are cathartic. In addition to the pines, the inner

TROPICAL WATER LILY   TEMPERATE WATER LILY

Eat young seed pod

Seeds

Rootstalk

Flowers-White, Yellow, Red, Blue

Pod (vertical section)

Fig. 2.19. Water Lily.

bark of willows, poplars, and birches has been used as food. Strip off the outer brown bark and use only the green and white portions of the inner bark, which can be eaten raw or roasted over a slow fire.

NUTS

Nuts are the most concentrated of natural foods. Figure 2-20 shows some widely distributed nuts; you are probably familiar

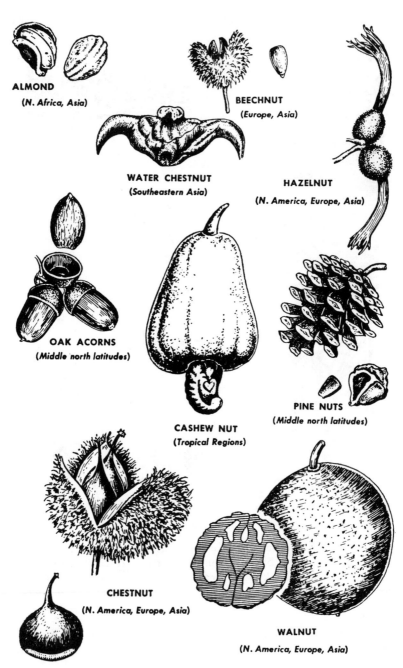

ALMOND
(N. Africa, Asia)

BEECHNUT
(Europe, Asia)

WATER CHESTNUT
(Southeastern Asia)

HAZELNUT
(N. America, Europe, Asia)

OAK ACORNS
(Middle north latitudes)

CASHEW NUT
(Tropical Regions)

PINE NUTS
(Middle north latitudes)

CHESTNUT
(N. America, Europe, Asia)

WALNUT
(N. America, Europe, Asia)

Fig. 2.20. Edible Nuts.

with others. Nuts that have a bitter taste, such as acorns, should be ground into flour and leached with water until the bitter taste is gone. Many evergreens, especially the pines, have edible nuts. If the cones are partially open the nuts can be shaken loose, but if closed, heat the cones to open, then shake the nuts loose.

BERRIES

Many berries are poisonous, although the majority are not. Stick to berries you can recognize.

MUSHROOMS AND FUNGI

Only a relatively few of the fungi are poisonous but there are enough of these varieties to make mushroom hunting a hazardous sport. The novice is advised to shun mushrooms as possible food; their value as such is not worth the gamble. Some edible fungi and the more dangerous poisonous varieties are illustrated in Fig. 2-21 as an aid to identification for those who already have some knowledge of mushrooms.

COOKING

The complete survival kit should contain a good-sized pot that can also be used as a container for rations or other survival items. If you can't carry a pot, carry a large sheet of heavy aluminium foil of the type used to wrap foods for freezing. With this you can do wonders in food preparation. The foil can be wrapped about roots or tubers, which can then be thrown directly into the fire for roasting. Small animals, fish, and birds can be cooked in the same manner as can any piece of meat; or the foil can be used to line a hole in the ground which becomes a pot for *stone boiling*. In stone boiling, stones are heated in the fire then put into the pot with water and food to provide the heat for boiling. The heavy foil can also be shaped into small pots and pans for cooking over the fire or to make a reflector-type oven.

Even without a pot, foil or other cooking gear you should be able to cook anything you can catch, pick, or dig up. Roast foods such as tubers, roots, and fish in the flames or coals of a fire by first coating them with mud or clay. You can also roast foods directly on the coals but you will lose the outer portion by burning. Fish prepared with a clay coating need not be scaled—the skin will come off when the baked clay is removed.

Many foods can be cooked under the fire. Before laying the fire prepare a shallow pit and line it with leaves, or damp cloth.

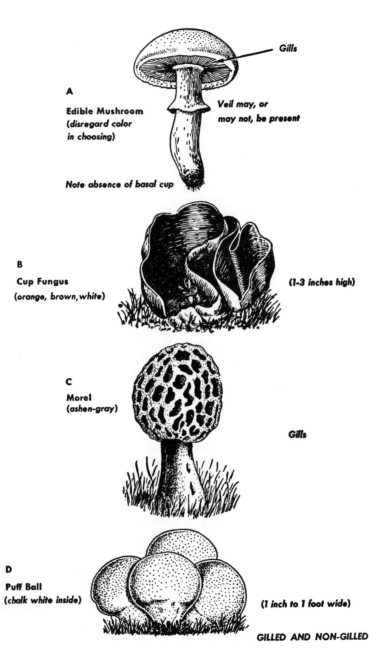

A

Edible Mushroom
*(disregard color
in choosing)*

Gills

*Veil may, or
may not, be present*

Note absence of basal cup

B

Cup Fungus
(orange, brown, white)

(1-3 inches high)

C

Morel
(ashen-gray)

Gills

D

Puff Ball
(chalk white inside)

(1 inch to 1 foot wide)

GILLED AND NON-GILLED

Fig. 2.21. Kinds of Edible Fungi.

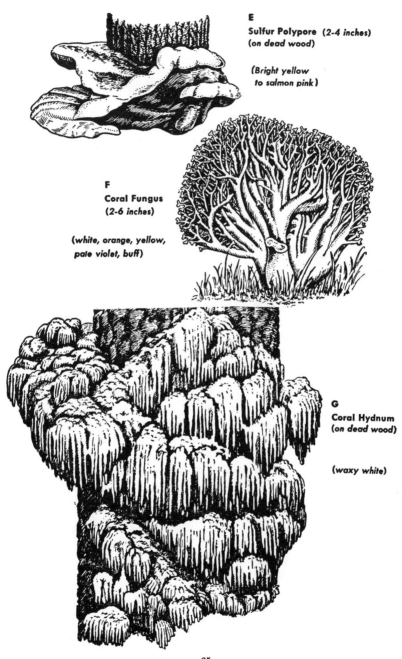

E
Sulfur Polypore *(2-4 inches)*
(on dead wood)

*(Bright yellow
to salmon pink)*

F
Coral Fungus
(2-6 inches)

*(white, orange, yellow,
pale violet, buff)*

G
Coral Hydnum
(on dead wood)

(waxy white)

65

Place the food in the pit, cover first with a layer of leaves or cloth, then with a layer of sand about one-half inch thick. Build the fire directly over the pit and clear away when the food is done. Time for cooking must be determined by experiment. This method is best applicable to foodstuff of small size, such as fresh-water snails.

Heated stones can be used for stone boiling as explained above or to steam cook, clambake style. For steaming dig a pit, place the heated stones at the bottom, lay the food to be cooked directly on the stones, then cover with wet leaves, grass or sea-weed and a layer of sand or dirt. Shellfish, which gape open when thoroughly cooked, need no protection when placed on the stones. Other foods should be wrapped, the nose and appetite serving as guide to cooking time. Most game can be spitted and cooked over an open fire or glowing coals, barbecue style.

Storage of food, especially animal food, is difficult under survival conditions. Recook animal food that you carry over from one meal to the next to avoid any possibility of food poisoning. Cook all meat and fish as soon as possible after killing. Keep fish and shellfish alive as long as possible—by storing fish in a box submerged in water, and keeping shellfish crabs and lobsters in water or in moistened seaweed. Clean fish immediately after killing. Never eat fish with slimy gills, flabby flesh or skin, or an unpleasant odor.

Hang meat high to keep it away from animals and cover it to keep away blow flies. The presence of mold on meat does not mean that it is spoiled; simply brush off or wash off the mold before cooking. Venison and other meat can be sun dried or smoked. Cut it into thin strips for drying. Remember, thorough cooking is the best insurance against food poisoning.

ORIENTATION

Once the survivor of a crash or bailout is sure that he will live he asks himself "Where am I?" If he cannot answer this simple question, too often he rushes off blindly, hoping to find someone who can give him the answer. This is how men become lost—permanently.

If you ask yourself this question and can't come up with a fast answer, sit still and ask yourself, "Where should I be?" This you should know or be able to deduce. You know your point of departure, you know your destination, you know the course you intended to follow, and you know your time on course and your approximate ground speed—so you know where you *should* be.

Pull out your map (if you have one) or draw a map on any available piece of paper or on the ground and mark that spot as the place where you should be. The chances are that you are somewhere close to that point. How close will depend on many factors, such as changes in forecast winds, instrument errors, poor choice of landmarks, and the like. Estimate the maximum error in miles that these factors might have introduced into your computation, and draw a circle with a radius equal to this mileage error around the previously plotted point. You now know you must be within that circle. With this positive knowledge as a starting point, take a look at the terrain. Where within that circle you have plotted would you find this particular landscape? From here on you are on your own—but now you are thinking, not giving way to panic; and by eliminating the places you couldn't be you will probably arrive at a very good idea of where you are.

The process outlined above is essentially *ex post facto* dead reckoning navigation and pilotage. What about celestial navigation? Can't you use the sun and stars to find your position? You certainly can if you are a navigator and if you have a sextant, a watch with the correct time, and the proper navigational tables. But you can't improvise a sextant. In surplus stores you may find some of the survival sextants which were carried in life rafts and aircraft survival kits during World War II. Of several types the most common is the bubble circle sextant developed by the U.S. Naval Observatory. A book of instructions will be packed with these sextants, together with the necessary tables. When used according to instructions some of these little sextants can take sights accurate to within 20 to 30 minutes of arc. If you are interested in navigation get one of these sextants for your survival kit, and for added insurance spend some time learning how to use it.

Although there is no simple procedure by which you can get an accurate position (latitude and longitude) from the sun or the stars, you can establish direction, check the variation of your compass and in some locations establish your approximate latitude and longitude. These procedures are given below.

DIRECTION FROM THE SUN

You can find North by observing the sun when it rises or sets. Table 2-1 shows the true azimuth (true bearing) of the rising sun

TABLE 2-1

Azimuth of the Rising and Setting Sun													Latitude	
0	5	10	15	20	25	30	35	40	45	50	55	60		Date
113	113	113	114	115	116	117	118	121	124	127	133	141	1	JANUARY
112	113	113	113	114	115	116	118	120	123	127	132	140	6	
112	112	112	113	113	114	115	117	119	122	125	130	138	11	
111	111	111	112	112	113	114	116	118	120	124	129	136	16	
110	110	110	111	111	112	113	115	117	119	122	127	133	21	
109	109	109	109	110	111	112	113	115	117	120	124	130	26	
107	107	108	108	108	109	110	111	113	115	117	121	126	1	FEBRUARY
106	106	106	106	107	107	108	109	111	113	115	118	123	6	
104	104	105	105	105	106	107	108	109	110	112	116	120	11	
103	103	103	103	103	104	105	106	107	108	110	112	116	16	
101	101	101	101	101	102	102	103	104	105	107	109	112	21	
99	99	99	99	100	100	100	101	102	103	104	106	108	26	
98	98	98	98	99	99	99	100	100	101	102	104	106	1	MARCH
96	96	96	96	96	97	97	97	98	98	99	100	102	6	
94	94	94	94	94	94	95	95	95	96	96	97	98	11	
92	92	92	92	92	92	92	92	93	93	93	93	94	16	
90	90	90	90	90	90	90	90	90	90	90	90	90	21	
88	88	88	88	88	88	88	88	87	87	87	87	86	26	
86	86	86	86	85	85	85	85	84	84	83	82	81	1	APRIL
84	84	84	83	83	83	83	82	82	81	80	79	77	6	
82	82	82	82	81	81	81	80	80	79	77	76	74	11	
80	80	80	80	79	79	78	78	77	76	74	72	70	16	
78	78	78	78	78	77	76	76	75	73	72	69	66	21	
77	77	76	76	76	75	75	74	72	71	69	66	63	26	
75	75	75	74	74	73	73	72	70	69	66	63	59	1	MAY
74	74	73	73	73	72	71	70	68	67	64	61	56	6	
72	72	72	72	71	70	69	68	67	64	62	58	52	11	
71	71	71	70	70	69	68	67	65	63	60	55	49	16	
70	70	70	69	69	68	67	65	63	61	58	53	47	21	
69	69	69	68	68	67	66	64	62	60	56	51	44	26	
68	68	68	67	66	66	64	63	61	58	54	49	41	1	JUNE
67	67	67	67	66	65	64	62	60	57	53	48	40	6	
67	67	67	66	65	64	63	62	59	56	53	47	39	11	
67	67	67	66	65	64	63	62	59	56	53	47	39	16	
67	67	67	66	65	64	63	62	59	56	53	47	39	21	
67	67	67	66	65	64	63	62	59	56	53	47	39	26	

Table 2-1 (Continued)

Azimuth of the Rising and Setting Sun													Latitude	
0	5	10	15	20	25	30	35	40	45	50	55	60		Date
67	67	67	66	65	64	63	62	59	56	53	47	39	1	
67	67	67	66	66	65	64	62	60	57	53	48	40	6	
68	68	68	67	66	65	64	63	61	58	54	49	41	11	JULY
69	68	68	68	67	66	65	64	62	59	55	50	43	16	
69	69	69	69	68	67	66	65	63	60	57	52	45	21	
70	70	70	70	69	68	67	66	64	62	59	54	48	26	
72	72	72	71	71	70	69	68	66	64	61	57	51	1	
73	73	73	73	72	71	71	69	68	66	63	60	55	6	
75	75	74	74	74	73	72	71	70	68	66	63	58	11	AUGUST
76	76	76	76	75	75	74	73	72	70	68	65	61	16	
78	78	77	77	77	76	76	75	74	72	71	68	65	21	
79	79	79	79	79	78	78	77	76	75	73	71	68	26	
82	82	82	81	81	81	80	80	79	78	77	75	73	1	
83	83	83	83	83	83	82	82	81	81	80	78	77	6	
85	85	85	85	85	85	85	84	84	83	83	82	81	11	SEPTEMBER
87	87	87	87	87	87	87	86	86	86	85	85	84	16	
89	89	89	89	89	89	89	89	89	89	88	88	88	21	
91	91	91	91	91	91	91	91	91	91	92	92	92	26	
93	93	93	93	93	93	93	94	94	94	95	95	96	1	
95	95	95	95	95	96	96	96	97	97	98	99	100	6	
97	97	97	97	97	98	98	99	99	100	101	102	104	11	OCTOBER
99	99	99	99	99	100	100	101	101	102	104	105	108	16	
101	101	101	101	101	102	102	103	104	105	107	109	112	21	
102	102	103	103	103	104	104	105	106	108	109	112	115	26	
104	104	105	105	105	106	107	108	109	110	113	116	120	1	
106	106	106	107	107	108	109	110	111	113	115	119	123	6	
107	107	108	108	108	109	110	111	113	115	117	121	126	11	NOVEMBER
109	109	109	109	110	111	112	113	115	117	120	124	130	16	
110	110	110	111	111	112	113	114	116	119	122	126	133	21	
111	111	111	112	112	113	114	116	118	120	124	128	135	26	
112	112	112	113	113	114	115	117	119	122	125	130	138	1	
112	112	113	113	114	115	116	118	120	123	126	132	140	6	
113	113	113	114	115	116	117	118	121	124	127	133	141	11	DECEMBER
113	113	113	114	115	116	117	118	121	124	127	133	141	16	
113	113	113	114	115	116	117	118	121	124	127	133	141	21	
113	113	113	114	115	116	117	118	121	124	127	133	141	26	
113	113	113	114	115	116	117	118	121	124	127	133	141	31	

Table 1 NOTE: When the sun is rising, the tabulated azimuth is reckoned from North to East. When the sun is setting, the tabulated azimuth is reckoned from North to West.

and the relative bearing of the setting sun for all the months in the year in the Northern and Southern Hemispheres.

An example of how to find North from the rising sun is as follows: On January 26 your position is 50° 00′ N and 165° 06′ W. Entering Table 2-1 at that date and under 50° N latitude, you find the azimuth of the sun to be 120°. Since the sun is rising, you know that this is the true azimuth of the sun from North. Therefore, North will be to your left 120° when you are facing the sun.

To find North from the setting sun, consider the same problem as above. However in this case the azimuth of the sun is not the true azimuth, but a relative bearing. Since the sun sets in the west, North must be to the right of the sun. Therefore North will be 120° to your right when you face the sun.

Table 2-1 does not list every day of the year nor does it list every degree of latitude. If you want accuracy to within one degree of azimuth, you may have to interpolate between the values given in the table. However, for all practical purposes, using the closest day and the closest degree of latitude listed in the table will give you an azimuth which will enable you to hold your course. For example: If you are at 32° north latitude on April 13, the azimuth of the rising sun is actually 79° 22′; however, by entering the table with the closest day listed, 11 April, and the closest latitude, 30°, you get 81° as the azimuth of the rising sun. This value is accurate enough for field purposes.

DIRECTION FROM THE STARS

Polaris. In the Northern Hemisphere one star, Polaris (the Pole Star), is never more than approximately 1° from the Celestial North Pole. In other words, the line from any observer in the Northern Hemisphere to the Pole Star is never more than one degree away from true North. We find the Pole Star by locating the Big Dipper or Cassiopeia, two groups of stars which are very close to Celestial North Pole. The two stars on the outer edge of the Big Dipper, called pointers, point almost directly to Polaris. If the pointers are obscured by clouds, Polaris can be identified by its relationship to the constellation Cassiopeia.

The angular distance of Polaris from the meridian of the observer (the North-South line passing through the observer's position) can also be determined by the relative positions of Cassiopeia and the Big Dipper. Figure 2-23 shows positions of maximum error and minimum error of Polaris. For positions between these

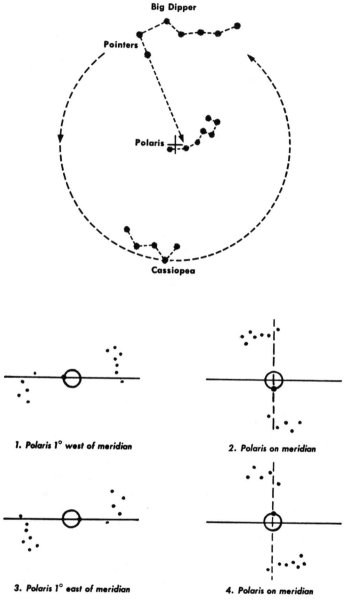

Fig. 2.23. Relationship of Polaris to the Big Dipper and Cassiopea.

extremes, you can make a mental interpolation to find the angular distance of Polaris from the Celestial Pole.

Orion. The constellation of Orion consists of seven stars. The three closest together are called the Belt of Orion (Fig. 2-24). The star through which the North-South line on the diagram passes is exactly on the Celestial Equator. No matter where on earth you are, this star rises due east of you and sets due west.

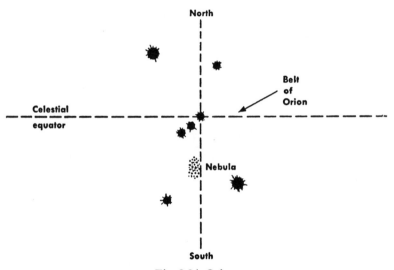

Fig. 2.24. Orion.

Southern Cross. Polaris is not visible in the **Southern Hemisphere**; there the Southern Cross is the most distinctive constellation. As you fly south, the Southern Cross appears shortly before Polaris drops from sight astern. An imaginary line through the long axis of the Southern Cross or True Cross points toward the South Pole. The True Cross should not be confused with a larger cross nearby known as the False Cross, which is less bright although its stars are more widely spaced. The False Cross has a star in the center, making five stars in all, while the True Cross has only four. Two of these are among the brightest stars in the heavens; they are the stars on the southern and eastern arms. Those on the northern and western arms, while bright, are smaller.

There is no star above the South Pole to correspond to Polaris above the North Pole. In fact the point where such a star would be, if one existed, lies in a region devoid of stars. This point is so dark in comparison with the rest of the sky that it is known as the Coal Sack.

Figure 2-25 shows the True Cross and to the west of it the False Cross. Hold the page above your head for orientation and note

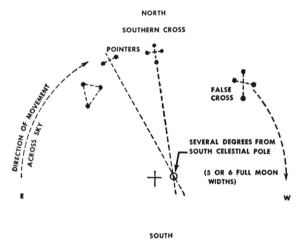

Fig. 2.25. Locating the South Pole.

two very bright stars just to the east of the True Cross. With them and the True Cross as guides, you can locate the spot within the Coal Sack which is exactly above the South Pole.

COMPASS CHECKS

You can use the directions you obtain from sun and stars either directly or as checks on your compass. To check your compass, sight on the heavenly body you are using as a reference (Polaris or the sun) and note the magnetic azimuth of that body. The difference between this magnetic azimuth and the true azimuth of the body will be the magnetic variation at your position. Note this variation and check it with the variation given on your map. (For example, the magnetic azimuth of the sun at midday is 190°. The true azimuth is 180°. 190° minus 180° is 10°. The variation is 10° W. Subtract 10° from your magnetic azimuths to get true azimuth.) If the difference is less than 3°, check again before changing your map. If even a small difference is constant, adjust your map to correspond with your observations.

Checking magnetic variation can be very important to a man down in poorly mapped territory. Much of the earth's surface—especially the arctic—has not been well mapped magnetically. Small local variations which would not trouble an airplane traveling 300 miles an hour can be of great concern to a man traveling 20 miles a day.

If you find a great discrepancy between the variation shown on your map and the variation you observe, first make sure that no iron or electrical fields are close to your compass. Iron may be present in the rocks around you, so look carefully to see whether varying the distance from compass to rock will change your compass reading.

LATITUDE BY THE LENGTH OF THE DAY

When you are in any latitude between 60° N and 60° S, you can determine your exact latitude within 30 nautical miles (½°), if you know the length of the day within one minute. This is true

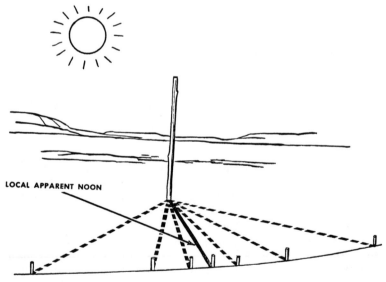

LOCAL APPARENT NOON

Fig. 2.26. Stick-and-shadow method of determining local apparent noon.

throughout the year except for about 10 days before and 10 days after the equinox—approximately March 11-31 and September 13-October 2. During these two periods the day is approximately the same length at all latitudes. To time sunrise and sunset accurately, you must have a level horizon—a land horizon cannot be used.

Find the length of the day from the instant the top of the sun first appears above the ocean horizon to the instant it disappears below the horizon. This instant is often marked by a green flash. Write down the times of sunrise and sunset. Don't count on remembering them. Note that only the length of day counts in the determination of latitude; your watch may have an unknown error and yet serve to determine this factor. If you have only one water horizon, as on a seacoast, find local noon by the stick and shadow method shown in Fig. 2-26. The length of day will be twice the interval from sunrise to noon or from noon to sunset. Knowing the length of day, you can find the latitude by using the nomogram in Fig. 2-27.

LONGITUDE FROM THE SUN

You can find your approximate longitude (within 2° or 3°) by timing the moment when a celestial body passes your meridian. The easiest body to use is the sun. Use one of the following methods.

(a) Put up a stick or rod as nearly vertical as possible, in a level place. Check the alinement of the stick by sighting along the line of a makeshift plumb bob. (To make a plumb bob, tie any heavy object to a string and let it hang free. The line of the string indicates the vertical.) Sometime before midday begin marking the position of the end of the stick's shadow. Note the time for each mark. Continue marking until the shadow definitely lengthens. The time of the shortest shadow is the time when the sun passed the local meridian or local apparent noon. You will probably have to estimate the position of the shortest shadow by finding a line midway between two shadows of equal length, one before noon and one after.

(b) If you get the times of sunrise and sunset accurately on a water horizon, local noon will be midway between these times.

(c) Erect two plumb bobs approximately 1 foot apart so that both strings line up on Polaris, much the same as a gun sight. Plumb bobs should be set up when Polaris is on the meridian and has no east-west correction. The next day, when the shadows of the two plumb bobs coincide, they will indicate local apparent noon.

Mark down the Greenwich time of local apparent noon. Green-

TABLE TWO
EQUATION OF TIME

Date	Eq. of Time*	Date	Eq. of Time*	Date	Eq. of Time*
Jan. 1	−3.5 min.	May 2	+3.0 min.	Oct. 1	+10.0 min.
2	−4.0	14	+3.8	4	+11.0
4	−5.0	May 28	+3.0	7	+12.0
7	−6.0			11	+13.0
9	−7.0	June 4	+2.0	15	+14.0
12	−8.0	9	+1.0	20	+15.0
14	−9.0	14	0.0	Oct. 27	+16.0
17	−10.0	19	−1.0		
20	−11.0	23	−2.0	Nov. 4	+16.4
24	−12.0	June 28	−3.0	11	+16.0
Jan. 28	−13.0			17	+15.0
		July 3	−4.0	22	+14.0
Feb. 4	−14.0	9	−5.0	25	+13.0
13	−14.3	18	−6.0	Nov. 28	+12.0
19	−14.0	July 27	−6.6		
Feb. 28	−13.0			Dec. 1	+11.0
		Aug. 4	−6.0	4	+10.0
Mar. 4	−12.0	12	−5.0	6	+9.0
8	−11.0	17	−4.0	9	+8.0
12	−10.0	22	−3.0	11	+7.0
16	−9.0	26	−2.0	13	+6.0
19	−8.0	Aug. 29	−1.0	15	+5.0
22	−7.0			17	+4.0
26	−6.0	Sep. 1	0.0	19	+3.0
Mar. 29	−5.0	5	+1.0	21	+2.0
		8	+2.0	23	+1.0
Apr. 1	−4.0	10	+3.0	25	0.0
5	−3.0	13	+4.0	27	−1.0
8	−2.0	16	+5.0	29	−2.0
12	−1.0	19	+6.0	Dec. 31	−3.0
16	0.0	22	+7.0		
20	+1.0	25	+8.0		
Apr. 25	+2.0	Sep. 28	+9.0		

* Add plus values to mean time and subtract minus values from mean time to get apparent sun time.

wich time is the time on your watch corrected for the time zone you are using. For example, if your watch is on eastern standard time (75th Meridian time) add 5 hours to your watch time to get Greenwich time. The next step is to correct this observed time of meridian passage for the equation of time—that is, the number of minutes the real sun is ahead of or behind the mean sun. (The mean sun was invented by astronomers to simplify the problems of measuring time. It rolls along the equator at a constant rate of 15° per hour. The real sun is not so considerate; it changes its angular rate of travel around the earth with the seasons.)

Table 2-2 gives the values in minutes of time to be added to or subtracted from mean (watch) time to get apparent (sun) time.

Now that you have the Greenwich time of local noon, you can find the difference of longitude between your position and Greenwich by converting the interval between 1200 Greenwich and your local noon from time to arc. Remember that 1 hour equals 15° of longitude, 4 minutes equal 1° of longitude, and 4 seconds equal 1' of longitude.

Example: Your watch is on Eastern Standard Time. It normally loses 30 seconds a day. You haven't set it for 4 days. You time local noon at 15:08 on your watch on 4 February.

Watch correction is 4 × 30 seconds, or plus 2 minutes. Zone time correction is plus 5 hours. Greenwich time is 15:08 plus 2 minutes plus 5 hours or 20:10. The equation of time for 4 February is minus 14 minutes. Local noon is 20:10 minus 14 minutes or 19:56 Greenwich. Difference in time between Greenwich and your position is 19:56 minus 12:00 or 7:56. A time of 7:56 equals 119° of longitude.

Since your local noon is later than Greenwich noon, you are west of Greenwich. Your longitude then is 119° W.

TRAVELING FOR AID OR RESCUE

If you have considered carefully all the factors involved and decide that traveling for help is better than staying where you are, then prepare as carefully as possible for the trip. Plot your expected route on your map. If you don't have a map, draw one—even if it is only two marks on a piece of paper.

If you have only an aeronautical chart copy the section of the chart covering your intended route, on a much larger scale. (Charts intended for aircraft that fly hundreds of miles an hour are hardly suitable for a hiker doing three miles an hour.) On the map mark your expected camp sites. Make a copy of the map to leave as a guide for the rescue party that may be looking for you.

Gather all your gear together and decide how much you want to take with you. You should travel as light as possible, yet not leave anything behind that you will really need, such as matches or a lighter, maps, compass, watch, signaling equipment, knife, canteen (full if possible), available food, first-aid kit, and extra socks. A gun and ammunition, fishing gear, extra clothing, gasoline for fuel, fabric from your parachute, wire and shroud lines from your chute are necessities in some environments but can be dispensed with in others. You may want to take your "Mae West" with you to help in crossing rivers. Keep the total weight of the items you select to below 30 lb., considerably below that amount if you can. After you have made your selection review the need for each item, keeping in mind that you will have to carry this gear each foot of the way.

Make a pack from your parachute harness and fabric or other available cloth. Use a piece of cloth large enough to double as a shelter. Arrange the pack so that the weight falls on your shoulders, not on your lower back. Rig a tumpline on the pack to take some of the weight off your shoulders, and walk around a bit with the pack in place before taking the trail. You will probably find that the pack needs adjustments. (See Fig. 2-22.)

Before leaving the camp site, construct ICOA Signal Number 7 (Fig. 2-4, page 29), indicating your direction of travel as a guide for rescue aircraft. This is most important and may save you many weary hours of travel by speeding up your rescue.

Assuming that you know the approximate course you want to follow, what is the best method of making that course good? In flat, featureless terrain you may be able to follow a compass course. In mountainous terrain, a compass course is usually not practical, so select landmarks along your intended route and travel from landmark to landmark. Whatever your method, be sure to keep an accurate record of your progress on your sketch map.

When following a compass course choose two easily visible points, trees or other prominent objects, exactly on the line you want to follow and as far apart as possible. Before reaching the first point select a third point in the same line, on reaching the second point select a fourth, and so on. Check your back trail occasionally to make sure you are traveling in a straight line and

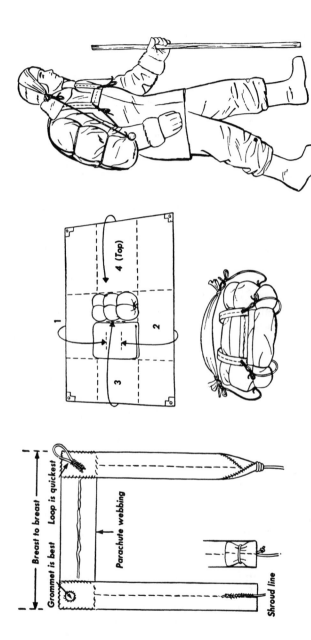

Fig. 2.22. Pack Strap—Pack—Tumpline.

79

to give you a view of landscape features you will want to recognize if you have to backtrack.

Since your object should be to arrive at your destination in good shape rather than to break speed records, take it easy. Travel a set period of time, then rest for a few minutes. When resting, keep faced in the direction you are traveling or mark your direction by a pointer of some kind. Keep up a steady pace when you are traveling—you'll go farther and last longer. Take the easy route up slopes, at a slant and zigzagging, instead of spending your strength in a straightaway climb. Usually you should go around obstacles rather than through or over them. Detour around swamps, mud flats, and heavy brush thickets. Go around ravines and gullies rather than climbing down and then up again. Whenever you do make such a detour, be sure to backsight to your last identifiable landmark to re-establish your course.

When traveling in a party keep together and adjust the pace to that of the slowest man. At rest periods count noses. Put one of the stronger men at the rear of the party to help anyone who lags behind. In poor visibility and during storms, make camp while there is still light and wait for better conditions before resuming travel. Get shelter up and your fires built before darkness falls. Unpack only what you need and keep your gear together so you can repack with a minimum of confusion in the morning. If you are traveling in a group, have tasks assigned to each person so that work will not be duplicated or important tasks left undone.

When crossing streams carry a pole and probe the stream bottom ahead of you to avoid holes. Avoid swamps when you can, but if you must cross one avoid slick spots and mud holes—step on clumps of grass and exposed roots. If you do get mired in the mud lie flat on your stomach and swim out of trouble. The mud will not suck you down as the old wives' tales would have it; in fact you will be more buoyant in mud than water, and "swimming" in mud, although somewhat messy, carries no risk of "drowning."

Use almost the same technique in quicksand that you do in mud—throw yourself flat on your back if you find yourself sinking. If you are carrying a pole (as you should be) put it underneath your shoulders for additional support, then pull your legs out of the sand and roll or crawl back to firmer footing.

In some areas, such as lowland jungles, rivers will offer the easiest and surest route to civilization. Use your rubber life raft if you have one, or build your own raft of logs. Good manageable dimensions for a raft are five to seven feet wide by 10 to 14 feet long. Use sound light logs six to eight inches in diameter cut to the same length as the raft. Check floating quality of each log before adding it to the raft. Bind the logs together with shroud lines from your parachute, wire salvaged from the aircraft, vines, or braided bark or grass. Erect a canopy of parachute cloth or brush to provide protection from sun and rain.

When using a raft travel only during daylight hours, and keep close to shore, staying out of rough water and sheer-walled gorges. At the slightest hint of trouble head for shore. On a raft use a pole in shallow water and an oar in deep water.

3

Arctic and Subarctic: Geographical and Environmental Considerations

THE FAR NORTH

The Far North is commonly divided into an arctic region and a subarctic region—that is, not by the Arctic Circle (lat. 69° 33′ N), but by climatic differences. (See map, Fig. 3-1, page 83.)

Arctic Region. The boundaries of the arctic region are usually delimited on the basis of temperature rather than latitude. It is the region in which the mean temperature for the warmest summer month is less than 50° F. In many places this temperature boundary is located only very roughly, but so far as is known it coincides fairly well with the northern limit of the forest. The North American arctic region includes the northern coasts of Alaska and Canada, the Canadian Arctic Archipelago, much of Labrador, and all of Greenland.

Subarctic Region. The North American subarctic region is a belt of variable width south of the arctic region. Within it the mean temperature of the warmest month is higher than 50° F. Newfoundland, southwestern Labrador, most of Alaska, and most of interior Canada are subarctic.

Forests are characteristic of the subarctic region, though there are a few areas that are treeless. In the arctic region there are no forests. Shrub willows, however, are common and in some places they grow in clumps seven to eight feet high.

The arctic region is characterized by vast stretches of treeless land called "tundra." Tundra has a variable cover of grasses, lichens and shrubs. Unlike prairie country which it generally resembles, tundra to a large extent is poorly drained and marshy. Tussocks or hummocks of vegetation abound in the marshy areas and the soil is everywhere poor.

Most of the tundra and parts of the forested subarctic region are permanently frozen a few feet beneath the surface. During

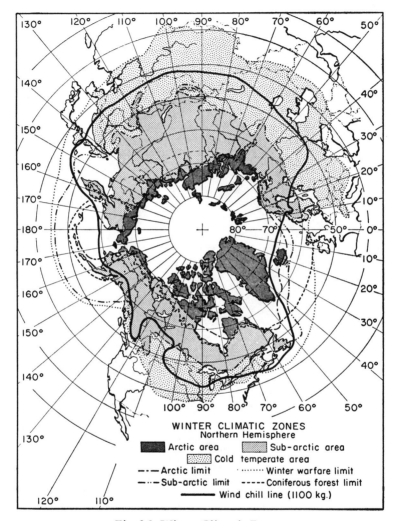

Fig. 3.1. Winter Climatic Zones.

the summer the ground thaws to a depth of a foot or more, but because of the underlying frozen ground water cannot sink below the thawed layer. Consequently the ground is kept moist in many places. Frozen ground (*permafrost*, Fig. 3-2) is thus responsible for the marshy character of the tundra and for the poor drainage

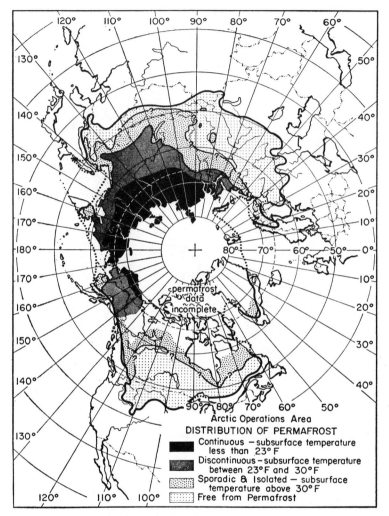

Fig. 3.2. Distribution of Permafrost.

of large parts of the Far North. Also, it is in part responsible for the many lakes.

The Yukon and Mackenzie Rivers, draining the Far North, are among the largest rivers in the world. Lesser streams are numerous, but most of them are quite small and wander aimlessly. This is particularly true of the areas underlain by permanently frozen ground. Following a small stream, therefore, may lead you nowhere at all.

Because drainage is generally poor and because permanently frozen ground prevents moisture from seeping far beneath the surface, both rain and melt water from snow or ice are likely to swell streams rapidly, causing frequent floods. Damming of a partly thawed stream or river by ice and debris almost invariably causes an already swollen stream to overflow its banks and inundate a large area on either side. Therefore spring with its melting snows and break-up of rivers and lakes is generally the time when floods are most common—and the worst time of the year for travel on foot.

In the Far North lakes are abundant. Most of them are the direct result of poor drainage induced by the presence of permanently frozen ground. In areas where bedrock is at or near the surface, the major cause of the lake basins was the scooping action of the former great glaciers of the Ice Age that plowed their way across many far northern regions.

The numerous lakes are in large part responsible for the development of transportation and communication in the Far North. They afford favorable emergency landing sites and bases for pontoon-equipped planes in the summer, and for ski-equipped planes in the winter. For several weeks during the spring break-up and autumn freeze, lake and river landings are hazardous.

There are two basic kinds of glaciers—*ice caps* and *valley glaciers.*

Ice caps, as their name implies, cover large areas of land without regard to the underlying topography. An outstanding example is the Greenland Ice Cap, the largest in the Northern Hemisphere. Much smaller ice caps cover parts of Baffin Island, Bylot Island, and Ellesmere Island, in the eastern part of the Canadian arctic. The western part of the Canadian arctic is free of them, with the possible exception of Meighen Island in the far northern section.

Valley glaciers are essentially rivers of ice confined to valleys. A valley glacier may be connected with an ice cap much as a stream is connected with a lake, or it may be an independent unit. Valley glaciers occur wherever there are ice caps; they also are found in the mountains of Alaska and the Yukon. All glaciers move with a slow flowing motion, some almost imperceptibly and others at the rate of ten feet or more a day.

The brittle surfaces of both ice caps and valley glaciers are characterized by great gaping cracks called *crevasses*. They may be from ten to a hundred feet in depth, and are caused by the slow flowing movement of the ice far beneath. Generally speaking, the steeper the slope and the more irregular the bed of the glacier, the greater the profusion of crevasses. They are the more dangerous because they are often covered with snow. A fall into a deep crevasse is usually fatal.

NATURAL SUBDIVISIONS OF THE NORTH AMERICAN ARCTIC

THE STATE OF ALASKA

The greater part of our 49th state is not arctic but subarctic. The truly arctic part is more or less confined to a broad zone that includes the coast from the Seward Peninsula to Point Barrow, and eastward to the International Boundary at Demarcation Point. The Brooks Range is part of this zone, as is Seward Peninsula, whose tip, Cape Prince of Wales, lies only 57 miles from Siberia on the opposite side of the shallow Bering Strait.

Coastal Region. The arctic coast of the State of Alaska is generally low and flat except for parts of Seward Peninsula and the vicinity of Cape Lisburne. For example, Cape Prince of Wales has an altitude of 2300 feet, while the altitude of Cape Lisburne is 850 feet. In the vicinity of Point Barrow the low coast reaches its greatest width. Here there is a wide triangular plain with the tip of the triangle near Barrow on the north and the base abutting against the Brooks Range on the south. The region near the coast is said to have considerable oil reserves. Harbors are few along the entire coast from Seward Peninsula to Demarcation Point. In many places, too, the bottom is gently shelving so that large boats have to stand off some distance from shore.

Brooks Range. The Brooks Range extends roughly east-west in the northern arctic area of the state. Actually it is not a single range but a series of ranges, some of which reach altitudes of more than 8,000 feet. Both the western and eastern ends of the range approach close to the coast, the western end being near Cape Lisburne and the eastern end near Demarcation Point. The middle section, however, lies farther inland, being about 125 miles south of Point Barrow. The Brooks Range is not well known, but should be counted among the great mountain ranges of North America.

CANADA: GENERAL

Arctic Canada includes the Canadian Arctic Archipelago and most of the north coast of Canada. Both regions as a unit are commonly divided into the western arctic and the eastern arctic. The boundary between the two is rather indefinite but is generally regarded as lying along the axis of Boothia Peninsula and Somerset Island. The basis of distinction between the western arctic and the eastern arctic is twofold: first, the regions themselves differ topographically and second, they usually are approached from different directions and there is almost no travel between them except by air.

Western Arctic. The western Canadian arctic comprises the mainland coast from Demarcation Point to Boothia Peninsula, and the islands to the North. The largest of these is Victoria Island—second in size in the entire archipelago and about as large as Great Britain. Other important islands are Banks Island and Melville Island.

Most of the western Canadian arctic is low-lying. There are few mountains and consequently hardly any glaciers. In a few localities, however, there are perennial snowbanks. The mainland is rocky in many places, except around the mouth of the Mackenzie River, most of the rock being granite or gneiss. On the other hand, the islands consist chiefly of sedimentary rocks widely concealed beneath tundra vegetation, mud, and sand.

Boat travel to Canada's western arctic is chiefly via the Mackenzie River, and to a much lesser extent via the arctic coast of Alaska. Commercial flying is well developed, the Mackenzie Valley being the major air route. A branch route goes to Coppermine on Coronation Gulf just south of Victoria Island. Within the western Canadian arctic there is active communication by boat as far east as Cambridge Bay at the southeast end of Victoria Island and much less frequent communication as far east as Boothia Peninsula. Since the establishment of the DEW (Distant Early Warning radar net) line there is much east-west traffic between stations.

Eastern Arctic. The eastern Canadian arctic comprises most of the mainland coast from Boothia Peninsula to Labrador, and the islands to the north. Of these, Baffin Island—about two and a half times as large as Great Britain—is the largest in the Canadian arctic, Ellesmere Island the third largest.

In contrast with the western Canadian arctic, the eastern Canadian arctic is generally high and in places very rugged. The east coast of Baffin Island and the eastern and northern parts of Ellesmere Island have mountains whose maximum altitudes approximate 8000 feet on Baffin Island and 11,000 feet on Ellesmere Island. Both islands have numerous valley glaciers in their mountainous parts, together with small ice caps. An ice shelf fringes the northern coast of Ellesmere Island. Glaciers are also present on Bylot Island, Devon Island, and Axel Heiberg Island. Well-developed fiords penetrate the coasts of most of these islands, especially Baffin Island and Ellesmere Island. Bare rock surfaces are more common in Canada's eastern arctic, particularly in the mountainous areas, than in the west, yet low tundra-covered regions also occur. On the mainland, for instance, the entire west coast of Hudson Bay is low, flat, and in most places characterized by tundra.

Travel to Canada's eastern arctic is by railroad to Churchill on the west side of Hudson Bay, by boat past the Labrador coast, or by airplane. Surface travel within the region itself extends as far west as Fort Ross, a Hudson's Bay Company post on Bellot Strait. This strait divides Boothia Peninsula from Somerset Island, and was the chief point of contact with the western Canadian arctic before the establishment of the DEW line.

Northeastern Labrador. Although Labrador lies entirely south of the Arctic Circle, its northeastern part is truly arctic. This part of Labrador, like much of Canada's eastern arctic, is mountainous, particularly in the northern part where the Torngat Mountains reach a maximum altitude of just over 5000 feet. Fiords, which penetrate the coast in many places in the northern half, are relatively rare in the southern half, but one—Hamilton Inlet—is several times as large as any other in Labrador. Although no trees grow in the northernmost part of Labrador, the southern part is forested. Practically all of Labrador is formed of granite or gneiss.

GREENLAND: GENERAL

Greenland is not only the largest of the arctic lands but also the largest island in the world. More than three-fourths of it is occupied by an ice cap that covers all of the interior and leaves only a relatively narrow ice-free strip along the coasts.

Ice Cap. Next to the Antarctic Ice Cap, the Greenland Ice Cap is the largest in the world. It is roughly dome-shaped, reaches a maximum altitude of about 10,000 feet, and is constantly but very slowly flowing outward. Not much is known concerning its thickness except that in some places it is probably 6000 to 7000 feet thick. Near the margin of the ice cap there are numerous crevassed areas, which make travel very dangerous and in some localities almost impossible. Crevasses have also been reported from a few places in the interior. Many valley glaciers, extending outward from the icecap to the coast, are the outlets through which the slowly flowing ice is discharged from the icecap into the sea.

Coastal Region. Most of the Greenland coast extends out beyond the ice cap, although there are a few stretches, especially in northwest and northeast Greenland, where the ice cap descends directly to the sea. Much of the coastal zone is mountainous. On the east coast individual peaks rise to altitudes of 10,000 to 12,000 feet. Watkins Gunnbjorns) Mountain (lat. 29° 50', long. 68° 55') with an altitude of 12,139 feet is the highest known, but there may be others not yet measured that are even higher. On the other coasts maximum altitudes are generally less than 6000 feet. Here and there isolated peaks (*nunataks*), surrounded by ice, project through the margin of the icecap.

Fiords cut deeply into the Greenland coast, many of them with glaciers at their heads. These glaciers discharge large icebergs which drift out to sea and become dangerous to navigation. The East Greenland fiord system is one of the most imposing in the world. Scoresby Sound, which extends inland more than 150 miles, is the longest fiord in the world, and Franz Josef Fiord with its precipitous varicolored walls exceeds the splendor of the Grand Canyon.

NATURAL SUBDIVISIONS
OF THE NORTH AMERICAN SUBARCTIC REGION

ALASKA: GENERAL

The subarctic part of Alaska, which comprises most of the State, is divided into two main regions—the subarctic coastal region and the interior region, each differing in topography and climate.

Subarctic Coastal Region. The subarctic coastal region comprises the territory south of the Seward Peninsula, the Aleutian Islands, the Alaska Peninsula, and the south coast of Alaska.

The region south of the Seward Peninsula is generally low-lying. It includes the broad deltas and alluvial plains of the Yukon and Kuakokwim Rivers. The Aleutian Islands and their continuation in the Komandorski Islands form an almost perfect arc, concave to the north, stretching across the northern Pacific Ocean to Kamchatka. Formed of volcanic rocks, the islands are generally rugged and mountainous. Altitudes of 4000 to 5000 feet are common, several mountains being considerably higher. Glaciers radiate from many of the peaks, most of which are volcanic cones, of which some are still active.

The Alaska Peninsula, a mainland continuation of the Aleutian Islands, is much like the island arc in general character. Altitudes, however, are commonly greater. For instance, Mt. Illiamna, a volcano, and some other peaks are more than 10,000 feet high.

The south coast of Alaska is composed of rocks different from those of the Aleutian arc and has no recent volcanoes; it is, however, even more mountainous. The Kenai Mountains rise to more than 5000 feet, and Mt. Marcus Baker in the Chugach Mountains farther inland is 13,250 feet in altitude. Farther southeast the St. Elias Range boasts Mt. Logan (in neighboring Yukon Territory) and Mt. St. Elias with altitudes of 19,850 and 18,008 feet respectively. This region contains large glaciers, including the great Malaspina and Hubbard Glaciers.

Interior Region. The mountains of the southern coastal region of Alaska continue into the interior, forming an arc known as the Alaska Range. Mt. McKinley, the crowning summit of this range, has an altitude of 20,300 feet and is thus the loftiest peak in North America. Farther north the broad valley of the Yukon River is the major feature of the Interior Region. The river itself, with a length of about 2000 miles, is one of the major waterways of the world and is navigable into Yukon Territory by steamboats of Mississippi type. The valley is fertile in many places and is the center of population.

CANADA: GENERAL

A very large part of the Canadian mainland is subarctic. Even the north coast is, in a few places, subarctic rather than arctic.

The principal natural regions are the Western Mountains and the Interior Lowland, the latter comprising the Mackenzie River Valley and the broad expanse of generally flat country that characterizes the rest of the subarctic mainland.

Western Mountains. The little-known Mackenzie Mountains and some other ranges of northwestern Canada, together known as the Western Mountains, represent the northward continuation of the Rocky Mountains of the United States and southern Canada. Altitudes of 7000 to 8000 feet are common, and some of the peaks carry snow the year round.

Interior Lowland. The Mackenzie River, like the Yukon, is one of the great rivers of the world. It is navigable for steamboats from the Arctic Ocean to Fort Smith on the Slave River south of Great Slave Lake, a distance of 1300 miles. In many places the Mackenzie Valley is well forested and fertile, and in the vicinity of Fort Norman it is rich in oil. Gold and other mining developments are located near Great Slave Lake and to a lesser extent near Lake Athabaska. Gigantic Great Bear Lake, noted for its radium ore, is separated from the Mackenzie Valley proper by a short low range of mountains. Other smaller lakes are scattered throughout the region of the Mackenzie Valley.

East of the Mackenzie Valley lies a broad, nearly flat plain whose surface has a maximum altitude of about 1400 feet and slopes gently downward to sea level around Hudson Bay. The northeastern part is treeless and truly arctic. The subarctic remainder is forested and forms a broad basin around James Bay, the southern extension of Hudson Bay. Most of this part of the interior lowland is characterized by granite, gneiss, and other similar rocks. Some of these rocks are so highly mineralized that they support several of the richest mining camps in the world. Countless lakes constitute another notable feature of the region.

Southwestern Labrador. Unlike much of the northeastern (Arctic) part of Labrador, the southwestern subarctic part is well forested. It is also less mountainous, and gradually merges with the subarctic interior lowland of Canada.

Newfoundland. The island of Newfoundland has a very irregular shoreline, similar to that of Labrador. However, the coast itself is generally much less abrupt, and the island as a whole is low-lying in comparison with Labrador. The most marked topographic feature, aside from the irregular fiordlike shoreline, is the Long Range, which extends northeast-southwest along the west coast, and reaches altitudes of 2000 to 3000 feet.

THE NORTHERN SEAS

General. The principal northern seas of the Western Hemisphere are the Arctic Ocean, Greenland Sea, Bearing Sea, Baffin Bay, and Hudson Bay. The first three also are common to the Eastern Hemisphere. Each of these seas occupies a distinct basin or otherwise easily delimited region, and each is essentially arctic.

Arctic Ocean. The Arctic Ocean is by far the largest of the northern seas. Parts of it are given local names such as the Beaufort Sea on the north coast of Alaska and the East Siberian Sea north of Siberia. The Arctic Ocean fills the arctic basin, which in turn occupies the central part of the polar region. In this respect the arctic differs markedly from the antarctic, whose polar region is a high continent rather than a basin. Surrounding the arctic basin is a continental shelf over which the ocean extends which lies at a depth of several hundred feet and is of varying width. Off Siberia, abreast of the New Siberian Islands, it is 435 miles wide, but off Point Barrow its width is only 60 miles. Most of the Canadian arctic islands lie on this shelf.

Greenland Sea. North of Iceland and between East Greenland and Spitsbergen lies the Greenland Sea. Although its surface waters have a broad connection with the Arctic Ocean, it occupies a distinct basin, and for this reason is regarded as a separate body of water. Its maximum depth is almost 16,000 feet.

Bering Sea. Bering Sea lies north of the Aleutian Islands and separates Alaska from Siberia. It is divided into two parts—a southwestern basin with depths as great at 13,000 feet, and a northeastern shelf with an average of only about 330 feet. Bering Sea connects with the Arctic Ocean through the Bering Strait, which is both narrow (57 miles wide) and shallow (not much more than 150 feet at the narrowest part).

Baffin Bay. Baffin Bay separates Baffin Island on the west from Greenland on the east. It has an independent basin more than 6000 feet deep. On the north and west, Baffin Bay connects with the Arctic Ocean through various channels of the Canadian Arctic Archipelago, and on the south it joins the Atlantic Ocean through Davis Strait.

Hudson Bay. Hudson Bay is strictly a shallow inland sea. It reaches the North Atlantic Ocean through Hudson Strait, a lane 500 miles long that separates Baffin Island from Labrador. Foxe Basin, a northern continuation of Hudson Bay, connects through the narrow Fury and Hecla Strait with the channels of the Canadian Arctic Archipelago. Depths in Hudson Bay are generally less than 650 feet. The bottom is gently shelving so that the water is shallow for some distance off shore. As a result, retreating tides uncover extensive mudflats.

ICE OF THE NORTHERN SEAS

General. There are two principal varieties of sea ice—one that is constantly moving (*pack ice*), and a generally immobile kind (*fast ice*). Both types consist of frozen sea water and are therefore salt to begin with, but, both eventually lose their salt content and become fresh. They are *not* icebergs, which are always fresh and are commonly more massive than sea ice.

Fast Ice. Fast ice remains immobile except when it breaks up during the summer. It forms in bays and straits free of strong currents that otherwise would keep the ice in motion. Generally fast ice affords better foot travel routes and emergency landing places than does pack ice.

Pack Ice. One of the outstanding features of arctic seas is the ever-moving pack ice. This includes not only individual ice floes (cakes of ice a few feet to a few hundred yards in diameter) but also great icefields whose limits cannot be seen from a high masthead. No matter how extensive, the pack ice is always moving under the influence of currents. Sooner or later during their movement, fields and floes crack apart and develop narrow *lanes* and broad *leads* of open water, even in the middle of winter. However, winter leads soon freeze over, forming smooth patches of ice. Sometimes instead of being pulled apart the fields and floes are telescoped together by the currents, with a force strong enough to crush the stoutest ship.

SUBARCTIC TOPOGRAPHY—EURASIA

PLAINS, MOUNTAINS AND DRAINAGE

Plains. The subarctic plains of Eurasia are of the same essential character as those of North America, the differences in vegetation being minor. The largest continental subarctic plain in this area is found in western Siberia.

Mountains. Many of the Eurasian mountain ranges extend from the subarctic to the arctic zone. The differences between these zones become apparent only gradually; tree lines are at lower altitudes, and the vegetative cover becomes more sparse until it is nearly nonexistent in the higher elevations of the arctic.

The Kjolen Mountains, which form the boundary between Norway and Sweden, change vegetative cover northward from shrub and low bush to tundra. The arctic and subarctic regions west of the Yenisei River have been exposed to continental and alpine glaciation. The highlands of northwestern Europe extending into the Union of Soviet Socialist Republics are an ice-scoured rocky plateau with glacial lakes and poorly drained, boggy land in the lower areas. The Ural Mountains, north-south parallel ranges approximately 6000 feet in elevation, extend northward to Novaya Zemlya, which is a glaciated plateau.

The central Siberian plateau east of the Yenisei has a general elevation of 2000 feet, with 6000-foot mountain ranges in the southern portion, rounded or flat-topped, and heavily forested within the taiga belt.

The Siberian plateau east of the Lena River has a north-south mountain mass of about 8000 feet in elevation. Its western slopes are alpinelike with deeply glaciated valleys, while the eastern slopes descend gradually to the level of the plateau. Mountains of 10,000 feet farther south have steep slopes with high, sharp crests.

In the uplands of Scandinavia, glacial scouring has exposed the rock base, and ice gouging has caused endless connecting lakes intermingled with glacial debris. In unglaciated central Siberia, the rivers and their tributaries are swift-running during the spring and summer months, and become raging torrents through the melting of snow on the mountains in the southern highlands. Farther north, this causes flooding and ice jams in the lowland areas.

Drainage. Because of the nearly level gradient of the Siberian Plain, the land adjacent to the middle and lower courses of the Ob and Yenesei Rivers is marshy, with poor drainage and braided channels. This is also true of the lower reaches of North Dvina, Pechora, and Lena Rivers.

ARCTIC TOPOGRAPHY—EURASIA

PLAINS, MOUNTAINS AND DRAINAGE

Plains. Arctic plains are found in western Siberia, both east and west of the Urals, bordering on the Arctic Ocean, south of the

Gory Byrranga, and along the coasts of the Laptev and East Siberian Seas. Additional plains occur on isolated lands such as Ostrov Kolguyev, Severnaya Zemlya, and Novosibirskiye Ostrova.

Mountains. In the northeastern part of Siberia the mountains have an average elevation of about 7000 feet, with the highest peak of volcanic origin reaching 16,000 feet above sea level. The entire area is generally covered with tundra, and streams flow seaward over permanently frozen subsoil. In some areas, valley glaciation can be found and snowfalls are heavy in the mountains to the east.

Drainage. The arctic rivers remain frozen until late in the spring; some years the river ice at their mouths does not thaw, as is frequently the case with the Lena River. Because of the nature of the soil above the permafrost, the drainage is slow and its pattern not deeply indented. Glaciers flowing from high elevations dissect the coastal margins and in summer provide the ice-cap drainage system.

WEATHER AND CLIMATE

It is most convenient for climatic description to subdivide the arctic according to the general vegetation zones: icecap, tundra, and taiga (northern coniferous forest).

The ice caps of the arctic have long and extremely cold windy winters, and short, cold summers. The tundra likewise has long and severe winters and short, cool summers. In winter, strong winds and snowstorms prevail; in summer, overcast skies, fogs, drizzle, and mist, sometimes mixed with snow or hail, are rather frequent. Although the annual precipitation varies from five to 16 inches, the relative humidity is high most of the year and the evaporation is slight. As the snow cover is thin over much of the wind-swept area, the ground freezes to a considerable depth in winter and thaws in summer to the depth of one to four feet.

The taiga belt in the interior has a continental climate. Such regions are characterized by a wide seasonal range of temperature with colder winters and warmer summers than coastal or maritime regions of the same latitude, due to the lack of tempering sea breezes. During the warm summers, coniferous trees and other hardy vegetation thrive. The annual precipitation is somewhat lighter than in the coastal regions, averaging between 10 and 20 inches.

WINTER

In winter, periods of clear skies, intense cold and light winds are interspersed with periods of somewhat warmer temperatures, strong, gusty winds and variable cloud cover. A rising wind velocity may raise temperatures as much as 40 to 50° F in a few minutes through mixing the radiationally cooled air near the surface of the earth with the warmer air which lies just above it. The coldest surface temperatures occur at the end of the long winter nights when clear skies allow the earth's heat to radiate into the atmosphere and when calm or light winds prevent any stirring of the air at low levels.

From the standpoints of body comfort, health, and personal safety, winter is the most unpleasant and hazardous season for man in the arctic. Periods of intense cold and strong stormy winds in the coastal tundra belts, together with continuous periods of extremely cold but light winds or calms in the interior accentuate the problem of maintaining the comfort, sanitation, and safety necessary for the efficiency of men and equipment. The duration of winter varies from practically the whole year on ice caps to three or four months in the warmest portions of the southern part of the area.

Temperature. The lowest temperatures are observed on ice-caps and in continental interiors, especially in closed basins where the cold air stagnates. The lowest known Northern Hemisphere temperature of −90° F was recorded in the Yana River Basin of Siberia in the subarctic in 1892; the lowest temperature ever recorded in North America was −81° F at Snag Airport in Yukon Territory, Canada, in 1947. The stratification of the cold air in basins, particularly those of mountainous areas, is such that the temperature at the bottom of the valley or basin is much lower than that along a mountain slope. For example, Fairbanks, Alaska, at 440 feet, has a January average temperature of −11.3° F, about 14° lower than the average of 2.1° F of McKinley Park at 2092 feet.

Winter temperatures along the tundra coasts are higher than those of the interior but are subject to wide fluctuations in midwinter, even with occasional thaws in some sectors. In spring, because of the great masses of adjacent sea ice, the temperature of the tundra coast rises more slowly during the period of increasing sunlight than that of the continent; conversely in autumn, with decreasing amounts of sunlight, the continent cools off more rapidly than the tundra coast which is still under the influence of the unfrozen sea.

A frequency data map of weather elements is more realistic in visualizing climatic conditions than the usual climatic map based on mean averages. Figure 3-3 indicates those areas of the North-

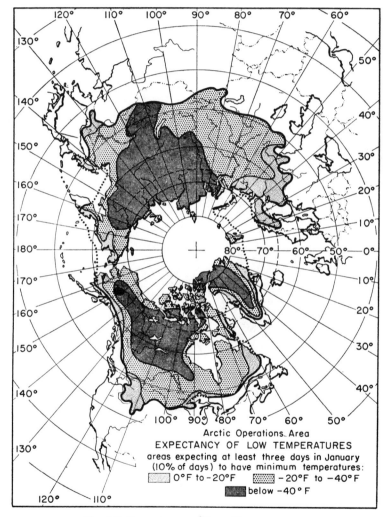

Fig. 3.3. Expectancy of Low Temperatures.

ern Hemisphere where the daily minimum temperatures are expected to go below −40° F on three or more days in January, the coldest month over most of the area. Figure 3-4 indicates, in addition to the low temperatures of the Yana River Basin and Snag, the extremely low temperature of −66° F recorded in the

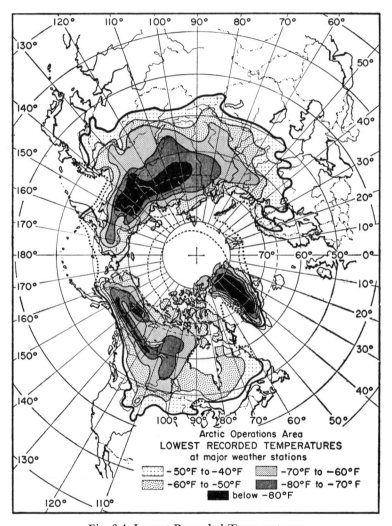

Fig. 3.4. Lowest Recorded Temperatures.

Yellowstone National Park, and other areas where extreme temperatures of −50 and −40 F have been observed.

Wind. There are few regions where winds as a single element are likely to cause acute discomfort. A few arctic coasts such as those of Greenland, Bering Strait, and the Kara Sea have wind speeds in excess of 70 or 80 miles an hour which hinder military operations. Extremely low temperatures and high winds rarely occur together.

Combinations of wind and low temperatures harmful or painful to man occur most frequently during the passage of cyclonic storms which are often accompanied by blowing snow. Usually with the passage of such storms, the temperature rises with warm and humid winds, then suddenly falls with a shift to colder winds which may be strong for hours or days. The storms along Labrador, Greenland, and the Soviet sectors of the arctic can become violent. Drifting snow can cause serious problems, since it is so fine that it penetrates the smallest openings in clothing and equipment.

Windchill. Most people notice that cold weather seems colder when the wind is blowing, but few realize how seriously harmful the resulting physiological effect, or windchill, can be. Windchill is the "rate of cooling," or "the rapidity with which body heat or the latent heat of vehicles or equipment is dissipated." For example, a 20-mile-per-hour wind with a temperature of 5° F is more effective in cooling the bare skin than a two-mile-per-hour wind with a temperature of −40° F. (See Fig. 1-2, Windchill Nomogram.) The coastal fringes of the arctic operations area, particularly the coast of Greenland, the shores of the Kara Sea, and the coasts of Bering Strait, produce the greatest windchill for places of low elevation. Windchill for the intermediate and upper mountain slopes can be much greater than that of the valley floor. The tundra coast and the open portions of the continental interior are periodically subject to severe windchill during the inrush of air masses during the colder portion of the year. Sheltered basins and depressions, which are free of wind, trap the extremely cold air.

SUMMER

Over the tundra coasts the rise in temperature in early summer is delayed by the huge expenditure of the sun's energy required to melt sea ice, whereas over the continent the ground warms up rapidly. The thawing of the snow cover, frozen soil, and absence of downward drainage because of underlying permafrost results in waterlogged conditions which are steadily maintained by high humidity and frequent drizzles or light rain over wide portions of the area.

In the interior of the continent the rise of temperature is more rapid in spring and summer, and the wind speeds are lower than those along the tundra coast. Here hordes of insects are encountered for a longer period than in those areas exposed to strong winds. For two to four months during the warmer portion of the year protection against mosquitoes and black flies is a major problem along the tundra coast and over most of the continental areas.

Temperature. The highest summer temperatures in northern regions are in the continental interiors where the ground warms up much more rapidly than the tundra coast adjacent to the cold or ice-covered seas. For example, Ostrov Diksona (Dickson Island) has an average July temperature of 48° F, while Verkhoyansk in the interior has an average of 68° F. At Fairbanks, Alaska, the average daily maximum temperature in July is 71° F, but at Nome on the Bering Sea—approximately at the same latitude—it is only 56° F. The average July temperatures at most stations in the Canadian Arctic Archipelago are either in the low forties or upper thirties.

The very lowest summer temperatures in the arctic—other than those of the Polar Basin—are observed along the high-latitude coasts. Pond Inlet in the Canadian Arctic Archipelago has an average temperature of 36° F in July and August; Point Barrow, along the north coast of Alaska, is slightly colder with an average of 33° F for the same two months. In both cases the average daily maximum temperatures are about 45° to 48° F, although only a few days have subfreezing weather.

In the interior and southern parts of the arctic the temperature may reach 90° F and even occasionally go above 100° F. The highest summer temperatures that occur in the prairies south of the evergreen forests are accompanied by lower humidities than those of the tundra. These high summer temperatures are most comfortable.

Wind. Summer winds present no great problem in most of the arctic operations area, although the greater wind speeds along the coasts and on icecaps, in combination with the low temperature, accentuate the perception of cold. Usually the summer season is somewhat less windy, and storms are much less numerous than in other seasons.

Transition. Spring and fall advance rather slowly along the tundra coast and more rapidly over the continent. Over the latter the ground warms up quickly during the increase of daylight in spring and similarly cools off quickly when the period of darkness lengthens in autumn. Both seasons are marked by great variability of weather and temperature from day to day; it may be very cold one day and mild the next. In many parts of the area, autumn or late summer is the period of maximum precipitation.

Break-Up and Freeze-Up of Rivers. As the advance of the spring and autumn varies widely from year to year, the times of break-up and freeze-up in the river ice vary correspondingly.

The most critical time for cross-country movement is spring, when the ice in streams and lakes has deteriorated to the point where it is unsafe yet blocks movement by water. Where the terrain is mountainous, the swollen streams are difficult or impossible to cross, and bridges may be swept away. High waters that continue into late spring and early summer come from the melted snow along the upper courses of the rivers. (See Figs. 3-5 and 3-6.)

In autumn, when the stream volume and current velocities are less, freeze-up of rivers closely follows the earliest autumnal drops in temperature in the interior portions of the continental land masses.

Snowfall and Snow Depth. Snowfall is generally light along the tundra coasts. Only along windward slopes of uplands such as the western slopes of the Urals, of the Middle Siberian Plateau of the Taymyr Peninsula of the mountainous areas of Kamchatka and the Okhotsk Sea region, and the southern Labrador highlands, is the accumulation of snow excessively deep with numerous snowstorms every year. In the continental interior where the air is very dry and cold the snow cover is thin and the soil freezes to great depths. (See Fig. 3-7.)

Along the tundra coast, the snow is almost constantly blowing about, even during winds of six to eight miles an hour. As a result the snowdrifts pile up near obstructions, while only a thin cover remains over the wind-swept areas. The force of constant strong winds combined with cold snow causes the snow surface to become extremely hard. Small serrations known colloquially as "wind anvils" are formed, the surface becoming so hard that

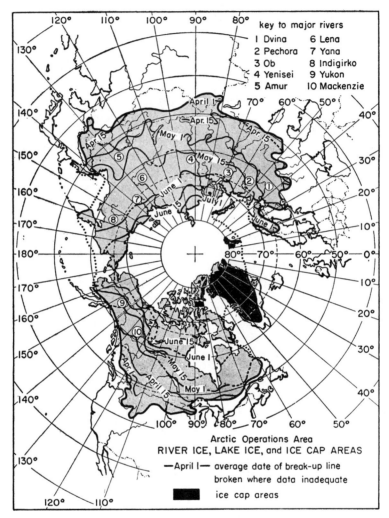

key to major rivers

1 Dvina	6 Lena
2 Pechora	7 Yana
3 Ob	8 Indigirko
4 Yenisei	9 Yukon
5 Amur	10 Mackenzie

Arctic Operations Area
RIVER ICE, LAKE ICE, and ICE CAP AREAS
—April I— average date of break-up line
broken where data inadequate
■ ice cap areas

Fig. 3.5. River Ice, Lake Ice, and Ice cap Areas—Break-up.

a heel mark will not appear on the surface and making the use of skis impractical. The abrasive effect of snow increases with lowering temperatures; sleds become increasingly difficult to pull, and runners wear out rapidly.

Rain and Drizzle. Summer generally is the wettest season in the

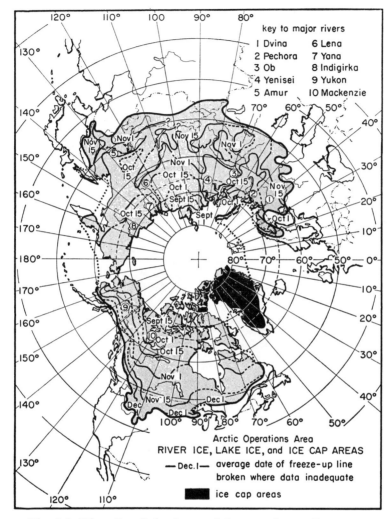

Fig. 3.6. River Ice, Lake Ice, and Ice cap Areas—Freeze-up.

arctic, with comparatively light precipitation along the tundra coasts compared with that of the temperate regions. The tundra coasts are continuously wet and miserable with frequent occurrence of mist, overcast sky or fog, and lack of evaporation.

At low temperatures the air is able to hold only a little mois-

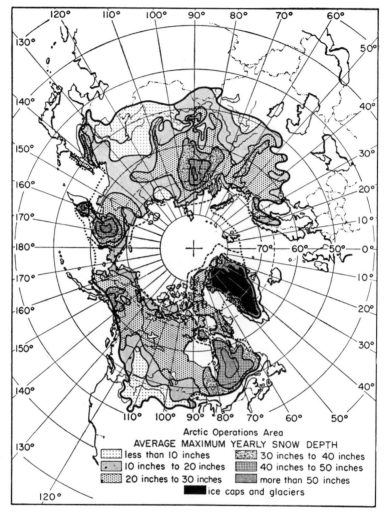

Fig. 3.7. Average Maximum Snow Depth.

ture; consequently the amount of precipitation in any one storm
is light. In places where the relative humidity is high, especially
along the tundra coast, it is difficult to keep active, perspiring
men in dry clothing. Laundry dries either very slowly or not at
all. During an extremely dry period, when the actual amount of

moisture in the air is slight, a common arctic complaint is that of dry and sore nostrils, an ailment which at times makes normal breathing painful.

Foggy weather is most frequent during summer months along the tundra coast. Under conditions of fog or high humidity, condensation of body moisture under clothing, which lowers the insulation value of the clothing, is a constant annoyance and hazard to comfort, health and efficiency. In the field, frequent body ventilation, obtained by forcing the moist air out at the waist or collar, is necessary although it may be momentarily uncomfortable at low temperatures. Accumulation of body moisture on the inner side of clothing poses a difficult problem.

4

Cold Areas: Survival Considerations

The problem of survival in cold areas is a theme dear to the hearts of adventure-story writers and newspaper reporters writing about the arctic. But exactly what is a "cold area"? And where are these cold areas located?

Military climatologists recognize three degrees of environmental cold: *cool, cold,* and *very cold.* Environmental temperatures between 50° F and 32° F are classified as cool, those between 32° F and 14° F as cold, and those below 14° F as very cold.

Environmental cold can also be either wet or dry. If liquid water in any form is falling or if there is slush, water, or mud under foot the environment is *wet.* If there is no liquid water under foot or in the air the environment is *dry.*

If this definition is accepted most of the land masses north of 30° N latitude have cool or cold conditions during at least part of the year. North of 40° N either wet cold or dry cold prevails over much of the year, with at least some spells of very cold weather; north of 60° N, dry cold prevails over most of the year, with some wet cold seasons. And in mountainous regions the varying degrees of cold can be encountered even on the equator. (See Fig. 4-1.)

In other words, a survivor may have to face a cold environment almost anyplace in the world except in the tropical rain forest and savanna and in the hot deserts. Even in the hot deserts the nighttime temperatures may reach into the cool range. *Cold area* is not synonymous with *arctic.*

Chapter 2 discussed the various survival problems facing a survivor and their solution. The present chapter shows how to solve the same problems when they are complicated by cold, ice, and snow, and how to cope with the problems unique to the cold environment.

IMMEDIATE ACTION

In cold areas after a crash, take the same steps to safeguard your well-being as you would in any area, but at the same time

106

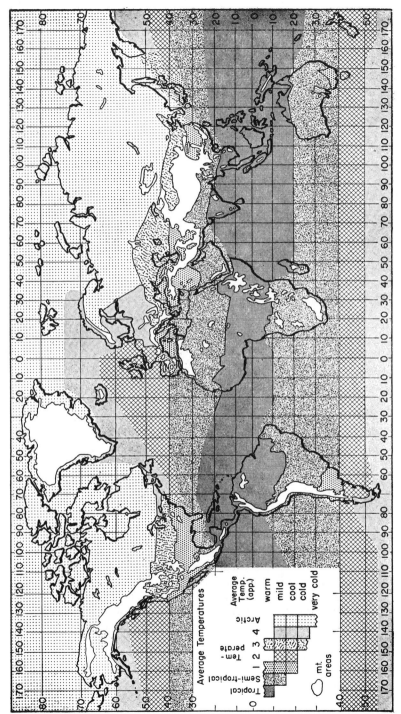

Fig. 4.1. Average Temperatures.

remember that protection from the cold is an immediate and ever-present problem.

Protection from the cold should begin with clothing suitable for the area over which you are flying. Pilots in Alaska and Northern Canada usually follow this rule and as a consequence very few of them ever suffer from the cold after a forced landing. Yet private pilots flying over the mountainous areas of the Western United States, where the same environmental conditions prevail, often fly in business suits—and, needless to say, forced landings in these areas often result in cold injury to the pilot and to his passengers.

In general, immediate action after a crash or forced landing in a cold environment must be extremely prompt. A fire must be started and a shelter constructed at the earliest possible opportunity. The same survival techniques apply as in warmer areas, but in the arctic you can't make mistakes without paying a penalty of discomfort or even injury.

Temperatures below freezing demand special protection for your aircraft too. If the aircraft is flyable, insulate the wheels from the ice or snow with tree boughs, boards, cardboard, canvas or any material available which will prevent a freeze-down. Remove the battery and take it into your shelter to keep it warm. Drain the oil into a container in which you can heat it before pouring it back into the engine. If the aircraft isn't flyable, drain the oil anyway so you can use it for fuel.

FIRST AID

The major first-aid problem in cold areas is to keep the injured men warm and dry and to treat wounds without exposing the victim to cold injury. Get injured personnel into sleeping bags and under shelter as soon as life-saving measures—such as stopping bleeding and artificial respiration—have been taken care of. Give conscious patients warm drinks. Provide extra heat for injured men by wrapping heated rock, sand, dirt, or any substance that will hold heat in several layers of fabric and put these packs around the patient. Be sure not to burn the skin. The most efficient spots for the packs are between the thighs, under the armpits, on the small of the back, and the stomach.

Frostbite is easier to prevent than to cure but often crash victims become frostbitten while unconscious or immobilized. Frostbite is difficult to define but easy to identify. Frostbitten tissue is hard and grayish or yellowish white.

The frostbite victim should be placed in a heated shelter if possible, and the frozen parts thawed as rapidly as conditions permit—a painful experience for the victim but one that results in less damage to tissue than the slow-thawing methods formerly advocated by medical authorities. If possible, thaw the frozen parts in warm water (not *hot*) at about 107° F. If warm water is not available wrap the frozen parts in heavy fabric and apply heat packs.

On minor frostbite or when other means are not available, thaw with body heat: place your bare warm palm against a frostbitten nose or ear, or place frostbitten hands against your chest, between your thighs, or under the armpits. Put a frostbitten foot between a companion's thighs or against his stomach.

Don't forcibly remove frozen shoes, mittens or clothing. Thaw in warm water or with heat packs until soft, then remove gently.

Don't rub or exercise a frozen part. You may tear the skin and cause further damage to the tissue.

Don't apply snow or ice. This causes more cold injury.

Don't soak frozen parts in gasoline or kerosene. The cold liquids will cause more cold injury and will irritate the skin.

Immersion Foot, also called *trench foot,* is a cold injury caused by exposure to wet cold at temperatures just above freezing. In immersion foot the extremities become red, swollen and painful. Like frostbite, immersion foot is easier to prevent than to cure. The only treatment is to keep the affected part warm, as dry as possible, and resting in a horizontal position to increase circulation.

HYPOTHERMIA is the medical term for the physiological condition caused by exposure of the entire body to cold, with a subsequent lowering of body temperature. Hypothermia can result from even a short immersion in cold water or by prolonged exposure to low air temperatures. The remedy is to rewarm the entire body. The preferred treatment is to give the victim hot drinks to provide a store of warmth in the care of his body and then to give him a hot bath. In survival conditions, get the victim into a sleeping bag and feed him hot liquids. All military survival manuals condemn the use of alcohol in hypothermia, yet most experienced arctic travelers recommend, and use, *small* amounts of brandy or whisky to warm up chilled men.

Snowblindness is a painful condition of the eyes brought on by exposure to glare, specifically light reflected from snow. The only treatment is rest and darkness. Keep the victim in a dark room or have him wear a lightproof bandage. The pain can be relieved by cold compresses if the air temperature is above freezing.

Don't use eye drops or ointment of any kind. They will not speed recovery and some types popularly used in the north will cause irreparable damage to the eyes.

Carbon Monoxide Poisoning. Poisoning from carbon monoxide is a common danger when liquid fuels are burned in poorly ventilated shelters. Often the victim becomes unconscious without any warning symptoms; treatment consists of getting the victim into the fresh air at once, applying artificial respiration if necessary and oxygen inhalator if available. (See section on *Health Hazards,* page 121, for hints on how to prevent the injuries described above. Prevention is the best first aid.)

SHELTER

You can survive under certain conditions, without a shelter in cold weather, but why run serious risks and cause discomfort or illness to others? Most cold areas provide the materials for building shelters; the intelligent pilot or passenger should learn to use them.

In cool climates, the cabin of a downed aircraft may provide adequate shelter. In cold or very cold climates the aircraft will be inadequate unless it is well insulated and has a functioning heater system and plenty of fuel. The reason is that the metal fuselage of the aircraft acts as a radiator and rapidly conducts the heat from the inside of the cabin to the outside air. Accordingly survivors should avoid depending on the aircraft and instead build a temporary shelter which will be easier to heat.

If possible, make your camp in timber to be near fuel and to get protection from the wind. The simplest shelter to construct is the lean-to, shown in Fig. 4-2. It can be made entirely of timber, using boughs to cover the framework, or with a pole framework and a parachute cloth or canvas cover. If you use boughs, put them on shingle-fashion, starting at the bottom. Face the open end of the lean-to downwind and build a long fire with a reflector opposite the entrance. A lean-to stays warm while the fire is blazing but gets a bit breezy when the fire is out.

Less work to construct than a lean-to is the tree-pit shelter, also shown in Fig. 4-2. This shelter can be made only in deep snow

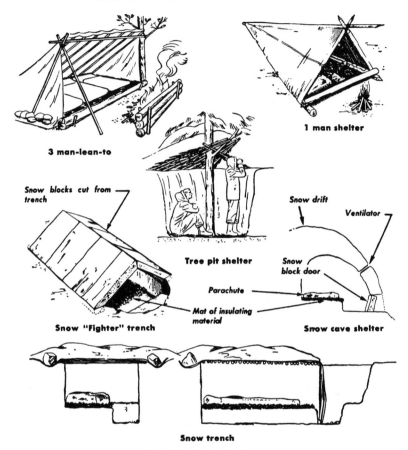

Fig. 4.2. Arctic Shelters.

and merely requires that the natural depression surrounding a tree trunk be enlarged and covered over with boughs. Pile snow on the bough covering for additional insulation.

If you have a parachute and are in wooded country make one of the paratepees described and illustrated previously in Fig. 2-5. The paratepee, a remarkably efficient shelter, easily erected and not too difficult to heat, has proved to be a lifesaver to Air Force personnel in Alaska and Labrador. Several crews who have gone down in those areas have used them in the dead of winter. One of their added virtues is that with a fire inside, the paratepee lights up like a Japanese lantern and acts as a beacon for rescue parties.

If you can't find timber, remember that snow is an excellent insulator. In deep snow you can make a snow cave simply by digging into a snowdrift, hollowing out the right size cave, and lining the floor with grass, brush or parachute fabric.

The ideal plan for a snow cave is to dig a tunnel sloping upward, then level off a floor. Build a sleeping platform about 18 inches above the floor and, if you have time, wall it in to conserve body heat. Make a ventilation hole through the roof and another one at the door so that any carbon monoxide generated by your fire will escape; since ventilation is important try to select a site which will not be buried by snow slides or by drifting snow. The best site is high up a valley wall underneath a snow cornice. In shallow snow, dig a trench and cover it with the blocks you dig out or with your parachute. In very shallow snow you may have to build a shelter from snow blocks. The classic shelter of this type is the igloo but if you don't have the architectural ability for this, a simple rectangular structure with a flat snow block or parachute-fabric roof will serve the same purpose. A snow cave will take two or three hours of hard work with a long knife or a digging tool. A snow trench won't take quite so long, but a novice working alone may require several hours to construct a snowhouse.

In any shelter you will need an insulated sleeping platform. An inverted, inflated life raft will do—or use boughs, seat cushions, or any other available material that will provide insulation between you and the snow.

When traveling in cold areas you should carry a sleeping bag, preferably of down-filled "double" construction. If you don't have a bag you can still survive even in extreme cold by sleeping in a heated tent or in front of an open fire. In 1939-40 the Finnish army operated without sleeping bags in temperatures down to $-40°$ F; U.S. soldiers have proved that they can do this, too. You may not be a soldier but your body obeys the same natural laws as that of a trained ski trooper.

Before using your sleeping bag, fluff it up to insure maximum insulation. Remove your outer clothing and use it as added insulation under the bag to block the flow of heat from your warm body to the cold ground or snow beneath you. You actually reduce the effective insulation of the bag by sleeping with all your clothes on—extra clothing increases your bulk, places tension on the bag and compresses the insulation, thus reducing its efficiency. You should fit loosely into your bag.

Don't breathe inside your bag or you will fill it with moisture that may freeze in short order. Leave a space at the top for your mouth and nose. If your face gets cold, cover it with a muffler or sweater—not with the bag.

Ventilate the bag after each use. Open it wide and pump fresh air in and out. Frost will accumulate in your bag from perspiration no matter what precautions you take; once a day, therefore, turn the bag inside out and beat the frost loose. If possible dry the bag in front of a fire.

When constructing a snowcave or snowhouse, avoid getting overheated. You may work up a sweat that can actually kill you by getting your clothes so wet that they won't dry out. To avoid this killing sweat, slow down and remove as much of your clothing as you safely can. Put it back on when you stop working.

When you go into the snow cave take your knife or digging tool along. No matter how carefully you have selected your site you may get buried by a heavy snow and have to dig your way out.

In any snow shelter check to see that the ventilation holes are open before lighting your stove.

Brush off all the snow you can before entering the shelter, and once in remove the rest before sitting or lying on the sleeping platform. Loose snow soon melts inside a shelter and a little water can nullify the insulation of your clothing or sleeping bag.

Keep movement in and out of the shelter to a minimum to conserve fuel—plan your movements and don't make any unnecessary trips outside. Assign a place for each item of equipment inside the shelter and keep it there. In moving about the shelter look before you step; you may accidentally kick over the pot containing your dinner.

To sum up, life in an improvised shelter demands constant attention to details. Forget a few details and you will be uncomfortable. If you continue to forget them you will be extremely uncomfortable or (in subzero weather) perhaps dead.

SIGNALING

Preparation of visual signals in cold weather is but little different than in warm weather. In general the cold will slow you down a little and you will take a little longer to do the job, but you can use the same signals described in Chapter 2. Snow on the ground will make moving about difficult but snow provides the perfect background for improvised signals.

Your aircraft is itself a good signal. Clean all snow and frost off the aircraft so that it contrasts sharply with the background.

In wooded areas, get signal fires prepared at once. On snow, build your fires on a log platform so that they will not melt the foundations under them. Small trees standing apart from others, as at timberline, can be made into signal fires without cutting them down. Build a "bird's nest" of inflammable material in the lower branches and light it when you see or hear an approaching aircraft.

In snow, tramp out signals, and if possible fill them with boughs, brush, or any other available material to provide contrast. Sea-marker dye sprinkled on the snow makes an ideal visual signal; the dye stains even dry snow a brilliant yellowish green, and will last until a heavy snowfall covers it or until the snow melts.

In snow-free areas, make your signals by cutting patterns in the vegetation or by digging shallow trenches.

If you have a paratepee shelter keep a fire lit all night. As previously noted, a paratepee lit from the inside is visible from great distances. In a snow cave or snow block shelter you probably won't be able to hear search aircraft, so that one of your party should stay outside at all times, weather permitting, to watch and listen. Build a windbreak without a roof for the man on guard.

Now that you have your signals out, relax and stay where you are unless you know your exact location and can walk to safety.

FIRE-MAKING *

In cold weather a fire may mean the difference between life and death, or at the least the difference between comfort and misery. Don't fly in cold climates without carrying matches or other fire-starting devices; keep matches or lighter in your pocket or in another easily accessible place, as you may need them in a hurry.

In snow, dig down to bare ground or build a log platform as a base for your fire. Otherwise it may melt into the snow and be self-extinguishing. Don't build a fire under a snow-covered tree

* See also pages 31-36.

without clearing the snow from the branches, otherwise snow may fall and put out the fire.

Fuel may be scarce. In the subarctic, dead branches of conifers are the best fuel and can be broken off standing trees. Where trees are scarce, burn any woody shrub—roots as well as branches. Dry grass will burn, but you will need a lot of it to maintain a fire; gather it in bunches and knot them to make the grass burn longer.

Oil from your aircraft is usually the best available fuel. In very cold weather drain the oil out immediately so that it doesn't congeal in the engine. You can drain it directly into the snow if you don't have a container.

Animal fat or any oil can be burned; all you need is a container and a wick, as indicated earlier on page 36. Soak the wick in the oil and light the end projecting outside the container. You can regulate the heat by trimming the lit end of the wick. A thick or broad wick burns more fuel than a thin or narrow one.

Some fats will have to be melted before they can burn efficiently. Place chunks of fat on a perforated tin can with a wick of greasy cloth or sphagnum moss underneath, then light the wick. The heat from the burning wick will melt the fat, which will fall on the wick and feed the fire. The same type of fire can be made using a bone, stick, or wire framework to hold the fat.

Candles are surprisingly efficient sources of heat in a well-insulated shelter such as a snowcave or snowhouse. For maximum efficiency, burn the candle or candles inside a tin can, with the level of the flame below the top of the can. Punch holes in the can to provide a constant supply of oxygen for the flame.

FIREARMS

For cold-weather use, strip your rifle, shotgun or other weapon completely and wash off all lubricants with gasoline or some other dry solvent. In cold weather, normal lubricants slow down the action of the weapon or cause it to jam.

Cold firearms brought into a warm shelter will soon "sweat" or show a layer of moisture on all metal parts. This is caused by the condensation of moisture in the relatively warm air of the shelter on the cold metal. When these weapons are again taken out into the cold the film of water freezes and may immobilize the action of the gun. Cover your weapons and leave them outside the shelter. However, if your shelter is only slightly warmer than the outside air you can bring the guns inside and store them at floor level where the temperature is lowest. When cleaning a gun in cold weather let it "sweat" for an hour, then remove all moisture before cleaning.

Keep all ice and snow out of the working parts of your gun and out of the muzzle. Carry a small stick with you to clean out the sights and breech block, and if possible, improvise covers for the muzzle and breech block.

If a part freezes in place, warm it gently and then gradually work it loose. Before loading, work the action a few times to insure that it is functioning properly.

Be careful not to touch the metal parts of the weapon with your bare flesh. Cover metal parts of the stock with cloth or adhesive tape. As with other activities, using a gun in cold weather is no more difficult than using it in warm weather—you simply have to pay attention to details that may be unimportant in other climates.

CLOTHING

Your body, even at rest, generates heat continuously. If you lose that heat to the environment at the same rate you generate it you feel comfortable, whereas if you generate less heat than you lose you feel cold. Conversely, if you generate more heat than you lose you become uncomfortably warm.

In a cold environment the primary purpose of clothing is to cut down the rate at which your body loses heat to the outside air. Clothing does this by (a) providing insulation between your body and the colder air, (b) keeping you dry, and (c) keeping the wind from direct contact with your skin.

Since production of body heat varies with activity, you need less insulation (i.e., less clothing or looser clothing) when you are moving about and working than when you are sitting still. If you work in the same clothing which keeps you comfortably warm while sitting still, your body will try to lose the excess heat by sweating. In cold climates, sweating is dangerous because the moisture accumulates in your clothing and often freezes *inside* the clothing.

Wet clothing, aside from being a nuisance, actually increases loss of heat by the wearer and reduces its value as insulation. Sweat collected in the layer of clothing next to the skin continues to evaporate and remove needed body heat even after the sweating process has stopped. The water or ice in the clothing also fills up the dead-air spaces that would otherwise provide insulation.

When you are engaged in manual labor in cold climates, reduce the amount of sweating by opening your clothes at the neck and wrists and loosening them at the waist. If you still feel warm, take off some of your outer clothing or remove your mittens or cap. When you stop working, put your clothing back on and reduce ventilatin. Try to stay cool, but not cold, and you'll be warmer in the long run.

According to physiologists, the best arctic clothing is the fur clothing of the Eskimo. A typical Eskimo costume weighing 12-18 pounds provides as much or more insulation as the best 20-30 pound factory-made clothing ensembles. Unfortunately fur clothing is not generally available to pilots and passengers; even if it were, we would find it unsuitable for most normal activities. So in cold climates we compromise by wearing *several layers* of clothing, adding and removing layers as we need more or less insulation.

The first layer next to the skin should be loose-fitting so as to trap air when the wearer is sitting and standing still, and to allow ventilation when moving about (and thus generating more heat). This loose-fitting inner layer is the secret of the efficiency of Eskimo clothing.

Over the loose inner layer wear as many additional layers as you need to keep warm. The outer layer of your clothing should be either a lightweight windproof fabric or a heavier fabric with a windproof cover.

Selection of cold-weather clothing is pretty much a matter of taste. The needed protection can be provided by a variety of combinations but the best clothing will not keep a man from freezing in subzero weather unless he uses it properly.

Wear enough clothing to keep in heat balance but not enough to sweat. Remove clothing while you are working and put it back on when you stop. Above all, don't "work up a sweat."

Hands and feet present special problems. Physiologists and clothing experts have determined that no hand covering can keep hands warm indefinitely when at rest in cold climates. Mittens are much better than gloves but even the best mittens will not keep a resting man's hands warm for more than two hours at −10° F. To keep your hands warm, exercise them or put them inside your clothing.

Your feet are more vulnerable to frostbite than any other part of your body—except your nose and ears—because feet get wet so often, either from sweating or from walking in water, and because circulation in the extremities is often restricted. The ideal footgear for cold-weather wear has not yet been perfected. Most experts recommend a loose-fitting boot worn with an insole and two or more pairs of heavy socks. In wet cold areas you will need a waterproof boot such as a shoe-pac or an oiled leather boot. In dry cold, felt boots or canvas mukluks are warmer than waterproof boots because they allow moisture to escape from the boot.

The sealed insulation boot, marketed under several trade names, proved quite successful in cold weather during the Korean war. This boot is worn with light socks or without any socks. Users report that although their feet feel clammy they do not freeze. If you use these boots, check the manufacturer's instructions on what socks to wear, and what temperature restrictions, if any, should be observed.

The preceding discussion has assumed that you are prepared for cold weather by the fact that you are wearing, or have available, suitable arctic clothing. But what should you do if you are suddenly flung into an arctic environment wearing temperate climate clothing?

The first thing to do, as previously noted, is to get a fire going and get under shelter—at least out of the wind. Next, improvise footgear from the best available materials. Men have made very acceptable arctic mukluks by wrapping canvas or parachute cloth stuffed with dry grass or other insulating material around their feet. In addition, wrap a scarf or piece of parachute fabric around your head and face. Be sure to protect your ears. Use parachute cloth as a blanket and roll up in it. When you get cold, move about, generate body heat, then cover up again quickly. Don't wait until you are completely chilled before exercising. If you get cold enough to shiver you are too cold; besides, shivering will actually burn up more calories than mild exercise.

HEALTH HAZARDS

The secret of good health in the arctic lies in prevention of illness, not in cures or remedies. Simple preventive measures that anyone can apply will keep you in good health until rescued.

Cold injuries, which include frostbite, trench foot, or general chilling of the body are all due to one cause—lack of insulation against the arctic environment. Your clothing will protect you if you use it properly, as outlined on page 117.

FROSTBITE AND IMMERSION FOOT

Frostbite, discussed in general terms on pages 108-109, is the freezing of some part of the body. It is a constant hazard in subfreezing environments, especially when the wind is strong. As a rule, the first sensation of frostbite is numbness rather than pain. You can see the effects of frostbite—a white spot on the skin— before you can feel it. Unless already a casualty and unable to help himself, *only a negligent person gets serious frostbite.*

It is easier to prevent frostbite or stop it in its very early stages than to thaw and take care of badly frozen flesh. To prevent severe frostbite, (1) dress to protect yourself against cold and wind—in high wind and when exposed to aircraft prop blast, protect your face; (2) *keep dry*—avoiding sweating as much as any other wetness; (3) in extreme low temperatures, be careful not to touch metal with your bare skin.

In addition exercise exposed parts of your body frequently. Wiggle your face, fingers, and toes from time to time to keep them warm and to detect any numb or hard areas. Move your ears with your hands from time to time for the same purpose. Watch your companion's face to see if any frozen spots show, and have him watch yours. Thaw any frozen spots immediately, using your bare hands or other source of body heat.

Although you must constantly be on guard to avoid cold injury in an arctic environment, you can console yourself with the observation, made by an eminent physiologist who has spent most of his life studying the effects of cold on man, that "many are cold but few are frozen."

Immersion Foot, also called trench foot, is a cold injury resulting from prolonged exposure to temperatures just above freezing. In the early stages of trench foot the feet and toes appear pale or bloodless, and feel cold, numb, and stiff. Walking becomes difficult. If preventive action is not taken at this stage, the feet will swell and become very painful. In extreme cases of trench foot, the flesh dies and amputation of the foot or of the leg may be necessary.

Because the early stages are not very painful, you must be constantly alert to prevent the development of this serious malady. (1) If possible keep your feet dry by wearing waterproof footgear and by keeping your shelter dry; (2) clean and dry your socks and shoes at every opportunity; (3) dry your feet as soon as possible after getting them wet—warm them with your hands, apply foot powder, and put on dry socks; (4) when you must wear wet shoes and socks, exercise your feet continually by wiggling your toes and bending your ankles, and avoid wearing of tight shoes.

SUNBURN

Paradoxically enough, you can get sunburned even when the temperature of the air is below freezing. On snow, ice, and water, the sun's rays strike both from above and below, and in a valley they come from every direction. Sunlight reflected upward from the bright surface attacks where it hurts most—around the lips, nostrils, and eyelids. Make a habit of carrying a chapstick in your pocket and apply it especially to those parts of your face exposed to reflected light. Do not use too much soap on your face; it removes natural oil that protects the skin from the sun. If you get blistered, get first aid immediately, since blistered areas, and especially lips, may become badly infected.

SNOWBLINDNESS

Snowblindness is easily avoided but once experienced it can make the sufferer miserable and susceptible to further attacks. When exposed to the glare of snow or ice, it does not take long for the eyes to start burning, watering, and seeing double. In snow or ice-covered areas keep your dark glasses on and carry an extra pair. Even on overcast days you can get snowblindness because there is still an enormous amount of reflection from the snow and ice. One handy substitute for glasses is a piece of wood, leather, or other material with narrow eye slits cut in it tied in front of the eyes. These are good in a blizzard because the slits can be kept clean by brushing them off, whereas glasses may become frosted over. The best cure for snowblindness is prevention by wearing dark glasses whenever the danger is present.

DEHYDRATION

The body requires water in order to function properly. If you do not drink enough water to maintain the proper fluid level in your body, you become dehydrated. Even slight dehydration lowers your efficiency, causing you to feel listless and to tire easily.

Dehydration also affects your morale in that small things will upset you easily. (See pages 201-207 for a detailed discussion of dehydration.)

Drink at least two quarts of water a day, even in cold weather. If you are doing any manual labor, you will need more than this amount. In warm weather, of course, you will need still more. Don't wait until you are thirsty to drink water. You can be partially dehydrated and still not feel thirsty.

CARBON MONOXIDE POISONING

Whenever a stove, fire, or gasoline heater is used indoors there is danger of carbon monoxide poisoning. Therefore a steady supply of fresh air in your living and working quarters is vital. Carbon monoxide is a deadly gas even in low concentration and is particularly dangerous because it is odorless.

Carbon monoxide burns with a blue flame and is freely generated by a yellow flame. If your stove or heater is burning with a yellow flame, either adjust the air intake to provide oxygen sufficient for complete combustion or raise the cooking pot high enough (usually about three inches above the top of the burner) so that the gases can burn completely. Remember, *a yellow flame means that carbon monoxide is being formed.* Take care of it immediately and check your ventilation.

Generally there are no symptoms. With mild poisoning, however, these signs may be present: headache, dizziness, yawning, weariness, nausea, and ringing in the ears. Later on your heart begins to flutter or throb. But the gas may hit you without any warning whatever. You may not know anything is wrong until your knees buckle. When this happens, you may not be able to walk or crawl. Unconsciousness follows, then death. You may be fatally poisoned as you sleep.

BODY PARASITES

Body parasites are very common in the populated areas of the north because of the crowded facilities. When you are in the midst of a native population or occupying shelters that have been used before, you must inspect your clothing and body each night for body parasites.

If you find that your clothing has become infested with lice you can get rid of them in various ways. While extreme cold does not kill lice, it paralyzes them. Hang up your garments in the cold; then beat them and brush them. It will help to rid them of lice but not of louse eggs. DDT powder and other chemical means can also be used to free your body and clothes of parasites.

INSECTS

Mosquitoes. The arctic is justly infamous for the abundance of its mosquitoes—because of the numerous swamps and lakes, and because the long, sunny days with slight variation in heat from night to day provide ideal conditions for insect incubation. Most arctic mosquitoes are vicious biters. As you try to protect yourself against them, it may be some comfort to you to know that both malaria and yellow fever, transmitted by mosquitoes in other parts of the world, are unknown in the arctic.

Midges. These extremely small bloodsucking insects, also known as "punkies," "no-see-ums," and "creeping fire," are found locally in such numbers that they become a terrible pest. Midges are most abundant in middle and late summer and breed in decaying leaves and along stream margins or even in holes in trees. They bite chiefly on cloudy days, in the evening, and very early in the morning; in bright daylight they seek the shade. Their most troublesome aspect is their small size; they easily penetrate even the finest mosquito netting and are restrained only by 60-mesh silk bolting cloth.

Blackflies. Small, chunky, blackish gnats called blackflies or buffalo gnats swarm about in large numbers in the northern early summer, chiefly in subarctic forests. They breed in swiftly flowing streams. They hover about eyes, ears, and nostrils, making little noise, but promptly alighting and sucking blood wherever the skin is exposed, especially behind the ears. While their bites are not especially painful, sensitive persons are affected by subsequent itching and swelling of the sites. Blackflies are usually active only in daylight and generally are most numerous during June and July.

"Bulldogs." In the north there are three kinds of large flies which together are called "bulldogs"—deerflies, mooseflies, and horseflies. All these "bulldogs," like the blackflies, frequent marshes and bogs on hot bright days. Strong winds do not keep them down, but cool weather sends them to cover. They are extremely annoying to man because of their continual circling and buzzing as well as their vicious bites. Under certain conditions, deerflies are capable of transmitting tularemia.

Preventive Measures. Protective covering for the entire body is the best method of combatting insect pests. Repellents in the form of oils and ointments are invaluable against some kinds of insects. In camp, smudges can be used but are of doubtful value. Insect-proof shelters are often a necessity.

Clothing should be so thick or so closely woven that insects cannot penetrate it. Zippered or pull-over shirt fronts are preferable to those with open fronts. In the interior, clothing with maximum protection against insects and minimum warmth is recommended. To prevent flies from attacking your ankles, wear high shoes, shoe-pacs, or leggings—or wrap your trouser bottoms around the ankles and tie them with strips of cloth. Gloves are necessary and must be long enough to close the wrist opening. Wear either a hat with mosquito net sewed on around the brim, or one of such shape that a headnet can be slipped over it. It should be a wide-brimmed hat, such as the fatigue or service hat, so that the netting will be held away from your face. Be sure the netting is dark—it is almost impossible to see through a white net. The bottom of your net should have a lightweight cloth carrying a drawstring by which the net can be drawn around your collar to close the neck opening. If you do not have a headnet, or prefer not to wear one, wear goggles with screened sides and apply insect repellent liberally.

No insect repellent has proved to be 100 per cent effective in all situations, but some very efficient preparations are now on the market. In general the "stick" type repellents that combine the active ingredient with a waxy substance which melts when spread on the skin are preferable to liquid repellents in survival kits. The liquids, no matter what the container used, have a tendency to leak and damage other components of the kit. *Don't* carry repellent in a metal or glass container with a screw top. The screw top will invariably corrode and require the use of pliers to remove.

FOOD

Every man may be his own expert when it comes to selecting food for an emergency ration, but in cold weather you will need, and want, more fat than you normally eat. Select food for your emergency kit that is high in calories, rich in fat, and, of course, palatable. All the old-time explorers used pemmican—a mixture of fats and lean meat that today evokes cries of horror from dieticians—as the staple in their diet. During World War II some dieticians compounded a fatty mixture, dubbed it "pemmican," and fed it to troops in a training situation. The men disliked the taste and some became violently ill. The dieticians claimed that the results of this test proved the unsuitability of pemmican as an emergency ration. But the fact remains that men have lived and worked for years at a time in rigorous environments using pemmican as the staple item of diet.

The following survival and trail ration is one of the successful ones to include pemmican. The whole ration was conceived and developed by Dr. Dana Coman, and Mr. Sigmund Gutenko, C.S.C., U.S.N. It was first used on the Byrd and Ellsworth antarctic expeditions of that year. Men have lived on this ration for 154 days in the antarctic undergoing the greatest hardships, meanwhile maintaining a constant high level of caloric expenditure. There have been no clinical pathological changes when this ration has been used. Constipation, so often resulting from concentrates, has not occurred.

TABLE 4-1

FORMULA AND PREPARATION OF PEMMICAN
AS DEVISED BY COMAN AND GUTENKO

Material	Per Cent
Pure oleostearin—melting point 118 F. (i.e. beef suet)	32.66
Whole milk powder	19.80
Dried bacon, 48-hr. smoked	17.57
Powdered beef liver, dehydrated	4.95
Granulated-roll dried beef, dehydrated	4.95
Tomato-vegetable concentrate, dehydrated	4.95
Soy bean grits, large mesh	4.95
Oatmeal, steel ground, quick cooking	2.47
Pea soup powder, dehydrated	2.47
Potatoes, shredded, blanched and dehydrated	1.48
Granulated bouillon	0.99
Brewer's yeast, type 50 B	0.99
Onion salt	0.74
Paprika	0.37
Lemon powder	0.37
Caraway seed, whole seed	.25
Cayenne pepper, ground	.025
Black pepper, ground	.025

PREPARATION

1. Bacon is sliced at least $\frac{1}{8}$ in. thick, and diced. The bacon is then rendered until the bacon grits turn to a light brown color, and are moisture-free. (The moisture is gone when the foam disappears.) Fat is strained from the bacon grits, the grits and fat then separated, weighed, and divided equally among the batches of pemmican made.

2. The oleostearin is now brought to its melting point and the bacon fat added, and the mixture thoroughly mixed.

3. The whole milk powder, powdered beef liver, and tomato-vegetable concentrate are next added, and mixed well, followed by the pea soup powder, soy bean grits, brewer's yeast, granulated bouillon, onion salt, and lemon powder.

4. Then the black pepper, cayenne pepper, caraway seed, and ground paprika are added.

5. Finally the mixture is complete with the addition of the quick cooking oatmeal, diced bacon grits, granulated rolled dried beef, and the shredded potatoes.

The final make-up of the trail-and-survival ration is as follows:

SURVIVAL AND TRAIL RATION
(37 ounces per man per day—5,500 calories)

Material	Ounces
Pemmican	12
Biscuit, whole wheat type	6
Bacon	1
Butter	2
Oatmeal, quick cooking	2½
Whole milk powder	4
Lump sugar	2
Milk chocolate	4
Fruit, dried and powdered	1
Orange or lemon powder	¾
Peanuts, almonds, etc.	1
Cocoa	¾
Salt and pepper mixture (about $\frac{1}{10}$ ounce)	

NATURAL FOOD RESOURCES

In some areas of the arctic edible plants and animals are abundant at certain seasons of the year, while in other areas very little game or edible plant life can be found at any season of the year. In no part of the arctic are native animals and plants a reliable source of food. However, if you have an opportunity to bag some game or pick some berries or greens, do not pass it up. They will add variety and nourishment to your menu.

ARCTIC ANIMALS

Caribou or Reindeer. The caribou is the most abundant and widespread of arctic game animals. In shooting, aim for the shoulder or neck rather than the head (Fig. 4-3). Caribou should

Fig. 4.3. Caribou (Aiming Point).

be skinned promptly, especially in summer. Keep fat with the carcass, not with the skin. If you do not have time for skinning, at least remove the entrails and genitals.

Moose. Look for moose in or near lakes or swamps. In clear, cold weather you can best spot moose or caribou by climbing a hill or tree and looking for the animal's "smoke" (condensed body vapor) which rises like the smoke of a small camp fire.

Musk Ox. The musk ox is rather rare, but is found occasionally on the islands of the Canadian Archipelago, in the barren lands and on the northeast coast of Greenland. Keep on the lookout for tufts of its long, dark-brown hair, its soft wool on boulders and dwarf willows, and for tracks and droppings. Musk oxen are easier to stalk and shoot than caribou and tend to bunch together rather than run when alarmed. Shoot for neck or shoulder. Face and forehead shots are wasted.

Seals. Seals are widely distributed and generally common. Their flesh and liver are excellent food. (Do not eat the liver of a bearded seal. It contains such a high concentration of vitamin A that it is poisonous.) In summer, shoot the seals as they come to the surface of the water to breathe or as they are basking on rocks. Aim at head, neck, or shoulders (Fig. 4-4). A dead seal

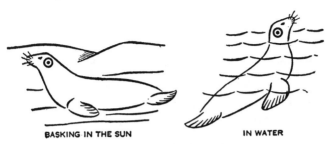

BASKING IN THE SUN · IN WATER

Fig. 4.4. Seal (Aiming Point).

usually sinks when shot in the water. You will need a harpoon to secure the body before it sinks out of reach. In winter, seals must be sought in the open leads in the pack ice. Hunting seals Eskimo style, through their breathing holes in the ice, requires harpoons or large three-pronged hooks. In the spring, seals lie on the ice next to their holes and bask in the sun. You will need a white camouflage suit to stalk them. Remove all blubber before you store seal meat or it will turn rancid.

Walrus. The meat and blubber of walrus are edible, as are the clams you may find in their stomachs.

Bears. All bears are edible although the flesh must be thoroughly cooked to guard against trichinosis. *Polar bear liver must not be eaten,* as previously stated in an earlier chapter—it is so rich in vitamin A that it is poisonous. All bears are dangerous and hard to kill; there should be two or more hunters in the party when hunting bears, and soft nosed bullets should be used. Aim for the neck or just behind the shoulder (Fig. 4-5). If the bear stands up, try for a heart or throat shot. The polar bear, as we have already noted, is always dangerous and is afraid of nothing.

Wolves and Foxes. Wolves and foxes are edible. Wolves follow

Fig. 4.5. Polar Bear (Aiming Point).

caribou herds; arctic foxes follow polar bears and eat their leav-ings. Foxes will hang around a camp or follow a trail party and try to steal food.

Rabbits and Hares. Rabbits and hares can be snared or shot. Aim for the head or you will not have much meat left. Do not try to shoot a running animal; whistle, and it will probably stop long enough for you to get a shot. When you eat hare or rabbit add fat of some sort—the meat rarely has fat. Do not cut up or dress a hare with your bare hands if you can help it, for you may contract tularemia (rabbit fever) by contact with their raw flesh. Cooked flesh is safe to handle and eat.

Marmots. Marmots are woodchuck-like animals that live above the treeline in subarctic mountains. They make excellent food, especially in late summer when they are very fat. Wait until the marmot moves away from his den before shooting, or he will probably fall back into his burrow.

General. Porcupines, beavers, and muskrats are found through-out the subarctic. All these animals are fairly easy to secure, and provide an excellent emergency supply of food.

Ground Squirrels. Ground squirrels abound in parts of the arc-tic and are easy to catch. Look for their burrows and dig them out. They are especially common along streams with sandy banks.

Arctic Birds. All arctic birds are edible, as are their eggs. For about two weeks during the summer molting season most waterfowl lose their flight feathers and cannot fly. At this time they are easy targets and some can even be caught by hand. Cer-tain nonmigratory birds are found in the northland in winter-time. Several species of grouse, like the ruffed, sharp tail, spruce, and ptarmigan (which turn white in winter) are common. To obtain the greatest food value from birds, pluck rather than skin them.

Arctic Fish. Fish form a large part of the native diet and are almost the entire diet of work dogs in the north country. On the coast, salmon, tomcod, and needle fish are plentiful. Inland, salmon, pike, and lake trout are the principal fish. All arctic fish and shellfish are edible, with the exception of the black mussel of the Pacific coast which is poisonous in the summer. *Avoid mus-sels entirely in Pacific waters.* Mussels are easily distinguished from clams and oysters by their orange-pink flesh. Cook shellfish by throwing them into boiling water.

Only the egg mass of the sea urchin is edible. Cut open the sea urchin and scoop out the eggs, which can be eaten raw. To prepare sea cucumbers, remove the insides and scrape the surface of the flesh with a knife to remove the slimy skin. Parboil the flesh and then chop up, or cook in a stew, or fry. It requires considerable cooking to make it tender.

Arctic Plants. In forested areas food plants are most abundant along streams, seashores, and in clearings. On the tundra, they are largest and most plentiful in wet places and in depressed areas protected by the wind. Do not be discouraged by the bare appearance of northern vegetation; food is often hidden. Many plants have starch stored in roots. Small low-growing bushes have many berries hidden under them. Look carefully for plant foods. Watch feeding habits of animals, particularly birds—they will lead you to food you might otherwise overlook.

All northern berries are safe to eat except the *baneberry* which grows in southeastern Alaska and western Canada. You can easily recognize berry bushes in the forest, but on the tundra it is easy to overlook them because they are dwarfed. Many grow flat on the ground and are partly covered by mosses and lichens. Look carefully when hunting for berries—a small bush may supply a handful. In the autumn, the leaves of some berry bushes turn brilliant red or yellow; look for these bright spots in both mountain meadows and on the tundra.

On the arctic tundra you can eat any plant with safety except one mushroom, the *emetic russula*. Recognize it by the color of its "umbrella" which is pink or rosy when young, red or yellowish when older. In the subarctic forest you can eat any plant except some mushrooms, water hemlock, and baneberry. *Do not eat mushrooms from the subarctic forest unless you know them.* All puffballs are edible but very young stages of some poisonous gill-bearing fungi may be mistaken for puffballs. Do not eat the mushroom if when you break open the ball you find gills. In the subarctic forest, two fungi are especially poisonous: *deathcup amanita* and *the fly agaric* (Fig. 2-11). The *amanita* is usually completely white, but the cap may have tints of olive, purple or brown. When fully grown the cap is four to six inches wide. The white gills on the under side of the cap are not attached to the stem. The stalk is white and brittle, and has a spherical base that is buried beneath the ground, resting in a soft white cup which is not visible unless the entire plant is exposed. *The whole plant is poisonous.* The *fly agaric* is a handsome fungus with yellow-orange or red-mottled cap, whitish or yellowish scales, and white gills.

WATER SUPPLY

Anyplace in the arctic is near water in one form or another. Potential sources are streams, lakes and ponds, glaciers, fresh water ice, and last year's sea ice. Freshly frozen sea ice is salty but year-old sea ice has the salt leached out. It is well to test freshly frozen ice when looking for water. In some areas where tidal action and currents are small there is a layer of fresh water lying on top of the ice, the lower layers of which still contain salt. In some cases this layer of fresh water may be two to four feet in depth.

If possible, get water from running streams or lakes rather than by melting ice or snow, which wastes fuel. In winter cut a hole through the ice of a stream or lake to obtain water; cover the hole with snow blocks or loose snow to retard freezing. In extremely cold weather break the water hole open at frequent intervals. Mark your water hole with a stick or other marker which will not be covered by drifting snow. Water is abundant during the summer in lakes, ponds, or rivers. The milky water of a glacial stream will not hurt you—let it stand in a container until the coarser sediment settles. In winter or summer, purify water from ponds, lakes, and streams by boiling or by treating with water-purification tablets.

When liquid water is not available, you will have to get water by melting snow or ice. To save fuel, use ice or the most compact snow available. Gather snow only from areas which have not been contaminated by animals or men. Ice sources are frozen rivers or ponds, glaciers, icebergs, or old sea ice. Old sea ice is rounded where broken and is likely to be pitted and to have pools on it. Its underwater part has a bluish appearance, whereas fresh sea ice has a milky appearance and is angular where broken. In all environments, remember to guard your sources of water supply from contamination.

HINTS ON OBTAINING WATER

Avoid burning the bottom of your melting pot by "priming." Place a small quantity of water in the bottom of the pot and add snow gradually. If water is not available, hold the pot in the hand near the stove and melt a small quantity of snow in the bottom of the pot before filling it with snow. Compact the snow in your melting pot and stir it occasionally to prevent burning the bottom of the pot.

Keep pots of snow or ice on the stove when not cooking so as to have water available when needed. Pile snow or ice to be melted just outside your shelter, and bring in as needed.

TRAVEL IN THE ARCTIC

If the decision to travel has been reached after consideration of the requirements discussed in Chapter 2, make your preparations carefully and equip yourself as best you can. But remember, overland travel in the arctic is a last resort unless you know the country well and have proper equipment. Experience has proved that the odds are with the man who stays put and uses his energy to signal search aircraft. Don't travel in a blizzard or bitterly cold wind—make camp and save your strength until the wind lets up. Don't travel with poor visibility, even if the wind is not blowing.

TRAVEL AIDS

In winter carry a sleeping bag, parka, mittens, snowshoes or skis, and mukluks, if you have them available. In summer don't forget mosquito netting and repellent, extra clothing (socks especially), and shoe-pacs. Wear goggles. Keep feet dry, summer and winter.

If you are caught without traveling aids, improvise. Make snowshoes from willow branches, aircraft inspection plates, small metal panels, seat bottoms, or metal tubing. Shroud lines and control cables can be used for webbing and harness. Sleds can be made from cabin doors, cowlings, or bomb bay doors. Ropes can be made from parachute lines (each line has about 450 pounds tensile strength).

PLAN ACCORDING TO TERRAIN AND SEASON

Head for a coast, major river, or known point of habitation. Most settlements are near the coast or near large junctions, lake outlets, points of land, and mouths of streams. Travel downstream—in summer use a raft, if possible. Rubber life rafts and antiexposure suits have been used successfully in arctic rivers, but don't use them to travel through tide rips, or in high winds. In winter the rivers generally make good highways, but look out for thin ice. Travel is sometimes easiest on ridges, particularly in summer when lower land is wet.

In general, plan to travel during the period from early morning to early afternoon; you will then have plenty of time to build a shelter and a fire. Dry your clothes, and prepare your evening meal, which should be hot and the biggest of the daily meals. Get into your sleeping bag early to conserve fuel and energy. Start again next morning as soon as it gets light.

Glaciers. On the other hand, when you are on glaciers, or on snow-covered terrain in the spring, travel from midnight to noon to avoid run-off streams. Surfaces are better for travel at night, and rest periods are more comfortable during the warmer day. On valley glaciers, watch out for falling rocks early in the evening.

Other Obstacles. Obstacles to summer travel are dense vegetation, rough terrain, insects, soft ground, swamps and lakes, and unfordable large rivers. In winter the major obstacles are deep, soft snow, dangerous river ice, "overflows" (stretches of water covered only by a thin layer of ice or snow), severe weather, and a scarcity of native foods.

The snow lies deep in the timbered areas, and travel is exceedingly difficult without snowshoes or skis. Progress is generally better when frozen rivers can be followed and the wind has packed the snow hard. However, winter river travel also has its dangers. These are discussed farther on in this section.

North of the timberline major vegetation thins gradually until it finally lies only along creeks and river beds. Here, travel along ridges is often preferable to following rivers unless they are large and fairly clear of snow. In summer, ridge travel is by far the best. The terrain is drier and the ground firmer under foot. Furthermore, if a breeze prevails, it is strongest on the ridges, blowing the mosquitoes down into the valleys and timber.

Rivers and Coastal Plains. A glance at any map of the arctic will reveal that the majority of towns and settlements are located on rivers or on the coast. The reason is obvious. Waterways are the highways of the arctic. In summer, boats are often the only transportation. In addition, food and fuel are usually available along the inland waterways. Vegetation, brush, and timber line the river banks; fish and bird life are in or on the waters. In short, the natural resources necessary to sustain life are to be found more readily along the rivers, either in winter or in summer.

The freezing of arctic rivers is a battle between the cold air and the current of the river, a battle which never ceases throughout the winter. The current constantly cuts the ice away from below, while the outside air carries away heat, to maintain or increase the thickness of the covering ice. Snow is on the current's side in this battle, forming an insulation which tends to prevent the escape of heat. Thus all snowbanks, especially those on cut banks, are apt to lie on thin ice or no ice at all.

Overflow often occurs where gravel bars exist in the bed of the river. Such bars freeze solidly and dam the river. The water then seeks an outlet, generally along the bank under a snowdrift or around a log or rock, about which the current is faster. In extremely cold weather these overflows "smoke" and can readily be mistaken by the uninitiated for the smoke of a habitation. Overflow often lies under deep snow on the surface of the ice and cannot be seen until a person sinks in it.

Because of these hazards, you should travel the barest portions of the river and avoid all obstacles protruding through the ice. Keep to the inside of all curves and away from undercut banks where the current is swiftest. As the river progresses to areas where the fall is slackened, the current is slower and the ice is thicker. However, overflow can also occur there, because the ice freezes deeper and blocks the shallower parts of the river bed. Very often after a freeze-up the source of the stream or river dries up so rapidly that an air pocket is formed under the initial ice, a particularly dangerous condition for the traveler. Probe the ice ahead of you with a pole.

One danger area still remains on any river anywhere in the arctic—the junction of two streams. Here the resulting whirlpool keeps the water open longer than anywhere else, except swift rapids. In by-passing all junctions of streams, cross well downstream from the mouth of the joining stream. Cross glacier-fed streams early in the morning when the water level is lowest.

When floating down a stream, watch out for "sweepers"—trees that lean nearly horizontally and may brush personnel or equipment off the raft.

Take special care when crossing thin ice. Distribute your weight by lying flat and crawling across. If traveling in a party, rope each man across. If one breaks through, pull him out and get him under shelter at once. Build a fire and dry his wet clothing.

TUNDRA TRAVEL

Winter travel over barren lands is very demanding. Without snowshoes or skis progress can be difficult, even impossible. Gales of such force that they are impossible to face may sweep unchecked. There is no natural shelter except that provided by scattered high banks and willow thickets about lakes and along stream beds. Game is very scarce, and fires cannot long be maintained on the fuel generally found in the middle of winter. Most of the rivers follow ancient beds which wind and twist. Survivors who must travel fast cannot afford to follow these old streams, which double and quadruple the distance to be covered.

Because of blowing snow, fog, and the lack of landmarks, a compass is an absolute requirement for barren-land travel. Even with a compass, one man has difficulty steering a straight course by himself, and variations in the higher latitudes are extreme.

Break-up and Freeze-up. The spring break-up, the summer, and the fall freeze present far greater travel difficulties than does the winter season. Travel must be accomplished on foot without the aid of skis or snowshoes, and equipment must be carried on the back. The masses of soggy vegetation on the tundra cause the traveler to slip and slide; lake systems must either be crossed or circumnavigated. Use antiexposure suits, if available, in crossing lakes. Be careful in crossing sand bars and mud flats at the mouths and junctions of rivers, and lakes and lagoon outlets. Quicksands and equally dangerous bottomless muck may trap you. Mosquitoes rise in hordes. It is true that there is a much greater possibility of catching fish and shooting birds in summer than there is in winter, but the physical demands of summer travel are more exhausting than those of winter. Rain and fog prevail during break-up and freeze-up; thawing days are followed by freezing nights. The problem of keeping dry, even with rainproof equipment, is almost insurmountable.

If a river flows in your desired direction, use it to float downstream rather than attempt to travel cross-country. Time spent in constructing a raft will be quickly regained.

The months of July and August are the best for cross-country travel in the arctic, because less rain falls during these months.

MOUNTAIN AND GLACIER TRAVEL

In mountainous country it is sometimes best to travel on ridges —the snow surface is probably firmer and you will have a better view of your route from above. Look out for snow and ice overhanging steep slopes; avalanches are a hazard on steep snow-covered slopes, especially on warm days and after heavy snowfalls.

Be especially careful on glaciers. Watch out for crevasses (deep cracks in the ice, that may be covered by snow. Travel in groups of not fewer than three men if possible, roped together at intervals of 30 to 40 feet. Probe before every step. Always cross a snow-bridge crevasse at right angles to its course.

Find the strongest part of the bridge by poking with a pole or ice axe. When crossing a bridged crevasse, distribute your weight by crawling if you are not wearing snowshoes or skis.

Crevasse Types. The three types of crevasses most common on glaciers are transverse, longitudinal, and marginal crevasses. The most common type are the transverse crevasses,. which are simple tension cracks occurring at approximately right angles to the direction of flow of the glacier—in other words, lying *across* the slope of the glacier. Also common are longitudinal crevasses which run downslope, or parallel to the flow of the glacier; these are formed when the snow and ice spreads *outward* at the mouth of a valley. Marginal crevasses are formed near the *edge* of a glacier, but may sweep in arcs all the way across some valley glaciers. They point diagonally upslope toward the center of the glacier, usually at an angle approximating 45 degrees.

Some crevasses are as deep as 100 to 150 feet, but the majority only reach 50 to 75 feet. Crevasses in the snow-covered parts of glaciers are the most dangerous. They are often hidden by snow bridges—layers of snow which cover the void. In temperate zones, travel is most dangerous in early summer after the snow bridges have begun to lose their strength but before they have collapsed or melted away sufficiently to define the surface outlines of the crevasses. In arctic areas such as the Greenland Ice Cap there is often too little melting to reveal the crevasse pattern, even in late summer. Hidden crevasses can often be recognized by slight depressions on the surface or by the slightly dull appearance of the snow over the crevasse. Sometimes only part of the snow bridge will have collapsed, revealing the direction of the crevasse.

In snow-covered areas, crevasses often have their maximum width a few feet below the surface. For this reason, extreme caution should be exercised near the edges of crevasses.

Crevasse Rescue. Rescue from a crevasse should be effected promptly. The first requirement is to firmly anchor the rope by which the man is hanging. The second is to relieve the strain on the hanging man by dropping the free end of the rope (or another anchored rope) with a loop made for him to stand in. This action not only facilitates the rescue but also eliminates the serious danger of suffocation from constriction by the rope. He can pass this rope through his chest loop as shown in Fig. 4-6 to prevent

Fig. 4.6. Rescue from a Crevasse.

his falling backward in the ascent. The work will be greatly facilitated if an ice ax or other object can be placed under the ropes at the edge of the crevasse to prevent the rope cutting into the snow, while both ropes have a turn around another ice ax, pole, or solid object for a belay.

The victim now grasps the climbing rope firmly and brings his feet up as high as possible, permitting the man above to take up the stirrup rope. He then stands up and repeats the process, ultimately reaching the lip, where some strong-arm work and a vigorous pull on the rope are necessary to get him over the edge.

If two ends of rope are available, an improvement on this method is to give the handing man two loops (double-stirrup method), one for each foot, as shown in Fig. 4-7. By alternately raising one foot and then the other while his comrades are taking in the ropes at the top, he can get out with less exertion.

Certain precautions should be observed. The exact edge of the crevasse should be ascertained by probing; it may overhang and drop the rescuers into the void if approached too closely. An overhanging lip should be cut away if possible, otherwise the rope will cut into it, and the man cannot easily be brought over the lip. If the edge is sharp ice, it should be rounded off so that the rope will not be cut. The handle of an ice-imbedded ax can be laid at the edge of the overhang to protect the rope.

Prusik Knot. The Prusik knot is a valuable means of saving yourself if you fall into a crevasse, or in climbing up a rock face. The knot will hold tightly when weight is applied, but it will slide easily when unweighted. The method of tying is shown in Fig. 4-8. Take a bight of line and turn it twice around the rope, then pull the loose ends of the line through the loop.

Fig. 4.7. Crevasse Rescue Double-Stirrup Method.

You can also use the Prusik knot for climbing a rope. Use three slings fashioned from lengths of line. Make two stirrups and a chest loop fastened by Prusik knots to the climbing rope, as in Fig. 4-9. There should be about five feet between the stirrup and the knot in order to have the knot in front of the chest in an easy handling position. Then, by moving first one stirrup and then the other, it is possible to climb the rope. At the same time, by pushing up the chest loop, the victim is secured against loss of balance and can take a rest by leaning back at any time.

Rockfalls. These are caused by thawing of the snow and ice that bind loose rocks together. At times of the day when thawing is in progress, avoid passing beneath loose rock faces. Evidence of danger is the accumulation of debris from previous rockfalls. When climbing on loose rock, take care to avoid dislodging rocks that may injure men climbing below.

Any snow slope steeper than 20° is subject to avalanching. After a heavy snowfall, avoid all steep slopes. If you must ascend

138

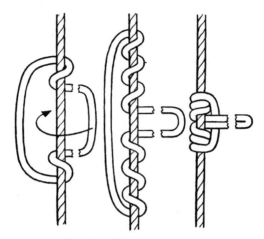

Fig. 4.8. The Prusik Knot.

them, do so in a single track directly upward. Concave slopes are less dangerous than convex ones. Avoid steep slopes in snow that is not firmly consolidated, because the track caused by the party may break the cohesion of the snow and cause it to avalanche. Avoid crossing below precariously balanced masses of ice; if absolutely necessary to do so, cross as rapidly as possible. Snow cornices overhang on the lee side of ridges; if approached from the windward side the true crest is difficult to detect.

Never approach the edge of a cornice. If you must follow a corniced ridge, ascertain the true ridge line and keep well below it on the windward side. Avoid traversing or climbing directly below a cornice. Not only is there danger that the cornice may become dislodged, but the snow mass immediately below it is particularly unstable. If you must cross a cornice, tunnel *through* it —don't try to go over the top.

Avalanches. If you are overcome by an avalanche, try to keep some part of your body, preferably your head, above the surface. Swimming motions will help to keep you afloat. Because an avalanche flows like a stream, the more horizontal you lie, the better. In a vertical or nearly vertical position, you are likely to be bowled over and buried by the upper layers of snow which move more rapidly than the lower. If you are on skis or snowshoes, discard them immediately. Should you become completely covered by snow, try to create an air space about your head and

Fig. 4.9. Use of Prusik Knot to Climb a Rope.

shoulders. By doing this, avalanche victims have survived many days. If a roped party is overcome by an avalanche and one or more members are able to remain above the surface, it is comparatively easy to extricate those who have been buried. If the party is not roped, survivors should begin searching at the point where buried members were last seen, and should continue on the course along which the avalanche would have carried them. If no clues exist as to the position of a buried man, begin the search at the lowest tip of the avalanche and probe the whole snow mass systematically.

OTHER TRAVEL HAZARDS

Quicksand. In many areas, especially after heavy thaws or spring break-up, steep earth banks may be dislodged and start landslides. Precautions and measures for escape and rescue are the same as for avalanches. Outwash fans of fine sand and silt at the mouths of glacial streams, as well as sand bars at river mouths, are frequently saturated with water. Avoid such areas and cross only when it is absolutely necessary, as you may sink in. If your feet get caught and you start to sink, throw yourself flat as you would in an avalanche, no matter how disagreeable this may be in mud. Later in the summer, flooded land is treacherous because gas bubbles from decaying vegetation soften up the saturated soil and you may sink in deeply. Snowshoes, skis, or any substitutes that will distribute your weight over a large area are helpful in crossing bogs in the summer or thin or rotten ice on streams or lakes. Snowshoes or skis also bridge small cracks and holes in the ice into which you might otherwise slip.

Whiteout. When the sky is overcast and the ground is covered with snow, the lack of contrast makes it difficult to judge the nature of the terrain. Under such conditions men have walked off cliffs or fallen into crevasses or gullies without seeing them. Do not travel in these "whiteout" conditions.

In traveling, remember you are likely to misjudge distances to objects because of the clear arctic air and lack of familiar scale such as trees and other landmarks. Underestimates of distance are more common than overestimates. Mirage is common in the arctic.

Magnetic Compass Problems. The conventional magnetic compass reacts sluggishly throughout much of the arctic and may be almost useless within about 300 miles of the magnetic pole (which is located on Prince of Wales Island). There are several reasons for this compass deviation. First, the horizontal component of the earth's magnetic field is weaker in the arctic. Second, the compass needle tends to align itself with the earth's magnetic field, which dips into the ground at an angle that increases as the magnetic pole is approached. Most needles are weighted to compensate for this dip. A weight which counteracts the dip in the geomagnetic latitude of Washington, D.C., for example, is inadequate at a higher latitude, and the compass will not respond properly. Third, friction of the pivot on which the needle rests has a greater effect when the horizontal directive force is low.

For arctic regions, therefore, use a compass that is balanced for the geomagnetic latitudes in which you are traveling. Don't rely on one reading only; take several readings and average the results. Read the midpoint of the swing of the needle rather than the point at which it comes to rest; the friction of the pivot might cause the needle to stick at an incorrect position. Properly used, the magnetic compass is serviceable throughout most of the arctic, but you must remember its limitations.

TRAVEL ON SEA ICE

The decision to move across sea ice must be made only as a last resort unless land has been sighted. In both winter and summer, snow conceals thin ice and often hides cracks and holes in the ice.

Travel conditions on sea ice vary greatly from place to place and from season to season. The smoothest ice is that frozen in protected fiords or bays; the roughest are the pressure ridges found anywhere in the pack. Beware of the pressure ridges between the fast ice frozen to shore and the moving pack.

Usually solid sea ice, four to six inches thick, can be traversed, but for the inexperienced traveler, 10 inches is a safer minimum. On the other hand, fresh water ice is solider, and six inches is a safe minimum for travel across it. Snow-covered ice should be probed to determine its strength.

Navigation. The problems of navigation are almost identical with those on the barren lands, with one major exception: the polar ice pack is in constant motion because of current and wind. As a rule the sea ice is faster-moving during the summer months when the ice is loose than during the winter months when the ice is more firmly cemented. Determination of direction, therefore, may be particularly difficult. Landmarks in the form of high pressure ridges and hummocks are usable only over short distances, since it may be that they are located on other floes which are changing position. Add to this the fact that the magnetic compass is very unreliable in high latitudes, and the necessity for constant directional checks on the sun and stars becomes obvious.

Maintaining a straight course over sea ice is very difficult due to the lack of landmarks, blowing snow, and fog. Even with a compass one man has difficulty keeping to a desired course. If possible, build snow cairns or leave flags to mark your back trail and use as reference points for back sighting.

Floes. In winter there is generally very little open water except between the edges of the floes. In summer there is water on top of the floes, between them, and in large openings surrounded by floes. When crossing from one floe to another, jump from a point a couple of feet in from the edge of the ice, not from the edge itself. When the ice is closely packed, you can walk as though it were solid—using common sense, of course. You can easily tell if the touching or overlapping edges are solid enough to walk on.

When large heavy floes are touching each other, the ice between the floes is usually ground and powdered and can bear no weight, but moving with the powdered ice will be larger chunks that can hold you up. The powdered ice may be as much as 20 feet wide, but if you move *against* the ice, you will usually find a place to cross, especially when moving ice touches fast ice frozen solidly to shore.

When crossing pressure ridges, be careful to step only on solid ice. Bridges of snow that form between peaks of ice are not always solid.

Slush and Melting Ice. Springtime melting can make an ice surface very rough. Salty sea ice also becomes soft and honeycombed in spring, even though the air temperature remains below freezing. It is advisable to avoid areas of ice covered with melt water, because the surface beneath is likely to be pitted and rough. It is true, however, that melt water standing on ice is an indication of the soundness of that ice. As thawing progresses, the water disappears into the ice, indicating that it is honeycombed and therefore weak and unreliable. After the melt water runs off, the ice surface is dry, white, soft, and slippery.

In spring, water on the ice sometimes refreezes on the surface, leaving a layer of slush beneath. This hazardous condition is to be expected following a cold snap during break-up.

It is a good idea to wear an antiexposure suit when traveling over broken or slushy ice. It will keep you dry and warm even if you fall into the water. Move slowly to avoid perspiring.

In the very high latitudes, ice is comparatively solid in winter. Wherever the ice joins open water, however, the edges are always broken and subject to fairly rapid movement. As the sun returns, the ice recedes and there is open water along the entire arctic coast. Along the north coast, ice lies offshore, and with strong north or west winds floes are often driven ashore. Riding one of these floes is definitely a last-resort procedure, since there is no guarantee that the wind will continue until the floe grounds. The ice is honeycombed with holes and covered with lakes and water-soaked snow. There is practically no dry surface anywhere, even at the Pole. Fogs abound, and misting rain is frequent.

Icebergs. All icebergs frozen in the ice are likely to have open water around them. This is due to the force exerted by the current on the greater mass of the berg below the surface. Icebergs driven by the currents have been known to crash through ice over several feet in thickness. Towering icebergs are always a danger in open water. The area below the surface melts faster than that in the air. When the berg's equilibrium is upset, it topples over, and when this happens the adjoining area is obviously no place for survivors. The resulting waves throw the surrounding small ice pieces in all directions. Therefore, stay away from pinnacled bergs. Seek out low, flat-topped bergs for shelter at sea.

5

Deserts: Environmental Considerations

WHAT AND WHERE DESERTS ARE

The chances are only one in five that you will ever fly over desert country, for about one-fifth of the land area of the world is desert (Fig. 5-1). But if there is a desert accident in your future you'll be more likely to survive it if you know the facts about deserts and how to act in them.

As the term is used here, deserts are found on every continent except Antarctica. They vary in size from the great Sahara, which covers half the continent of Africa, to the Desert of Maine, which is only 500 acres in extent—about as big as two average sized American farms.

Although deserts occupy about 20 per cent of the earth's land area, only 4 per cent of the population inhabit them. That may explain why for centuries deserts have been cloaked in mystery and romance, synonymous with sand storms and mirages. Few people lived in deserts, still fewer had reason to travel there.

Today many deserts are regions of big business. Oil wells and pipelines, the discovery of important minerals and the search for new supplies have converted deserts into travel areas for technicians and scientists, executives, administrators and diplomats. Tourists are fascinated by their majestic scenery and awesome beauty. The modern importance of deserts increases the possibility that some day you may find yourself in need of desert information.

DESERTS DEFINED

One definition of a desert is a land area with less than four, five, or ten inches of annual rainfall. If the definition is based on low precipitation and vegetation, however, it includes large sections of the Arctic, which are not deserts in the accepted sense. Definitions which use temperature, rainfall and the moisture needs of plant life are more satisfactory. Even those, however, take in marginal regions which may be desert for one or two years

144

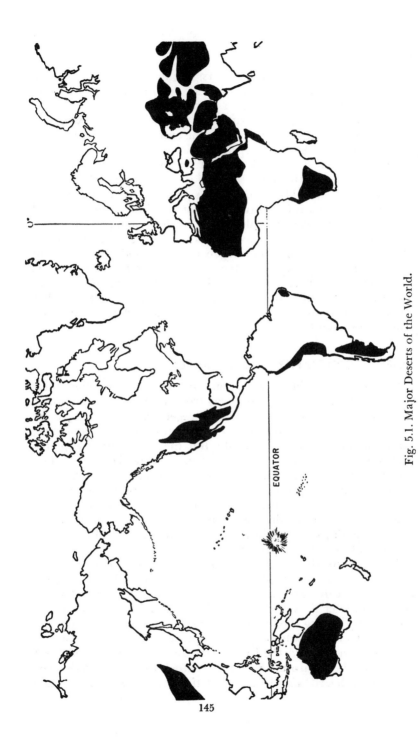

EQUATOR

Fig. 5.1. Major Deserts of the World.

145

and distinctly *not* desert other years, like much of Israel's Negeb.

Without attempting to give a specific definition, when we speak of desert in this book we mean a place of extremes. It's extremely free of lakes or streams of running water; trees are extremely few or nonexistent. Water is always the extreme necessity for man or beast in any desert or steppe.

The idea that a desert is a great sea of sand is ten per cent true. Only one-tenth of the Sahara is sandy (Fig. 5-2) and the same proportion holds for deserts in general. By far the greater part of the Sahara is flat gravel plain or *reg*, from which the sand has been blown away and piled up in the low, "ten per cent" area where the sand dunes are located. There are gravel surfaces in the Gobi of Mongolia, the Negeb of Israel and the Sahara of Algeria that are packed into true desert pavements. Salt deserts exist that are as hard as any roadbed. Rock deserts that extend for miles appear from the air as smooth as a dance floor. In other regions broken rock deserts look more shattered than an arctic river in a spring thaw.

DESERT TOPOGRAPHY AND CLIMATE

Desert hills and buttes and mountains rise abruptly from their surrounding plains like skyscrapers from a city street, an appearance that is partly due to the lack of vegetation. Where there are no grasses, trees or shrubs to soften the contours of the landscape, sharp angles are more noticeable. But there is another explanation too. Rains in desert regions are few and far between. When they do come, sparse or nonexistent vegetation cannot hold back the water and let it sink into the ground where it falls; instead the waters rush down every slope in a torrential flood. Broken rock and talus dirt at the base of hill or mountain are swept out onto the plain, scattered in a flat, dry delta. The solid hill is left to stand abrupt and naked, free of sloping talus.

In temperate climates, plant roots and freezing moisture break up rocks. These agents play only minor roles in desert weathering, temperature itself being more important. Dry air and scarce vegetation offer little shelter from hot sun. The result is the desert heats up during the summer day and cools off rapidly at night. In the Sahara the daily range of temperature is 45° F or more. It may be down around the low 30's at 5 a.m. in March, but by 1 p.m. it will be up around 80°. The poet who was going to be true to his sweetheart "till the sands of the desert grow cold" was a

Fig. 5.2. Location of Major Sand Deserts in Africa and Arabia.

fickle fellow indeed—he could change sweethearts every day at 5 p.m.

More important, however, is the fact that the daily range in temperature causes the rocks to expand in the heat of the day and contract at night. Daily expansion and contraction eventually breaks the rocks into smaller and smaller pieces until they are reduced to sand. As soon as the sand is fine enough to be moved by the wind it is blown away and piled up in the low places of the desert where the dunes are located.

SANDBLASTING

As the desert winds blast the sand toward the basins, rocks along the way are scoured and etched into weird shapes (Fig. 5-3).

Fig. 5.3. A camel caravan rests on this level stretch of sand near Hofuf, Saudi Arabia. The odd anvil-shaped structure in the background is an eroded hill. Expansion and contraction from sudden changes of heat and cold are important causes of desert erosion. Rain and wind carry away the talus from eroding buttes like this but wind is responsible for sweeping clean the desert floor. (*Aramco Photo*)

Pebbles lying on the desert floor are polished. The sandblast of the desert seldom cuts or mars objects more than six feet above the floor. If you ride the desert trails and examine the concrete marker posts you can see for yourself how true that is. Near the ground it can scour the paint from your automobile and polish the metal, but those particles which are carried high into the desert air are too light and soft to do much cutting. Close to the ground you'll want protection for yourself and your transportation. Those natural sandblasts will reduce the transparency of a windshield, roughen a propeller, or sting your bare skin like hot needles.

DRAINAGE PATTERNS

Anyone who flies the desert will see vivid drainage patterns of streams now dry and filled with sand. Some of these arroyos, oueds, wadis, or dry washes are the skeletons of ancient drainage systems and often mark the course of underground water. After rare desert rains they carry flash floods a few miles to a basin or salt flat, where the waters lose themselves in a few weeks, either sinking into the sand or evaporating. Desert winds lift the fine silt from the basins and leave smooth flat areas, some of which are hard and firm enough for aircraft landings. Others are thin crusts over soft mud-pie fillings—safe enough for a wheels-up landing, although walking out of such a salt marsh can be difficult.

Internal basins and wheel-spoke drainage patterns add beauty to the desert from the air, but are reminders that following a stream bed will seldom lead to the sea. Even along the Mediterranean coast of the Sahara the dry wadis run inland to desert

Fig. 5.4. Flat desert floors among the sand dunes are swept clean by prevailing winds. Patches of vegetation grow where water from intermittent rains has accumulated on the dune edges. (*Aramco Photo*)

basins, although they start a few hundred yards from the sea.

Flat-floored basins are also found in the large sand-dune or *erg* areas of Sahara (Fig. 5-4). They are many acres in extent and as permanent as the dunes themselves. Maps made of the Sahara *erg* regions a hundred years ago show the *gassi* or flat basins just where they are today. The contour waves of the dune tops shift back and forth while the basins change but little. Permanent dune patterns are good directional guides but you must know the specific pattern for the area you are flying, since it varies for different regions.

SHIFTING SANDS

There are areas where dunes shift or move considerable distances in the course of a hundred years, so as to engulf buldings or oases. In other oases the population has been able to remove sand from around their trees and houses as fast as it blows in. Sand dunes that buried a church in Denmark* were completely blown away in a period of 30 years. No sandstorm, however, ever buried or suffocated traveler or caravans; although many people have been lost in sandstorms and died from lack of water, desert sandstorms are not like Dakota blizzards—sand doesn't accumulate as fast as snow.

OASES

Seen from the air, desert oases stand out sharp and clear (Fig. 5-5). Patches of palm trees make a dark blotch against the barren desert. Map makers haven't yet given such patches a suitable symbol. They show oases as named dots no more significant to a map reader than the dot and name of an isolated well. Maps also give symbols for the dry river beds and intermittent lakes, but the blue markings are, unfortunately, more vivid on the map than the reality is on the ground. The dark irregular outlines of an oasis are identifiable, and to an aircraft in trouble a most welcome sight, but as yet there is no system of symbols for air-to-ground identification. Deserts are wide expanses of terrain, and even at 150 or 200 mph, the pilot or passengers can observe few identifiable features.

* There are several deserts in Europe with complete absence of plants, great range of daily summer temperature, extreme cold in winter and no open water.

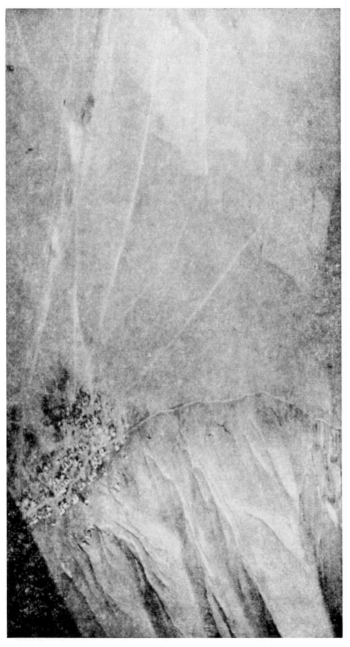

Fig. 5.5. Desert Trails are visible from the air. They lead to oases, native settlements, and water holes. Wells are located along the trails in every desert of the world. If you fly the desert learn the trail pattern. Note the patch work fields in this dry farming area of the Syrian Desert. (*Photo by Alonzo W. Pond.*)

TRAILS

One type of landmark that everyone who flies should notice, however, is the trail system. It is generally possible to drive an automobile anywhere in the desert. Dune areas, mountains and rough going usually can be detoured. It is also possible to land an aircraft in vast sections of all deserts. But unless you land near a trail your chances of finding help are extremely limited indeed. As you fly keep the trail pattern in mind, and when you come down head for a trail if possible.

General Laperrine, who knew the Sahara like the palm of his hand, was lost in one of the earliest desert air crashes. His pilot tried to fly the short route, but crashed a few miles away from the trail. Even though an extensive ground search began as soon as the plane failed to meet its ETA (estimated time of arrival), the general died of dehydration before rescue arrived. You can profit by the mistakes of General Laperrine, and of Bill Falls, whose tragic story is given on page 168.

When you fly the desert, look for the trails. They are clearly visible from the air, as shown in Fig. 5-6. People use them; they lead to water, to oases, to contact with the world. Desert trails are the most important landmarks for the man who flies the desert. Make a mental note if you cross them. Best of all, keep them always in sight if your flight plan will permit.

DESERT WEATHER

When you face the desert on its own terms rather than on yours, you discover that deserts are intolerant of carelessness and merciless in punishment for mistakes. If you want to land and survive in the desert you had better be prepared for weather of every kind and description. If you go to the desert unprepared, you are quite likely not to come back in good health—if you come back at all.

ALL KINDS OF WEATHER

Sooner or later every desert traveler encounters nearly every type of weather imaginable. Hailstones and cloudbursts, polar cold and tropic heat, sandstorms, thunderstorms, and windstorms are frequent enough to prevent the weather from becoming monotonous, yet rare enough to be considered "most unusual."

In Monument Valley, Arizona, where it hadn't rained during

July or August for twenty years, there were showers every afternoon at four o'clock throughout an entire summer recently. Toward the end of August a cloudburst hit the area, creating a roaring torrent six feet deep that uprooted trees and rocks like a modern bulldozer.

In 1954 the producers of an Air Force desert survival picture attempted to film it in the Libyan Desert of North Africa, planning the shooting for the last week of May and first of June, alleged to be six weeks beyond the last possible date for rain, and hot enough to work in shirtsleeves. Actually it turned so cold that the cameraman had to buy a sweater, and one day heavy rains prevented shooting of scenes. On another day (June 2) the fog was so bad that scheduled aircraft had to land 40 miles away from the regular field.

Near In Salah in the Algerian Sahara, warm weather one year lasted right up to November 30, but December 1 brought the full blast of winter, with a frigid north wind hit that almost tore one from the camel's saddle. Even with woolen long-johns, wool shirt, whipcord trousers and a sheepskin-lined overcoat, the icy wind cut through the traveler like a knife. One would have been warmer in northern Wisconsin that winter than on December 1 in the middle of the Sahara. That same day, two hundred miles farther north, another party traveling by auto trucks was caught in a sandstorm that completely blotted out all visibility.

SUDDEN WEATHER CHANGES

Sharp changes from pleasant warmth to desert cold are as "typical" of desert weather as intense summer heat. Snow may fall in the Mohave between November and April, making a beautiful landscape. One winter in west Texas a blustering norther followed "unusual" shirtsleeve weather so suddenly it caught hunters unprepared, and four froze to death during the night. Mac Young, the chief mechanic for the Mongolian expeditions led by Roy Chapman Andrews, stayed too late in the Gobi Desert one fall; winter struck suddenly and froze his hands. Despite all the expedition doctor could do, Young lost part of his fingers, suffering excruciating pain rather than have his hand amputated.

Not all the sudden changes bring only cold. At 2 p.m. on July 30, 1928, a hard storm broke while members of the Central Asiatic Expedition in the Gobi were moving to a new camp site. Scientists and natives crawled under trucks for protection from the heavy rain but eventually tiny rivers in the trail made that position too uncomfortable. When the rain stopped, the party moved on, but in a little while discovered that they had halted on the edge of a much bigger storm. Farther on, the hillsides had been flushed by the downpour. Ponds stood all over the landscape. A well near a trail in the valley was completely drowned out. There was enough water in some of these new lakes to make a good swimming hole.

The next morning the expedition found windrows of hailstones at the foot of hills. Many of these ice pellets measured $1\frac{1}{4}$ inches in diameter 18 hours after the storm.

Frans Larson reports on a storm that occurred July 5 of the following year. Drought had continued so long in that part of the Gobi that Mongols were on the point of moving their herds to the mountains in search of pasture. The storm hit and created a sheet flood that swept all before it. People were drowned along with horses, sheep, and cattle.

"A few hours after the storm," says Larson, "the Gobi burst into bloom like a magic garden—green grass made a velvet carpet under the warm sun where, only a few hours before, dry, burned grass and dust covered the landscape."

RAINFALL

Deserts vary in the amount of average annual rainfall. In the Gobi of Mongolia some sections average as much as 10 inches per year with a range from 13 to five or six. Other areas average only two inches. Over much of the Sahara four inches is the yearly average but it is not unusual to have five or 10 years pass without a single drop. Then a flood comes to create the mathematical average, and the desert blossoms.

The American and the Arabian deserts—the middle-latitude deserts—generally get some rain every year; although the total may be very little, yet it surpasses the complete aridity of vast sections of the Sahara.

HUMIDITY, FOG AND DEW

Fog, dew, and high relative humidity, not popularly associated with deserts, do exist in some arid localities. Early morning fog has been observed at Dhahran, Saudi Arabia, thick enough to hide buildings a hundred yards away. This desert city is on the Persian Gulf, but the fog sometimes goes inland as far as 200 miles. Bahrein Island is only 22 miles out in the Gulf. It, too, is desert but winds pick up enough moisture on the short sea-crossing to give the island much higher humidity than the mainland.

The Mediterranean shores of Tripoli have morning dew rather often; it may be seen dripping from the eaves just after sunup. Fog, though rare, is occasionally observed in the Sahara, like other rare desert weather phenomena.

In the Negeb of Israel archeologists have noted rows of rock piles which were long unexplainable. Finally some observant soul discovered pieces of grapevine wood in the rock heaps, and reasoned that the rocks were piled around the grape roots to increase dew formation and add moisture to the plants. Now desert botanists are beginning to study the effect of desert dew and desert fog on plant life. As yet we have no measurements to show how much dew a pile of rocks will collect. The fact that dew does occur in deserts on the shores of warm seas like the Gulf of California or the Persian Gulf is worth remembering. Possibly it could have saved the life of Bill Falls (page 168) and others.

SEEING THINGS IN THE DESERT

Visibility is definitely an element of weather and climate in desert areas. It is generally a long way to the horizon in any desert and there is little to interrupt the view between the traveler and the distant junction of earth and sky. While in the aviation sense visibility is almost always good, it is often deceptive.

The Arabs say, "Three things you cannot hide in the desert: smoke, a man on a camel, and a man in love." A survivor is probably not vastly concerned with the latter, but observers may disagree with the second, for camels seem to disappear before one's eyes in the Sahara behind sand dunes or blowing sand, or through distortion of air densities. At any rate smoke and dust *are* visible.

The desert lowers the visibility of those not specially trained as desert observers. Difference in air density in the cool of early morning and in the heat of midday distort light rays and produce mirages. The more common one is the "lake with islands." The apparent water on our blacktop highways in summer is of the same type. These mirage lakes are so realistic in North Africa that auto passengers often refuse to believe there is no lake until the car ahead stirs up a cloud of dust where the water seems to be. Another type of mirage makes mountains appear three times as close as they really are. The distortion is further emphasized because the absence of trees or other features prevents comparisons which normally aid in judging distance. The third, the rarest and most romantic, is the "inverted city in the clouds."

Seeing mirages does not mean you are going crazy. The apparent objects may not exist in three dimensions where they seem to be, but optically they are real enough to register on camera film.

Differences in air densities also distort visibility. A woman on horseback in the Gobi may look to you like a telephone pole but the local Mongols will recognize horse and rider. Other objects may be similarly distorted so badly that you do not see them at all—like the camels that seem to disappear so suddenly.

Desert glare, short shadows, and the fact that desert buildings are built of the desert soil all tend to hide objects. The summer sun is so nearly overhead in many desert regions that shadows remain shorter before and after high noon than in regions farther from the equator. The absence or scarcity of vegetation increases reflected light and glare so that one's eyes do not recognize the shadows, especially if one is not wearing sun glasses. The glare may or may not be painful—individuals vary in their tolerance to glare. Whether it hurts the eyes or not, it does cut down effective vision, and the optical hangover reduces the ability to see at night. Don't take chances with desert glare; protect your eyes, for you will need them to identify ground features.

If you want to be invisible in the open desert during the day, keep a knoll or even a very slight elevation between you and possible observers—the mirage will then give you protection. Keep in the shade of dunes or other topographic and structural features.

DUST STORMS

The greatest visibility hazard is, of course, the dust storm. Dust storms sometimes last for days and are serious enough in some regions to halt surface traffic. Such intensity does not often last more than a few hours, although the dust storm itself may last several days.

For the air traveler a dust storm can completely blot out the ground. On a flight to Timbuctoo in June 1952 one of the authors and his party were flying at about 5,000 feet when they hit the dust storm. Both sky and ground were blotted out for two hours, and there was no way of checking the drift. Finally they

climbed to 10,500 feet and saw the sun. A series of sun-line observations showed that they had drifted about 40 miles off course.

The average desert dust storm has a reasonable top. It is best
to avoid one, if it is on your route, by delaying your flight. If
you are caught, you had better get above it. When reports are
available you can probably file a flight plan around the storm.

If a dust storm catches you on the ground in a survival situation, lie quiet and "sweat it out" as best you can. No one is going
to be looking for you until the air clears; a search party couldn't
see you or your signals anyway. Fortunately dust storms are not
too frequent. In the worst desert areas they do not come oftener
than five to seven times a year.

CHANGE OF SEASONS

Desert seasons differ with geographic location. In the Salton
Sink, plant growth can take place 365 days a year but in the Mohave there is a distinctly nongrowing winter of about 15 weeks.
Regardless of growing season, however, you will recognize at least
two distinct seasons in any desert. May to October is distinctly hot
summer in the Sahara and in deserts of similar latitudes. October
and November, March and April are pleasant, mild extensions
of summer. December through February is raw winter but a good
period for work. The Automobile Association of South Africa
considers the Sahara "closed to travel because of heat" from June
through October. In the north, however, October is considered
a passable month for desert travel. Thus low, southern deserts
have distinct winter and summer seasons but spring and fall are
more like mild extensions of summer.

Northern deserts have more clearly marked seasons. A good
example is the desert of Mongolia, where four seasons are characteristic: spring, summer, fall and winter, with usually a false
spring inserted at the end of winter. These seasons are distinct,
with very pronounced extremes of temperature—as much as
150° F between the hottest day in summer and the coldest day in
winter.

Spring in Mongolia usually begins about the second week in
April. For two or three weeks there is a period of delightful
weather—warm, sunny days with not too much wind. These are
good days for field work but they are the deceptively pleasant
days of false spring. About May 1, the tail end of winter returns.
Cold, blustery days of dust-laden wind are the rule then until
early or middle June. Some rain and even snow vary the mo-

notony of wind and dust. The latter part of the month, for two or three weeks after the blustering end of winter, is the real spring, which spreads its rather comfortable warmth over Mongolia. Occasional light rains help the grass to flourish, furnishing pasture for flocks and herds. The wind has not stopped entirely, but it has ceased to dominate the landscape and man's thinking.

July, or sometimes mid-June to mid-August, is summer. Hot days—some of them extremely so—burn weather-consciousness into the mind of the outlander, but the nights are cool, and wind and dust again dominate the landscape. Occasional hard rains dump water onto the plains, and hailstones pelt the earth. But mostly it is just hot and dry during the daytime, dry and cool at night.

Fall usually is recognized by the invigorating, bright, clear days beginning in mid-August and lasting until mid-September or early October. This is the time of year when man and beast feel best in Mongolia. Summer pastures have restored the winter loss of energy to the animals. Fat meat and abundant milk build strength in man. The clear air, bright sun, and crisp temperature make one glad to be alive.

Winter comes with a rush any time after the middle of September. One day you may be enjoying a pleasant temperature near the eighties. The next day, the air cools and in a few hours the thermometer has fallen below $50°$ F. A little later, cold rain changes to snow or blasting wind, and winter arrives to hold Mongolia in its below-freezing grip for the next six months.

Desert seasons, in Mongolia or elsewhere, do not always run on schedule. The above description is an approximate picture, but changes may come a week or a month off-schedule and be just as far out of character. A section of a northern desert may be without rain or snow for ten months, as actually happened at Ula Usa ($42°$ $30'$ N, $111°$ E) in 1923. A cloudburst may sweep the pastures in a torrential flood to drown flocks and herds, men, women, and children, as Larson described it for the Gobi on July 5, 1929. A dry continental climate replete with sudden changes and complete surprises—that is the Mongolian and Gobi climate. It also applies to the mid-latitude deserts in other parts of the world.

HOW HOT AND HOW COLD?

Temperature is an important feature of desert climate. In low- and middle-latitude deserts daily extremes and wide seasonal differences are characteristic. Summer daytime heat in any desert is not to be ignored.

One of the authors flew to Dhahran, Saudi Arabia, from Bahrein Island about midday in early September not long ago. His pilot started to let down over the desert field, then went around again. When they were on the ground the pilot apologized. "Sorry, we couldn't make it on the first pass," he said. "It is so hot today, I couldn't get down on my usual approach." The morning settings of altitude, speed and judgment points are not applicable at noon in the desert.

The hottest official free-air temperature so far recorded is 134.4° F in the Sahara at Azizia, south of Tripoli, Libya. Second official honors go to Furnace Creek Ranch in Death Valley, California, which has reached 134° F. Higher temperatures have been recorded from thermometer readings in the sun, but such readings actually indicate the temperature of the mercury, not of the ambient air, and have little value for comparative purposes. Official thermometers are protected from radiant heat and measure only the temperature of the free air.

Desert rocks and sand can burn your feet even through your shoes. Men have also been hospitalized for burns resulting from merely touching aircraft wings in the Sahara. Metal tools exposed only for a few minutes to desert summer sun get too hot to handle.

Three things about desert heat are worth remembering. First, the air is 30 degrees cooler a foot above the ground. Second, the ground is cooler a few inches below the surface. Third and most important, the desert is sure to get much cooler when the sun goes down.

HOW DESERTS VARY

A daily difference of 45° F between daytime heat and predawn cool is common in the Western Erg of Sahara. (Around 50° F in summer; 36° to 40° F in winter at In Salah.) In the Gobi 25° to 35° F is the normal daily range. Low-latitude deserts sometimes have a range of 60° F during a single day.

The published monthly and yearly average temperatures are practically meaningless for desert regions because the daily range is so great and—in middle-latitude deserts like the Gobi—so erratic. At Edsin Gol, Western China, in November 1931, the daily range for four consecutive days was 24, 3.8, 22.9, and 36.2° F, creating quite a problem for the Western traveler who tries to select suitable desert clothing.

However, on really hot summer days it is worth knowing that if the temperature is 125° F at 1:00 p.m. in low-latitude deserts like the Sahara it will drop to a comfortable 95° F a little after sundown and fall to 75° F or lower before sunup next day. Knowledge of that daily variation will remind you to keep your body covered day and night. Clothes protect you from sunburn and from too rapid sweat evaporation in daytime heat. More clothes will protect you from the contrasting night chill.

Seasonal variations are also great. Winter temperatures in the Sahara regularly go down around freezing, sometimes as low as 28° F, with ice forming in water pails in March.

Seasonal differences in the Gobi are about three times the daily range—that is, about 125° F difference between the hottest day in summer and the coldest day in winter. In the Gobi the temperature drops to a frigid −20° or −25° F. In the low-latitude deserts like the Sahara, the seasonal contrast is largely accounted for on the above-freezing side of the thermometer. Out in Turkestan at Kasalinsk the range in one year is said to be 158 degrees between hottest and coldest days.

However, when you feel the sun beating down unhindered by dry air, with its heat reflected from bare rock, gravel or clean sand piles, you'll know that desert heat is a killer. It will burn your skin if you are not properly dressed; it will sap your strength and cut your efficiency and that of your aircraft at ground level; it will drain the moisture from your body and thicken your blood unless you drink plenty of water. Do your homework in the cool of morning and evening, keep in the shade during midday heat, and by all means wear a shirt.

DESERT WINDS

Desert winds, unlike those that blow in other parts of the world, are something more than features of the climate. They are not just air in movement, or a form of physical force; they are such a *personal* entity that desert people give them special names.

The *ghibli* of Libya is a hot, dry and sometimes dusty wind originating over the desert. When it comes from the south or southeast the *ghibli* has more or less dust. If it comes as a continuation of the more inland summer *simoon* it is very dusty.

In Algeria the *sirocco* comes several times between May and

October, blowing from the south quadrant—that is, southeast, south or southwest. It is hot—oven hot—dry, and dusty.

The *haboob* of Egypt is another summer inland wind. During the spring months from February to May the *khamsin* blows at five or six mph to as high as 16 or 18 mph.

In the Arabian desert the stiflingly hot, dusty wind that penetrates Jordan, Israel, Syria, and Lebanon is called the *simoon;* in Mesopotamia the same wind is called *shamal.*

English-speaking people also have given names to the desert winds. In Australia the "brick-fielder" is hot, dry and dusty air from the arid interior. In West Africa it's the "doctor" or the "harmattan" which blows great quantities of dust out over the ocean to impede coastal navigation. In the states of Idaho, Oregon and Washington a dusty *Palouser* travels from the Palouser region to carry dust to cities and annoy the good housekeepers of the area. Just to make more work for the ladies the Palouser carries a bit of light rain too, and thus leaves a muddy smear instead of just clean dust.

"Dusters" and "black blizzards" were strong west winds on the Great Plains during the 1930's. They usually came from the west and southwest but sometimes they blew from northwest or north. Whatever the direction, a "duster" was always strong and dry.

The *Santa Ana,* that cold gale sweeping into California and the coastal waters near Los Angeles, is a winter wind bringing dust from the deserts of Nevada and Utah. It is better known than the Palouser of the northwest and is the only one of the famous desert winds that is cold.

Gobi winds are easily the most memorable. In that region WIND is as certain as death or taxes. It blows so constantly that a traveler from beyond the Gobi finds that it dominates his very thoughts. Fifteen to 25 mile-per-hour winds persist day after day, driving fine dust that penetrates cameras, watches, clothes, and sleeping bags.

In general, the wind dies down about sundown for an hour or two, and there is also a calm before sunrise.

The limited number of observations available indicates that Gobi winds are generally westerlies although there are times in spring and summer when the wind shifts to the east or southeast. This is the wind most likely to bring moisture and rain, and accounts for the greater amount of precipitation in the eastern Gobi and for the progressive drying to the west.

During the latter part of June, July, and early August, wind is less continuous or rather less noticeable than in April and May. In the Gobi and central Mongolia calm days are not numerous. Even at Ulan Bator, well north of the desert and sheltered by mountains from north and west, there are only four days out of ten that might be called calm.

Wind in the Gobi not only is a physical force which carries dust and sand into sealed mechanical parts and makes the cold more penetrating, but sometimes it becomes a psychological hazard. It keeps up so long and so continuously that nerves become taut and edgy from the strain. When the letdown comes, the sudden calm surprises one with the realization that the wind has stopped.

WINDS AND CLIMATE

Winds, of course, play a most important part in desert climate. The prevailing westerlies that dominate the Gobi have traveled so far across the Eurasian Continent that their moisture has been squeezed out before they reach the Gobi. Similarly, when you fly from the Atlantic coast over Morocco to the Sahara you notice that the knife-edge of the high Atlas Mountains marks the border between desert and the fertile land. The moisture drops on the west side of the mountains and there is seldom enough left to spill over on the Sahara side. Mountains also protect the deserts of Western United States from the moist winds of the Pacific. The South American deserts are likewise sheltered against moisture-laden winds from the east by the Andes.

WINDS AND FLYING

Several years ago Edward Churchill, in an article called "Desert Flying is Tough," * pointed out that you can climb faster on the sunny side of a desert mountain than on the shady side. Trying to go up a desert canyon or cross a pass with a headwind is like swimming up a waterfall. Unless you have the power of a leaping salmon you had better not try it. Only the most powerful planes can climb as fast as some of the desert downdrafts.

In the desert the temperature contrast between shade and sunlight is so great that there are many updrafts and downdrafts, which is another reason for flying high over desert country.

Thus we have seen that there are winds of all descriptions in

* *Flying*, May, 1948.

the desert. Whether you fly, ride an automobile, or walk, the desert winds are a matter for special and personal consideration.

PLANT AND ANIMAL LIFE

Plants and mammals, birds, insects, reptiles and lizards all have adapted to life in the desert. What these living forms have done you can do by using intelligence. Negroes, Mongolians, Europeans, American Indians, Australians, indeed all varieties of *homo sapiens* have the physiological ability to adjust to the heat load and to a wide range of desert conditions.

Plants and animals have found ways to survive under extremes of heat and scarcity of water. In all cases the adaptation to desert conditions is primarily an adjustment to living for long periods without water.

PLANT CHARACTERISTICS

Desert plants have several characteristics that enable them to make the most economical use of available water and to resist long periods of drought. Some have extensive root systems which reach a maximum area and quickly absorb the moisture that falls in their vicinity. Some apparently excrete material which keeps other plant roots at a proper distance.

The amount of moisture determines the density of the plant cover. A wheel-rut where water has stood as a little pool after a desert shower will have more plants per square inch than the surrounding plain. On a shaded north slope plants are larger than those of the same species growing in drier, more exposed places.

Root Systems. Other plants have developed long roots which reach down deep in the earth to the permanent water table. In the American deserts mesquite* is an outstanding example. Where it grows you can reach water if you dig, although you may have to dig down 30 to 60 feet! When the Suez Canal was dug, roots of desert plants were found 100 feet below the surface. Living plants definitely indicate water, but in the desert it may be

---

* Mesquite *Prosopis juliflora glandulosa*) is a many-branched shrub or small tree 15 to 20 feet tall, sometimes so largely buried under the sand dunes that only two to three feet of the brownish tips protrude. It is a water-indicating plant of highest value, its long roots penetrating at times 50 to 60 feet to moisture. (From Jaeger, Edmund C., *Desert Wild Flowers,* Stanford University Press, Calif. 1947.)

Eucalyptus also is a deep-water indicator in deserts.

rain water that fell several weeks or months past, now so deep that to reach it without a well drill would thoroughly exhaust you.

Some plants survive the summer only as roots or bulbs which have developed a great degree of viability. They store water during rainy spring and conserve it in the roots through the dry period. A bulb from Turkestan (Leontice Eversmanni) as large as a potato was exposed for three years and lost very little weight. It was still able to germinate at the end of three years.

The visible size of a desert plant is little indication of the root volume. Travelers who find a tiny, seemingly dead stick on the desert plain pull or dig out its root system to obtain enough fuel to boil their tea, although the uninitiated would not expect that a finger-thick, two-inch stub could be a supply of firewood. Root systems are often 10 or 15 times the length of stems and branches above ground.

Water Conservation. Desert plants have several ways of conserving water once it is obtained. Some shed their leaves in summer; others shed large leaves and develop tiny ones that stay green and carry on the food-making job in hot weather. Some plants become completely dormant in hot seasons, only the roots surviving until the next rain. Tiny green spines, wax-covered leaves and even green stems carry on essential vital functions in the heat, while keeping moisture loss to a minimum. A few plants, such as the tamarisk, have developed controls which regulate evaporation, reducing it in summer heat. In some plants a few branches die and break off in summer, thus reducing the evaporation area. There are many types of adaptations in the desert plant world, all tending to conserve water and resist heat.

Cacti. The cactus plants found in American deserts have thick stems instead of leaves which store moisture and in which the green chlorophyll carries on the work of manufacturing food. The cactus plants are native to American deserts but the common prickly pear has been imported to desert regions all over the world. There are other thick-leaved, succulent plants which store moisture in wet seasons to carry them through long dry periods. This type is found only where there are two wet periods per year. Such plants found near Tucson, Arizona are not found farther west where there is no summer rain.

There is only one plant of the moisture-storing group which accumulates enough water to be of use to a thirsty, desert traveler —the barrel cactus, or *bisnaga*. It is sometimes called the compass cactus because in Arizona it is said to lean to the southwest. Whether or not it is a reliable compass, there is no doubt that it holds drinkable water and has no competition among desert plants on that score.

Nondrying Seeds. One of the most interesting adaptations is the ability of some plants to produce drought-resistant seeds. When a desert rain does occur these seeds sprout quickly, grow rapidly, flower, and produce a new crop of seeds. They survive in the desert by avoiding desert dryness and "living" only when water is available. The speed and energy with which colorful members of the mustard family and others can take advantage of a sudden rain is startling. For years a patch of Sahara may be as bare and dry as a concrete pavement. A few days after a hard rain, the desert becomes a beautiful, flowered carpet of vegetation.

Plant Distribution. In spite of the many ways plants have adapted to desert conditions, they are not widely distributed. Scattered bunches of coarse grass and shrubs are found in dry river beds, shallow basins and hollows between sand dunes. This vegetation is so sparse that camels have a leisurely walk between bites when turned into these pastures. Some plants depend on the torrential floods to uproot and destroy the plant but at the same time to scatter its seeds.

ANIMAL CHARACTERISTICS

Some desert animals have adjusted the timing of their reproductive process to season changes of temperature, humidity and length of day so that rutting season comes in the fall and the young are born in the season of richest vegetation. Just as seed plants sprout only when there will be enough light, warmth and moisture to guarantee the seed production, so desert animals gestate only when vegetation is sufficient to produce offspring strong enough for the rugged hot summer.

Birds. Desert birds nest earlier than similar species in more humid regions, and also have fewer eggs. That is because the intense heat of the desert limits the area the adults can cover in hunting food for the hungry youngsters. Also, the old birds are forced to rest in the shade during a longer noon than birds in cooler climates.

Many diurnal creatures of the desert are black or partly black. Scientific studies thus far seem to indicate that their dark hue protects them from the strong ultraviolet rays of desert sunlight.

Avoiding the Heat. The most important adjustments animals have made are in relation to desert heat and the absence of water. All desert creatures avoid the midday summer heat. Some sleep it out in burrows a foot or more under ground; others stay in the shade of rocks, overhanging banks or on the north side of steep hills. A patch of artificial black shade will be as much as 36° F cooler than the same spot in the desert without shade. Those creatures who pass the heat of the day in burrows enjoy a really cool existence because they go abroad only during the cool desert night, when their underground shelters reach maximum temperature. Since there is a 12-hour lag in burrow temperatures, such animals as kangaroo rats and jerboas have 24-hour "air conditioning."

THE SHIP OF THE DESERT

The alleged ability of camels to endure desert hardships is of course legendary. The stories told and written about this odd creature are part true, part false, and part fantasy. In 1954 two biologists from Duke University, Drs. Bodil and Knut Schmidt Nielsen, dissected a number of camels at the Beni Abbes Research Station, Algeria. They also took camel temperatures, measured the water they drank, weighed them when they were thirsty and after they had drunk their fill. The Schmidt-Nielsen team finally came up with the first scientific facts and explanation of how camels have adapted to desert conditions.

It is true that in winter desert pasture camels can go weeks and months without drinking water. They get their required moisture from the vegetation they eat, just as the gazelle or desert antelope do. Under such conditions they are not working and the desert air doesn't get very hot. When there is enough moisture in the vegetation they eat, camels just don't get thirsty, and won't drink even when water is offered to them. If their food is dry in the winter they can go at least two weeks or longer without drinking. At the end of that time they begin to show an interest in drinking water and will drink enough to bring their weight back to normal.

In the month of June a camel lost 22 per cent of its weight in eight days but gained it all back in ten minutes by drinking 103 litres of water.

But, contrary to popular belief, the camel doesn't store water. Instead his body can tolerate wide temperature ranges and uses water economically. His body, which doesn't have to keep an even temperature like man's, cools down in the desert night; accordingly the camel can let his body temperature go up several degrees in the heat of the day before he has to sweat and thus check the body heat.

Camels' body temperatures can go as low as 96.6° F and as high as 108.6° F without damage, giving them an advantage in water conservation over man whose body temperature must stay pretty close to 98.6° F. When man starts sweating to cool down his body the blood thickens unless lost water is replaced, but the camel takes water from the rest of his body to keep his blood volume normal.

In the year's run, however, the camel uses about as much water as other animals of equal size. In a circus or zoo a camel drinks every day, like a horse or other mammal. In the Sahara the camel men start training their animals when they are calves to go four days without water. Then when they are on long, hot journeys they can go eight or 10 days without water but they must replace the deficit at the end of that time or they will die of "thirst."

Those caravan people who have slaughtered their camels to drink the contents of the stomachs probably have contributed much to the belief that camels store water. The stomach contents are natural body juices mixed with partially digested food. The liquid stinks and looks disgusting but if you can stomach the stuff it is nourishing and does contain moisture which may check your dehydration for a while. But it definitely isn't "hoarded" water.

6

Deserts: Survival Considerations

The average metropolitan U.S. newspaper frequently contains stories of emergencies that occur in American deserts with dismaying frequency. Those that appear in print are only the spectacular ones that are considered "news" to the major wire services. The sheriff's offices in Arizona, Texas, California and New Mexico can tell of many more. The rangers in Death Valley and Grand Canyon National Park will add others. Still more incidents occur each year in Arabia and North Africa. Tourists and businessmen, prospectors, geologists and those who fly for fun will continue to cross deserts in the face of known dangers. In an emergency landing they will find no shelter, no water, and no telephone to summon outside help.

SIGNALING

THE PRICE OF UNPREPAREDNESS

Bill Falls, age 22, climbed into a light plane in mid-September and took off from San Diego, California for Phoenix, Arizona. Three weeks later three fishermen flying home spotted Bill's plane 38 miles south of San Felipe, Mexico. His diary told the story. Lost, out of gas, he had survived a crash-landing on the desert against a lone tree but had gone eleven days on the desert without food, shelter, or water. Although planes flew over him every day, he didn't know how to signal them. For a while he bathed in the waters of the Gulf of California and in that way retarded his dehydration. A fishing village lay only 38 miles away but apparently he had neither map nor general knowledge of the area.

The men who found Bill Falls' body had trouble trying to take off in loose sand. Finally the pilot made it alone, then landed and tried again but blew a tire. Without food or water they walked a 60-mile land route to San Felipe. The first man pushed hard and reached the village in about 24 hours.

A signal mirror, a gallon or two of water, general knowledge

168

of villages along the Gulf! Such little things that Bill Falls needed and didn't have!

John De Castro was luckier on his first cross-country flight to Tucson, Arizona, when he ran out of gas and landed on an Air Force Gunnery range. He had no water but he did look for barrel cactus and tried to find signs of water. He finally followed jeep tracks for 35 miles to a roadside inn, a tall glass of water and 15 glasses of milk. Luckily his five days of hunger and thirst were in December so he was cold at night but not burned up by day. A signal mirror might have solved his problem because planes passed overhead very often.

The third incident occurred in June on the Mojave Desert. The score: two dead and two survivors; time, two days. Estimated temperature was between 120° F and 130° F. The four men whose jeep broke down were experienced desert travelers. They waited for the cool of the evening. One man started to walk the 15 miles to the highway; he made only five miles before he collapsed and died. The others walked about three miles to a dry lake bed where they were more likely to be seen. Water ran out next day. One man of the remaining three fell unconscious, another wandered in circles until he died. An airplane spotted the two living men early in the morning and a helicopter picked them up. A survivor said, "It was the worst thing I've been through in 20 years in the desert—but I've learned this: after so many years on the desert a fellow gets sort of careless."

An oil geologist exploring in the Sahara last year, fared better. Traveling with a companion in a jeep, he hit a World War II mine and was severely injured. His companion, thrown clear of the wreckage by the explosion and miraculously unhurt, rigged a shelter with blankets, left plenty of food and water handy, walked 35 miles to native help, and then pushed on to contact the proper authorities. The injured man was rescued after five days and a thorough wetting from a cloudburst—the only rain the area had had in many months.

A few years ago two men on a 400-mile cross-country flight between Los Angeles and southern Utah crashed in the desert. One of them was dazed after the crash and either slept or was unconscious during the night. In the morning he woke to find it raining. With fabric from the plane he trapped water to drink. The pilot was still unconscious. He took the mirror from the plane and put it in the pilot's pocket, then began walking down the mountain. He got to a rancher. Search planes were sent out and ground search was started. They couldn't locate the crash.

Later a search plane pilot saw a small flash of light about 18 miles from the wreck. He came down for a closer look. It was the lost pilot signaling with the mirror his passenger had stuck in his pocket. A signal mirror is the best, the simplest, the most important piece of survival equipment ever invented for the desert.

THE BARE ESSENTIALS

The Siamese twins of desert survival equipment are a gallon canteen of water and a signal mirror. Those are the bare essentials. Without them your desert survival is a matter of luck, fortitude, and seasonal low temperatures.

The equipment quintuplets of desert survival will be water, mirror, compass, flashlight (electric torch) and more water. Beyond those minimum items additional equipment should include shade-producing material, adequate clothing, more water, additional signal equipment (flares, radio) still more water, and finally some food.

If you survive in the desert you must keep your body properly hydrated either with adequate water or by keeping body heat production down and keeping desert heat (from sun, air, and ground reflection) out.

FLIGHT PLAN

Rescue in the desert depends on how well the authorities and your friends are informed of your whereabouts. In words of one syllable, FILE A FLIGHT PLAN. An overdue ETA (Estimated Time of Arrival) sets the wheels of rescue into motion. Too many private planes take off from minor flying fields without a flight plan.

The speed of your pickup will depend on your actions from the moment of take-off and every minute thereafter. Search will be centered along the route of your *filed flight plan*. It will begin near your last reported fix or check point. The more you are off course the longer it will take to find you. The longer it takes to find you the more important is your ability to signal searching planes.

SIGNAL MIRROR

"A column of smoke by day, a pillar of fire by night" is a Biblical quotation worth remembering for desert signaling. You may have trouble making a smoke by day but the blinding flash of a signal mirror will "knock a pilot out of the cockpit," and you can almost always stir up the *desert dust* to make a cloud if you see or hear a plane. Likewise there may be no fuel for your flame by night but even the tiny spark of an electric torch shows far in the blackness of a desert night.

Don't waste your flashlight batteries. Save them until you hear an aircraft at night. In the daytime you can use the signal mirror whenever there is sunlight; it pays to flash it at the horizon even when no plane is in view. Search planes have turned toward a mirror flash even when the survivor had neither seen nor heard them.

When you think your mirror flash has hit a plane be sure to hold it on him until he turns your way. Don't move the mirror erratically so that it can be confused with gun flashes. But if the pilot comes toward you don't blind him—once he is headed in your direction give him only occasional flashes to keep him on course. When he has landed on the desert remember he is trying to help you. All he needs is a guiding light, not a steady blinding glare.

THE WILL TO SURVIVE

There is, of course, one vitally important factor in every successful survival incident. Its absence has made tragedies of what should have been only minor incidents. That factor, of course, is your *will to survive.*

Without the will to survive men have died in deserts when water was within reach. With it, they have lived to reach safety under fantastic conditions and with no equipment other than their bare hands. A prospector in the deserts of northwestern Arizona traveled 150 miles in eight days without water in temperatures sometimes over 120° F. He lost 25 per cent of his weight —nearly twice the dehydration normally considered fatal at that temperature. He lived by the grace of God and his will to survive.

KNOWLEDGE VS. FEARS

You, too, might survive in the desert with nothing but your will to survive. It has been done, but you can increase your chances to live and tell about it if you have the three additional assets to survival:

Knowledge to survive
Equipment for survival
Intelligence to survive

Your *knowledge* should include as much know-how on outdoor living as you can accumulate. Air Rescue Service personnel say that country boys, or city boys who have had a lot of Boy Scout training, are the best survivors.

Your knowledge should include all you can learn about the area in which you are located and the areas over which you may have to fly. Knowledge of the people who live in those areas is excellent life insurance. Remember when you become a survivor you may be the foreigner in another people's "home town." It is up to you to *know their customs.*

You can carry *equipment* for survival when you fly. It is well worth the space it occupies. How much the equipment is worth depends on your knowledge of how to use it.

INTELLIGENCE vs. CARELESSNESS

It takes *intelligence* to survive in good health. Start planning on what you would do IF and WHEN. Plan to take advantage of circumstances.

Fear of the unknown; fear of discomfort; fear of people; fear of your own weaknesses—these fears handicap you like two strikes on a batter before he steps to the plate. You can eliminate fear with a little knowledge.

You'll find that discomfort can be endured, that it is seldom as bad as you feared. The people you were afraid of will usually turn out to be "good Joes" when you get to know them. The unseen wild animals that scare you by their noises at night will run from you in daylight. A little planning and thinking about survival now will eliminate most of your weaknesses and your fears.

Stupidity, or the inability to recognize and evaluate a situation even with all the facts in hand, is the greatest hazard of all. If you fail through negligence to take along a survival kit on your flight—or if you can't get on well with strange people or take advantage of the "breaks" that come your way—don't blame Lady Luck or the survival equipment.

Rest is important in survival. When you have a job to do or a problem to think out, you need energy. Plenty of rest will increase your efficiency, allow you to walk farther and think more clearly about escape from your dilemma.

Time is not a factor in survival if you land near water. Authorities and your friends will get you out if you do your part intelligently. It may take a week, or it may take six months—so you must rest and be patient.

WATER AND SHADE

One well-known crew that flew over all types of Sahara Desert terrain decided "If we ever get in trouble over the desert we'll ride the plane down. We'll need the water, the equipment and the shelter the plane can provide." These men have taken the first step toward a successful desert survival experience if they ever encounter one. They plan on having as much water as possible. They plan on utilizing the shade and the equipment that a grounded, even wrecked airplane can supply. They know the value of shade in extending their survival time and in reducing the body's need for drinking water.

The intelligent, foresighted traveler can live in the desert for days, weeks and months at a time—but always on his own terms, not on the desert's terms. He always plans in advance for possible and probable emergencies. He carries his shelter, sleeping bag, and supply of food and water. He learns in advance where wells or water holes could be expected and he keeps his friends posted on the area in which he is working.

You can do the same. As long as your radio works you can keep authorities informed of your location. You can see that your water supply is in the plane in nonleaking containers when you take off. You can check your survival kit, and learn how to use the things it contains. You can learn to use your signal mirror and emergency radio equipment. You can study the maps and learn the few landscape features, find out whether the dry river beds lead to the sea, or lead deeper into the desert (as they do on the north edge of the Sahara in Libya).

Don't sell the desert short. It is a rugged region but a fascinating one if you are prepared.

DESERT SHELTER, FIRES AND CLOTHING

SHELTER

Natural shelter is hard to find in most deserts. In general it is limited to the shade of cliffs, the lee side of hills or the overhanging bank of a dry stream bed. In some desert mountains you can find good cavelike protection under tumbled blocks of rocks broken from cliff sides. On rare occasions you may find a twisted, stunted bush or tree in the Gobi, Sahara or Arabian Deserts. Over these a survivor may spread his parachute for shade. In the Amer-

Fig. 6.1. Typical desert terrain—Aruma south of Riyadh, Arabian Desert. (*Aramco Photo*)

ican Southwest, cactus plants will serve the same purpose but out on the open plain of all deserts you must carry shelter, like food and water, with you.

During the Sahara winter (October to May) the absence of shelter is not serious. It gets cold at night, but not much below freezing, while daytime temperatures reach the 80's and low 90's. You will not suffer from exposure if properly dressed.

In the summer months with their hot days shelter from the midday sun is advisable. Natives on desert journeys carry tents either of skins or of woven wool cloth, as well as tent poles and stakes. These tents are about four feet high in the center, sloping to about 18 inches above the ground. During the heat of the day this gives good circulation of air and a cool place to rest. When it begins to get chilly in late afternoon or evening, matting is unrolled around the inside edge of the tent to keep out the breeze and retain the heat. Some nomad groups raise and lower the edges of the tent as the temperature rises and falls.

In Sahara oases, dwellings are thick-walled, flat-roofed adobe structures, often whitewashed and painted blue around the windows and doors, since blue reduces glare and seems to keep away some of the flies.

The Mongols of the Gobi have semipermanent dwellings called

Fig. 6.2. Mongol Summer Camp. The felt walls of winter yurts are raised in warm weather to allow air circulation. (*Photo by Alonzo W. Pond.*)

yurts (Fig. 6-2). These are circular with a willow or bamboo frame (purchased from China) over which is lashed a thick sheet of felt. The conical roof is also of felt with an open smoke hole like an American Indian tepee.

Mongol lamaseries are adobe structures built by Chinese laborers and decorated with red and gold. Many lamas, however, erect felt yurts in temple courtyards for their sleeping quarters. The felt yurt, like the adobe house, is well insulated against both the summer heat and the winter cold. The latter is a serious hazard in the Gobi where January and February temperatures are regularly down to $-15°$ F or $-20°$ F.

For traveling short distances, especially in summer, the Mongols use a light, cotton-cloth A-type tent, blue outside and white inside, also sloping to the ground at both front and back. Like the circular yurt, it offers minimum wind resistance. Tent poles and pegs are carried with the cloth, as no supports are available in the desert. During hot middays of July and August the edges of the tent are propped up to allow free circulation of air. When strong winds blow, extra ropes over ridge pole and sides are staked down to keep the tent from ballooning off across the desert.

DESERT FIRES AND FUEL

Cooking fires are not large in any desert. Fuel is so scarce that desert travelers learn to make efficient use of all such material they find. In semidesert regions any thorny bush or any vegetation that will burn is gathered and carried miles to camp sites for fuel. Stems of palm leaves and similar wood serve as fuel in and near oases. Out in the open desert dry roots or any bits of dead vegetation are carefully hoarded to boil tea or cook a meal. Dried camel dung is the standard fuel where woody fibers are lacking.

In the Gobi, dried heifer dung is the preferred fuel. You will recognize it by the symmetrical shape in contrast to the broad irregular pattern of cow dung. It burns with a hot blue flame in contrast to the smoky yellow flame of cow dung or sheep dropping. Bricks of hand-pressed dung are used to build winter corrals; as the cold becomes severe the top layers of the corral walls are used as fuel for cooking and for heating the yurts. *Argol* is the Mongol word for all kinds of dung. The natives have large argol baskets and argol forks which are used in collecting animal droppings for winter fuel supply.

DESERT CLOTHING

In summer heat, desert conditions call for head and body covering against direct sunlight and excessive evaporation of sweat. Natives in the Sahara prefer either white wool or white cotton. Even the Tuaregs, famous for their blue-black garments and face veils, wear white cotton undergarments regularly and white outer garments occasionally.

Gobi natives wear dark clothing, even in summer, and in winter add sheepskin overcoats. Gobi winters are cold, and bitter winds are common. During that season you will be comfortable only if dressed as for a Dakota winter. In spring and fall, the strong wind and dust penetrate ordinary clothing so that a sheepskin-lined garment is comfortable even though the temperature is not much below freezing.

During Sahara winters, natives wrap themselves in woolen burnooses or capes with hoods. Explorers often dress in woolen underwear, wool riding trousers, wool shirts, and sheepskin coats.

By 10 a.m. the coat is removed; by 1 p.m. the wool shirt is open at the neck and sleeves are rolled up. At 4 p.m. the process is reversed, and before long the wool-lined coat is welcomed again.

In either the Sahara or Gobi a good hiking boot, comfortable and suited to the taste of the wearer, is the best footgear for a man afoot. Desert surfaces are not often as hard as concrete, although there are many rock plateaus in most of the arid wastes. A good leather or composition sole will protect your feet from gravel and clumps of sharp-bladed grass. Generally loose trouser legs will be more comfortable than wraps or puttees in summer. Some men, however, prefer high leather boots or leather puttees even though they are hot in summer.

Sand-dune areas can be crossed barefoot in cool weather but in hot summer any desert surface will burn the soles of your feet. The average man's feet will sink less than an inch in the sand either barefooted or with shoes. Sand does slow your speed somewhat, compared to the level plains, but it is not a serious handicap. Nor is any special preparation required for keeping sand out of your shoes, as some survival literature would indicate.

DESERT FOOD

Food, like water, must be carried with you in the true deserts. When you reach an oasis you are no longer in the desert in the survival sense, for you have reached a populated area. Food is far less important to survival than water; you can get along without food for several days with no ill effects. In fact you can live several weeks without food, but only a few days without water.

You may find enough wild plant food in many deserts to supplement the concentrated foods in your survival kit, but don't plan on living off the native vegetation. In the American Southwest edible wild plants are more abundant than in the Sahara, the Gobi, or in Arabia but it may take more energy to gather the food than you'll get by eating it.

CACTUS PLANTS

The fruit of all cactus plants is good to eat. Some cactus fruit is red, some yellow when ripe, but all are soft. Any of the flat leaf cactus plants like the prickly pear can be boiled and eaten as greens (like spinach) if you peel or cut off the spines first. In severe droughts cattlemen burn off the spines and use the thick leaves for fodder. The prickly pear has been introduced to the

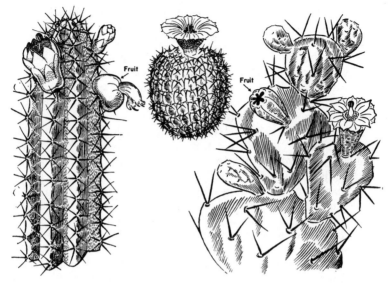

Fig. 6.3. The fruit of all cactus plants is edible. They are all native to America but the prickly pear (right) has spread to the edge of most deserts over the world.

desert edges in Asia, Africa, the Near East and Australia, where they grow profusely around native habitations. Natives eat the fruit as fast as it ripens.

True cacti are found only in the American deserts—unless, like the prickly pear, they have been imported to other deserts. There are other plants found in world deserts which look like cacti. The safe rule to follow is: If it looks like a cactus but has a milky juice, AVOID IT.

CELERY, CURRANTS AND CHERRIES

Wild celery, wild currants and choke cherries are all edible and are found in sections of American deserts. Indians living in those areas gather piñon nuts for food but it will try your patience to eat enough for a good meal. They are so tiny you can almost starve to death while eating them. Explorers have listed half a dozen edible plants which they have tasted while in the Gobi of Mongolia. All may be considered as agreeable supplements to your diet. They are neither plentiful enough nor sub-

stantial enough, however, to form your main food supply for
many days.

THORNBUSH

The young leaves can be eaten or steeped to make a drink like
tea. The pale green inner bark is edible and has a slightly sweet
taste, but a camel can eat outer bark, inner bark and twig. You
might find the twigs indigestible and the thin inner bark hardly
worth the labor to separate it.

DUNE-PLUMS

These are small, berrylike drupes, each with one seed. The
fruit is dark purple when ripe but may be eaten even when red,
and either raw or cooked. The flavor resembles that of an ox-
heart cherry. In some areas you can gather dune-plums by the
pailful.

RHUBARB

Two kinds of rhubarb, a lowland and a highland type, are
good to eat. The lowland type has a round leaf, about 1½ in.
in diameter. Its two to five leaves grow close to the ground where
summer rains have moistened the earth. It may be eaten raw or
cooked.

The highland rhubarb is found in the Altai Mountains above
2000 feet altitude. It has thick stalks like our garden rhubarb
(pie plant) and spear-shaped leaves. You find it on broken rock
and dirt on the slopes at the base of steep cliffs where moisture
is available.

ONIONS

There are two kinds of onions in the Gobi. A hot, strong type
like scallions grows in the desert in late summer. During this
season native mutton tastes strongly of onion flavor. These will
add pep to your food, but you won't want to make a meal of
them. The highland onions grow 2 or 2½ in. in diameter. You
can eat these like apples and can also eat the greens either raw
or cooked.

Onions and other bulbs are found in other parts of the world
besides the Gobi. If a bulb looks like an onion when cut in two,
but does not smell like an onion or like garlic, *don't eat it.*

PEAS

There are several kinds of desert peas with small seeds resembling lentils. These, too, may be eaten raw or cooked. Some species taste bitter unless roasted and then boiled. Pealike pods of plants are edible when young and tender. In mature pods the seeds and the gummy inside of the pod are both edible.

FLOWERS

Sometimes after a rain there are abundant flowers in many desert regions. You can eat any flowers of the desert except possibly those with milky or colored sap. Grasses are all edible. Usually you pull the grass blades away from the roots and eat the soft tender part of them. All grass seeds are also edible. During the time China was occupied by Japan before World War II many Chinese had little else but grass. One man kept a list of the more than 125 different species he had eaten.

OTHER PLANT FOOD

In the Arabian Desert there is a plant which the local people call *abal*. When it is in full bloom it has red tassels and small white flowers, which are edible and may be eaten raw. The dry twigs of the plant are crushed in mortars by the Bedouin to make a substitute for tea, which tastes somewhat bitter and is said to be constipating but serves as an antidote to the salts in the waters of such desert regions as the Naifa.

If there is rain during October in the Arabian Desert there will be truffles and mushrooms the following spring. They form a substantial addition to the food of the tent dwellers on those occasions.

Succulent plants are numerous in some desert and near-desert regions. These have thick, fleshy leaves with much moisture. Some of them even look like stones, so don't let their camouflage keep you from a juicy meal. Others are erect like the cactus. They have spines but no obvious leaves and their sap is milky. Those succulents with milky juice and those which are extremely astringent or bitter are to be avoided.

Natives, especially in the Sahara, have a notion that most plants are poisonous. Their fears are justified in the case of the oleanders. Even the smoke from burning green oleander sticks will cause nausea.

Citrullus colocynthus is a delicious-looking but poisonous

Fig. 6.4. Sahara Desert. Plant with poisonous fruit resembling citron.
It is called coloquinta by the French.

watermelon-like gourd of the Sahara and Arabian Deserts. It strongly resembles the little round watermelons sometimes seen in American supermarkets. It is not eaten by desert rodents, ruminants or jackals, apparently because it is violently purgative. *Citrillus* is the only plant in the Sahara with enough moisture to be of value to a thirsty traveler—but poison is poison, so don't be tempted.

The general rule regarding strange plants applies in the deserts as well as other parts of the world: avoid those plants with milky or colored sap. It is safe to taste anything otherwise, but if you don't like it, spit it out. A taste of a suspected plant won't kill you even if it is poison.

ANIMAL FOOD

Animal food will be difficult to find in the Sahara. Gazelles do exist but are constantly hunted out by the desert soldiers. Antelopes, however, are numerous in many parts of the Gobi; it is not uncommon to see herds of ten to a hundred animals, but you may also strike areas where there are none at all.

Wolves are found in rugged terrain near good antelope pasture. Around occasional springs or water holes in old river beds many birds are found night and morning. In spring and fall, ducks and other waterfowl are numerous. In fact, game is generally available in the Gobi, but so are domestic animals.

Thick-tailed lizards of desert areas are edible and meat is a more sustaining food than the scarce desert plants. Kangaroo rats and jerboas are also edible but hard to catch unless you are a skilled trapper. Snakes are certainly not numerous in the most arid deserts but, like other desert animals, they can be eaten when you do find them.

All desert animals are found only where there is some vegetation. You may find them far from water, however.

When meat is digested the waste products must be eliminated from your body through the kidneys. That takes water. If your water supplies are low it may be wise not to eat the rats, snakes, and lizard's tails even if you can get them. You can dry the meat and save it until you have a water supply; meat keeps very well if wiped dry and buried in desert sand.

The only important edible insects you are likely to find in the deserts are locusts. They develop in some localities and swarm out to distant parts where they devour anything green. Natives roast them and feast on them during the short season of availability—slight compensation indeed for lost crops and subsequent famine. They are rich in protein so unless your water supply is adequate, eating locusts will increase your dehydration.

PLANT FOOD

The American deserts of the Southwest are far better supplied with wild foods than Old World deserts. An American botanist found only 13 species of flowering plants during a month's trip in the Libyan Sahara. He contrasts that number with the fact that "many dozens of species from places no larger than an ordinary farm are found in a single canyon of the American Desert or on a single slope." Even in its deserts, American abundance surpasses that of other parts of the world.

NATIVE SUPPLIES

Food is available from friendly desert people when you approach them properly. They will recognize your sign language for "I'm hungry" even if they don't understand your words.

The natives of Mongolia live in scattered family units, like the Navajo Indians in the southwestern United States. They raise sheep, goats, horses, camels, and cattle. They also keep large, unfriendly dogs. Flocks and herds are guarded and are taken to water twice a day. In an emergency, it is better to appeal to the natural hospitality of the native than to risk his anger by destroying his property.

Once contact has been made with the natives in any desert, food and water are usually available; in normal times, desert people are hospitable. Native food in the Sahara and Arabia is both palatable and edible. The meat offered you may be goat, mutton, chicken, or in rare cases, camel. *Cous-cous,* or steamed wheat flour pellets, which looks like a great platter of rice, is really good eating. The vegetables that go with it will be familiar to most travelers.

The food available in the Gobi is also familiar rather than exotic. Natives eat cheese and butter and buttered tea, also some rice. In recent years under Russian tutelage they have been urged to eat bread and vegetables. You are less likely to enjoy native food in the Gobi than in the Sahara, as many Mongols pay less attention to cleanliness and sanitation than the Arabs and the Berbers.

SOURCES OF WATER

The one great truth about the desert is: Where there is water, there is life.

Desert oases are proof of that statement. As water becomes available through new wells or irrigation projects, date groves and garden patches spread into once barren desert. When the wells go dry, the desert reclaims the area. Man can live in the desert only as long as his water supply lasts. The measure of his adaptation to the desert is therefore his ability to get water.

WELLS

In all deserts, wells are the sources of most water. Hand-dug wells have furnished water to irrigate Sahara oases which are located in low places of the desert—in basins, dry river valleys and hollows in the dunes. The best of these are ancient river beds.

Tunnels. In the western Sahara the natives have dug elaborate tunnels for irrigation. Starting at the edge of a basin or in the bed of an old river, they dig a ditch toward the desert, keeping the bottom of the ditch on a gentle slope away from the basin. As the ditch extends out into the desert it soon becomes too deep to be maintained as an open trench. The workmen extend it as a tunnel as far as they can see without artificial light. Leap-frogging ahead along the same line, they set down a well and tunnel backward and forward. Then another jump is made and another well dug. Eventually these chains of wells, connected by a tunnel in the moist sand, extend for miles into the desert. Water collects in the underground channel and flows to the basin, where it irrigates the gardens. The same system has been dis-covered in central Asian deserts nearly 10,000 miles from the tunnels in the Sahara.

Foggera and Quants. These chains of wells, called *foggera* in the Sahara, are even more extensive in Iran, where they are known as *quants*. In Iraq they are *karez*, while the people of Morocco call them *khotteras* (*rheteras*). Similar well systems have also been reported in Mexico.

Wherever found, these chains of wells are the aviator's friend. They can be seen from the air and they lead to oases. In the Sahara they guide pilots to some of their regular, hard-to-find air fields. To the man alone on the ground they are shelter and a lifesaving water supply.

The Gobi is itself a great basin with only internal drainage so that water falling on its mountain edges, if it does not evapo-rate, replenishes the ground water supply. Wells dug in valley bottoms or other low places of the Gobi tap that water supply at a depth of 10 to 15 feet.

In northern Mongolia, wells are less numerous than in the south because there are more springs. All roads lead to water, however. You'll know you are going in the right direction when your trail joins another. The "arrow" formed by two connecting trails points in the general direction of the water.

WATER POINTS

In American deserts, water points are more often natural springs or seepages on the rock walls of canyons. Rains and melt-ing snow of the highlands seep down into the rocks and eventu-ally flow through porous layers until those strata outcrop on cliff sides. Moisture from these natural springs is quickly absorbed by vegetation and evaporation or else is soon lost in desert gravels. If you are desert-wise you may find these water points, but many early travelers in Death Valley missed them.

Natural cisterns, or "tanks" contain sweet water after the rains. These rock basins collect the natural drainage. Often there are several such tanks in a series. The higher one fills and overflows to a lower cistern, which in turn spills to one still lower.

During gold-rush days prospectors' trails led to these water points. Frequently they were so far apart that travelers couldn't cover the distance between water points and died of dehydration. Some made it to the lower tank, found it dry and died of thirst, although there was water in the higher tanks only a few hundred yards away.

IRRIGATION DITCHES AND LAKES

Great desert rivers like the Nile, Tigris, and Euphrates have been used to irrigate the desert for centuries. Shorter streams on the desert edges are also diverted into irrigation ditches (Fig. 6-5) to water gardens and the roots of palm trees. At other points where mountain streams lose themselves in desert sands, the

Fig. 6.5. El Kantara, in the northern Sahara, is an oasis irrigated from a river north of the desert. Houses are thick walled adobe and flat roofed; adobe is good insulation against summer heat and winter cold. (*Photo by Alonzo W. Pond.*)

natives plant their trees and crops right over the lost rivers so that roots can reach the water without difficulty.

There are shallow lakes in most deserts, many of them undrained, which have been without outlets for many thousands of years so that evaporation has concentrated the amount of salt in the water and has made them distinctly salt-water lakes. Some of the salt water tastes like table salt, but in other areas it may contain magnesium or alkali. If not too strong, such waters are drinkable even though they may have a laxative effect.

POISONED WELLS

One sometimes hears stories about poisoned wells. Many of these are based merely on experience with bad-tasting water rather than actual poison. The danger of poison from water in the Sahara can be cited only as a curiosity, for there are just two wells in this class. One is at Tini-Hara in Esh-Shish Erg, where the water has so strong a chlorine content that it will stain or chemically attack clothing. In the same village, General Laperrine found another well with such a high concentration of saltpeter that it caused vomiting. Occasionally in the Gobi and in some American deserts one will encounter a well so strongly alkaline that he will prefer to go the six or eight miles to a fresher water supply.

ROCK HOLLOWS

In the Sahara and Arabian Deserts deep hollows on rocky plains act as cisterns and collect surface water from the rare torrential rains. These tanks may be dry for 10 to 15 years, then suddenly have water deep enough for a good swimming hole (Fig. 6-6). This water is fresh and drinkable and may take several weeks or months to dry up. Unfortunately there is no way for the casual traveler or stranger to know of the existence of such water holes, nor is there any rule to guide one to them. They are natural drainage basins like any depression on a plain or plateau. If you know there has been a rain recently in your area, keep a sharp lookout for hollows or any protected cavity which would naturally collect surface drainage.

PLANTS AS SOURCES OF WATER

In the Gobi and Sahara, plants are not a source of water supply. American deserts are slightly better favored. The large barrel cactus does contain considerable moisture which can be

Fig. 6.6. Water hole 500 feet deep—Wadi Kharj, Arabian Desert. (*Aramco Photo*)

squeezed out of the pulp if you have the energy to cut through the tough, outer spine-studded rind.* The amount of water you get from a barrel cactus will depend on how long it has been since the last good rain.

WATER HOLES

In desert and near-desert regions, wells are gathering places for native peoples as well as stopping places for caravans. Permanent camps or habitation may be some distance away from the well— sometimes as much as two or three miles away. Passing caravans may camp within a few yards or a few hundred yards from a well. Campfire ashes, animal droppings, and generally disturbed surface will tell you that others have camped there. Such indica-

---

* In 1942 Edwin Waldislaus Zolnier, 1st Lt., USMCR, parachuted from his burning plane and roamed the Arizona desert for 5 days. He tried the juice of several cacti which were "very nauseating" before he discovered the barrel type. He "gouged large chunks out of the living cactus and chewed the water content out of it." The juice completely satisfied his thirst and the taste was pleasant at first but became monotonous after a few days. Chunks of the cactus were carried for several days and still had moisture in them. The marine also rubbed his body with the pieces he had chewed. This moisture helped keep him cool. (From his letter of July 31, 1944, quoted by Ladislaus Cutak in *Missouri Botanical Garden Bulletin*.)

tions will also tell you that a well is not far off. Paths leading from the camping area should also lead to the well.

Many desert water holes are not true wells but natural tanks or cisterns. These may be located behind rocks, in gullies or side canyons and under cliff edges. Often the ground surface near them is solid rock or hard-packed soil on which paths do not show; in such cases you may have to search for the water point. In the Libyan Sahara, doughnut-shaped mounds of camel dung often surround the wells. Unless you recognize the small mound ring, you can easily miss the well.

On some flat plains, wells that are not often used are covered against sandstorms. Even though there may be no sand in the immediate area, sandstorms will in time fill up uncovered wells. Desert people have learned to cover such wells a little below the top. You can dig out the cover and reach water easily in these wells, but be careful not to dump the sand into the cavity—there may be only a shallow pool of water in the well bottom.

OTHER SOURCES OF WATER

When you are away from trails or far from wells, you may still find water. Along the seashore or on sandy beaches of desert lakes, dig a hole in the first depression behind the first sand dune, where rain water collects from local showers. Stop digging when you hit wet sand; fresh, or nearly fresh, drinkable water will seep from the sand into the hole. If you dig deeper, you may strike salt water.

Shallow Wells. Damp surface sand anywhere marks a good place to scoop out such a shallow "well" from which you can collect water into your canteen or other receptacle. Among sand dunes away from surface water the lowest point between the dunes is where rain water will collect. Dig down three to six feet. If sand gets damp, keep digging until you hit water. If you dig in the dune itself, you may strike a foot or so of damp sand with dry sand below; when that happens, you had better look for a lower spot to dig your well.

In a sand-dune belt, water will most likely be found beneath the original valley floor at the edge of the dunes rather than in the easy digging middle.

Dry stream beds often have water just below the surface. It accumulates and sinks at the lowest point on the outside of a bend in the stream channel as the stream dries up.

In mud flats during winter you may find wet mud at the lowest

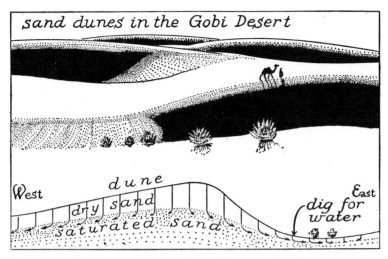

Fig. 6.7. In dune areas water collects after rains but in the course of months, sometimes even in a few days, it dries out or sinks down to deep rock layers beneath the desert floor. (*Drawn by F. K. Morris.*)

point. Wring mud out in a piece of cloth to get water—but don't drink if the water is too salty or tastes soapy.

"Soaks." Some watering places in Australia are known as "soaks." They are located in slight depressions, sometimes shaded by a scrubby acacia tree. The natives know these water points but often there is nothing to distinguish them from thousands of other similar depressions. The white man who finds himself alone in unfamiliar parts of the Australian desert will have trouble locating these rare water holes.

Sip Wells. Natives in the Kalahari Desert of South Africa have developed a technique of getting water from "sip wells." They locate a spot where the sand or river bottom still contains moisture from the last storm. They dig into the wet sand a foot or so and bury a bundle of grass or plant fibers; into the sieve thus formed they insert a hollow reed. By sucking hard on the reed they draw water out of the sand. The grass sieve keeps sand from blocking the reed and the native sucks water into his mouth without swallowing. He then spits the water into a container until enough is accumulated for immediate needs. One old native woman once supplied two white men and herself with water for several days when other supplies were exhausted.

Condensation. In the Arabian Desert near the Persian Gulf and the Red Sea and in the Libyan Sahara near the Mediterranean Sea, along the western South American coast and the Gulf of California there is considerable moisture in the air. This moisture will condense on cool objects. Often condensed moisture or dew will be heavy enough to drop from metal awnings or roofs on cool mornings. In Arabia, morning dew and fog extend inland several miles. Occasionally fog occurs as far out as 200 miles from the Persian Gulf.

If you find dew on the metal wings of your crashed plane you may collect the drippings in a container, or you might get more by wiping it off the cool metal with a clean handkerchief or soft cloth and wringing it out into a container.

Cool stones, collected from below the hot surface of the desert if placed on waterproof tarpaulin may cause enough dew to collect for a refreshing drink. Exposed metal surfaces like airplane wings or tin cans are best condensers of dew. They should be clean of dust or grease to get the best-tasting water. Dew evaporates soon after sunrise in the desert. If you expect a good drink you will have to collect the dewdrops very soon after sunup.

Surface Pools. Desert natives often know of lingering surface pools in dry stream beds or other low places, and cover them in various ways to protect them from excessive evaporation. If you look under likely brush heaps or in sheltered nooks you may locate such pools in semiarid brush country.

All birds need water; some fly considerable distances at sunset and dawn to reach water holes. If you hear their chirping in the early morning or evening you may locate their private drinking fountain. In true desert areas flocks of birds will circle over water holes.

The presence of vegetation does not always mean that surface water is available. Many plants have an extensive shallow root system, which enables them to make maximum use of water from rare desert rains. Other plants have long taproots that go down several feet to reach a permanent supply of ground water. In the American desert, mesquite is an outstanding example. The roots of this plant are known to grow to great depths to reach ground water.

Places that are visibly damp, or where animals have scratched, or where flies hover are more reliable spots to dig for water because they indicate recent existence of surface water there.

DESERT TRAVEL

The great deserts of the Old World have been crossed and recrossed by nomads and travelers for thousands of years, following definite routes along marked trails from oasis to wells and from wells to water holes or other oases (Fig. 6-8). In some areas

Fig. 6.8. Bedouin tent colony, sets up camp near troughs which provide water for the camels belonging to the nomads who travel across the Saudi Arabian desert. (*Aramco Photo*)

governments keep wells open or dig new wells, but most desert travelers are public-spirited enough to repair a damaged well, although their generosity doesn't extend to leaving a rope for the next traveler. Unless you are agile enough to climb up and down a chimney like Santa Claus, you had better carry a hundred-foot rope in the Sahara. Thirty feet will reach water in most Gobi wells.

Bandits and smugglers, especially in Asia, often search out old abandoned routes and even dig new wells to make difficult trails usable. Changes in governments and political boundaries sometimes produce confiscatory customs stations on desert routes.

Then caravans abandon the easy trails in favor of more difficult routes in unwatched territory.

TRAILS

Desert trails frequently resemble interlacing cowpaths, all lead-ing in the same general direction. Usually these networks of paths are only a few yards wide. In rough terrain there may be two or three paths close together, but in a pasture or region of some vegetation the trail may be half a mile wide. In either case trails are usually as clear and distinct as the cowpaths in a farm lane, and can be seen easily from an automobile but more easily from the air. Even abandoned trails that are hardly visible on the ground show clearly from the air.

Fig. 6.9. An Obo is a combination religious monument and lighthouse in the Gobi of Mongolia. Located on a high point it is built of stones and can be seen for considerable distance. Once a year food for the spirits is placed in the little openings among the rocks. Pieces of cloth with sacred significance are draped above the Obo to flutter in the wind and carry prayers aloft. As each Obo differs from all others in structure passing caravans use them as guide posts in their travels. *(Photo by Alonzo W. Pond.)*

In the Algerian Sahara, trail junctions are often marked with wooden signposts giving distances. Automobile routes are frequently well outlined with pebbles, for the trail makers actually swept the surface of the desert to mark the route. Gasoline pumps and rest houses have also been erected all across the Sahara, but they are supplied only when the tourist busses are expected.

Automobile routes in the Sahara do not always follow the camel routes. Frequently the auto trails traverse more barren country where water holes are great distances apart, while camel routes generally strike water every 20 to 40 miles. In the extremely dry Tanezroufts and in Tripoli there are waterless stretches of over 100 miles, although these are rare.

In dune areas wind soon obliterates camel tracks, but the trail can be followed by watching the accumulation of camel droppings in hollows just below the dune crests. On the open plain automobile tracks remain visible for years after a car has passed.

Caravan trails in Mongolia are well marked with piles of stone 6 to 10 feet high placed like lighthouses on prominent buttes and mesa edges. They are called *obos* and serve the double purpose of signposts to travelers and religious monuments (Fig. 6-9). Some have small openings in the stone structure where, once a year, the Mongol lamas place food for the spirits who inhabit the area. This is done at the time of a religious feast when the *obo* is decorated with silk prayer cloths. Desert winds soon whip

Fig. 6.10. A camel caravan traversing the sand dunes of the Arabian desert. (*Aramco Photo*)

the silk to shreds, but some bits of cloth will cling to the strings on the monument until the next ceremony and will waft lama prayers aloft to desert gods.

Transportation in the Gobi, Arabia and the Sahara has been by camel caravan for centuries. Where distances between wells or watering places are not more than one day's march in the Sahara and Arabia, the horse and little donkey are considered speedier than the camel. Those animals must be watered twice a day, however, which forces them to give way on long dry marches to the slower, more cantankerous camel, who isn't even inconvenienced by a two- to four-days' jaunt between drinks.

VEHICLES

Cumbersome two-wheeled ox carts covered with matting to protect the freight from rain and snow lurch over many Asiatic desert trails from June to the first snowfall (late August or September). Plodding oxen and heavy wheels cut deep into grasslands when rain soaks the trail. Then the route may be half or three-quarters of a mile wide, and motorcars swing wide from the trail to avoid the ruts.

In both the Sahara and the Gobi, as well as in much of the American desert country, travel by ordinary automobile is practical. Where the route leads down from a mesa, or where it crosses a dry wash, it is often wise to follow the "road," but otherwise one can drive almost anywhere—and even chase antelope—with a car. This statement does not apply to mountainous areas, sand-dune regions, or badlands, which exist in parts of all deserts. You may have to detour such places or be very selective of your path, but in general motorcars will take you where you want to go faster than camels or your own two feet. Motorcars may carry your rescuers today in any desert in the world.

Natives of the desert have little idea of distances. Once in the Sahara an American asked a sheik how far it was to the next oasis.

"Seventy-five kilometers," said the Arab.

"But we have an automobile," said the American, thinking perhaps that the camel route would be too rough and the car would have to detour.

"Oh, with an automobile it is only 25 kilometers," replied the sheik. Time and distance are thoroughly mixed in the native concept. To the sheik, kilometers are not a standard of measurable distance, but merely a way of expressing how long it takes

to travel from one place to another. Don't take a native's statement of *distance* too seriously, but if he tells you how many *days*
it will take you to walk to the next well, you can accept his estimate as fairly accurate.

FOLLOWING A ROUTE

Caravans travel at night in summer if visibility is adequate.
They also travel in the early morning or late afternoon. In hot
weather they almost never travel after 10 a.m. or before 5 or 6
p.m. There is more daytime travel in winter. At night a large
caravan may pass close by without your seeing it. If your ears are
keen, however, you will hear the creak of boxes on camel saddles
or the swish and rustle of rubbing bales and bags.

Walking is not at all difficult in deserts. Caravan men walk as
much as they ride and frequently wear only light sandals. Trails
avoid difficult terrain like loose sand or broken rocky areas.

Valleys, ancient stream beds or dry water courses lead to inland basins in desert areas. In the Libyan Sahara such valleys start
within a few hundred yards of the sea and run inland. Great,
through-going rivers like the Nile, Tigris-Euphrates, Rio Grande
and Colorado which flow all year lead, of course, to the sea. Even
some short valleys join the ocean, but you had better have a map
to guide you in any generalization about following stream beds
or valleys in the desert.

Maps of desert regions are notoriously bad. They give a general idea of terrain features but are often as much as 50 miles in
error on specific landmarks. Try to get an "estimated degree of
accuracy" from a reliable source for any map you carry, check
that accuracy *before* you have to use the map.

The Chinese have a saying that a journey of 1,000 miles begins
with one step. If after a crash or bail-out you find yourself afoot
in the desert, remember that the Chinese have been walking across
the deserts of Asia for two thousand years, and that the Arabs
have been walking across the Sahara and the Arabian Deserts for
many centuries. These peoples accomplish their journeys by
taking (and thinking about) just one step at a time, by following
century-old trails. Even American pioneers and gold-rush stam-
peders crossed American deserts one step at a time.

All deserts have trails. They are visible from the air. Keep
them in sight when you fly the deserts; keep them in mind when
you see them on your maps. Land on them if you have any
control of your landing.

Trails lead to water. Wells, water-holes, and oases are reached by trails. In the Gobi wells are often eight, 10 or 15 miles apart. In the Sahara they may be 15 to 40 miles apart. In some sections of both deserts there are longer stretches between wells, and your plight is serious if you come down in regions where there are no trails.

Deserts are big open spaces and a map—even a poor one—will help you locate trails or find water. Don't be without a map and a compass unless you have an Arab's memory for landmarks.

DESERT PEOPLES

Natives and people who walk the desert trails are friendly people. They know the hardships of the desert, and, like people living close to nature anywhere in the world, their natural sense of hospitality prompts them to help a fellow traveler, particularly if the stranger appears friendly and is not armed or threatening in his approach.

There are bandits and smugglers in some deserts. The former are usually not far from large centers of population where trails begin to converge. Such groups do not welcome threats or too many questions about their business, whereas a friendly approach will get you help in the right direction. Of course, if you look like a bandit or take a domineering attitude in the presence of desert travelers, their reaction may be one of self-protection instead of hospitality. A friendly fellow afoot in the desert, however, should meet up with friends on the trail.

HEALTH AND HAZARDS

Deserts are quite healthy places. Dry air is not favorable to bacteria. Wounds usually heal rapidly in the desert, even without treatment. Except in some oases of the Sahara, malaria does not exist in the desert. Venereal diseases, however, are prevalent in both the Gobi and Sahara, and are much more common in Mongolia than in Africa. But unless you lose all sense of proportion as to your immediate situation, you will not become involved in this aspect of desert life. Moreover, since Russian domination of Outer Mongolia it is reported that scientific treatment of venereal diseases has considerably reduced their incidence.

DISEASES

Contagious diseases are generally not as common in the Gobi and Mongolia as they are in densely populated China. However, several diseases are reported from Chahar on the southern border of Mongolia. Among these is trachoma, a form of conjunctivitis that can result in blindness—so keep your eyes clean.

Summertime dysentery can be avoided by watching your diet and by not eating or drinking uncooked native food. In the fall and early winter typhoid and paratyphoid are present, but your inoculation shots will give you normal protection from these.

Crowded living quarters in family *yurts* or in adobe lamaseries and inadequate diet during winter and early spring are probably responsible for the appearance of tuberculosis and the seasonal occurrence of scurvy among some natives. The Mongols believe that scurvy can be cured by drinking lots of milk. Proper diet, of course, is your protection against contacting either scurvy or tuberculosis.

Any man who follows natural habits of cleanliness and his normal ideas of diet will find the deserts of the world quite free from disease, probably safer in that respect than the crowded cities of the United States or Europe.

MOSQUITOES AND OTHER PESTS

Ordinarily mosquitoes do not travel far from their breeding place. They breed in quiet or stagnant water such as rain pools, swamps, water pockets in plants, old tin cans or similar places. Since their usual life span is 15 to 20 days (under some conditions even a couple of months), their presence does not mean that you are near a supply of water, because the water of the breeding place has had time to dry up. In 1942 sentries in the Libyan Sahara saw "a cloud of vapour coming from the north which looked like a duststorm by moonlight." The "cloud" was a swarm of mosquitoes, and the nearest breeding places were 18 to 20 miles to the northeast. A strong wind carried the insects into the desert. Possibly they could have traveled even farther,* although such mosquito journeys are indeed rare.

All mosquitoes are unwelcome company but only some species of the genus *Anopheles* carry malaria. You can usually distinguish *Anopheles* from other mosquitoes by the way they settle on your skin or other surface. *Anopheles* settle with the proboscis and long axis of the body in one straight line at an angle of 45° with its "landing field." The Culicine mosquitoes, which in general do not carry disease, land with the abdomen parallel to or in-

---

* Salt marsh mosquitoes will migrate 30 to 40 miles on strong winds and some wind-carried insects reach even greater distances.

clined toward the surface upon which it rests. Cold weather slows them down.*

"Singing" mosquitoes are not *Anopheles,* and do not generally carry disease. Malaria, yellow fever, dengue, filariasis (elephantaisis) and other ills are mosquito-borne.†

Unless the female *Anopheles* has bitten a patient with malaria or other mosquito-carried disease before she bites you, no harm is done. She is only a vector, not an originator. If a "silent" mosquito drills you at a 45° angle, play safe and reach for an antimalaria tablet or similar preparation. It will be a week before malaria develops if the mosquito has infected you.

Flies are sometimes found so far out in the desert that one wonders how they got there. In Egypt and Libya flies buzz and pry about any exposed part of your body with persistent malignity. They settle on your lips, the corners of your eyes, your ears. There is no rest from flies unless you cover your face and every part of your body when you are in a fly-infested desert.

Since World War II many areas have been treated against flies. If garbage is covered and kitchens, food-handling areas, and sleeping quarters screened, relief from flies is possible. If you travel in the desert they will probably "hitch-hike" on your back, but in time you can get rid of them, at least until you reach another inhabited area.

Other insects and arachnids are less numerous. In some regions you might shake a scorpion out of your shoes in the morning. On the other hand, you can spend months in the desert without seeing one.

In Arabia the nomad women keep down the lice population by washing their hair every week in camel urine; it is strong stuff which is indeed tough on the current generation of bugs; unfortunately a new generation supplants them before the week is out.

Snakes are not numerous in desert areas. Some individuals manage to see snakes where others see none at all. An American scientific expedition in the Gobi of Mongolia once camped near a nest of vipers. Every man in the outfit was killing snakes for

---

* Mosquitoes in arctic or subarctic regions will bite at much lower temperatures than desert or tropic insects.

† Recent discoveries indicate that mosquitoes of the genus *Haemagogus* and *Aedes,* which breed in rock pools and treetops, serve as vectors of yellow fever. Several species of *Aedes* also carry dengue fever. Certain species of all main groups of mosquitoes can transmit filariasis. *Culer* and *Aedes* transmit encephalitis; *Psorophora* carries dermatobia.

an hour or two, but other years the same group saw almost no live snakes. Cold weather keeps them sluggish, and you probably will not see one in wintertime even on southern deserts.

MINE FIELDS

A really serious hazard exists in the World War II battle-grounds of the Libyan Sahara. These are the mine fields that have not been cleared except to a limited extent on certain roads. The engineers who were assigned the clean-up job lost so many men that only necessary routes through the fields were cleared. The following list gives the location of some still dangerous general areas. In these localities you should exercise extreme caution.

TABLE 6-1

LIST OF MINE HAZARDS IN LIBYA

4 mi. SE of Tarhuna, 32-22° N, 13-41°E
8 mi. SW of Homs, 32-45° N, 14-15° E
3 mi. NW of Sedada, 31-20° N, 14-47° E
2 mi. NW of Gheddahta, 31-32° N, 15-15° E
2 mi. SE of Bungem, 30-35° N, 15-22° E
1 mi. South of Sirte, 21-12° N, 16-24° E
1 mi. South of Mizda, 31-26° N, 12-58° E
1 mi. NW of Hun, 29-14° N, 16-00° E
AREA 31-45° N, 14-12° E
AREA 31-20° N, 15-18° E
AREA 31-08° N, 14-32° E
Other fields are uncharted.

SANDSTORMS

Sandstorms are not a serious hazard unless you make them so. If you try to travel when visibility is zero either in black night or sandstorm you can get lost quickly. Desert nights were so black in World War II that sentries could not find their posts. Some even missed a white tent at 50 feet.

When wind and dust impede your progress or shut out visibility, stop traveling! Mark the direction you are going with an arrow scratched deep on the ground, a row of stones or other markers. Then lie down and sleep out the storm with your back to the wind. You may get some comfort by covering your face with cloth.

Don't worry about being buried by a sandstorm. Desert romance stories have to make the storms good, but no man was ever buried alive by a desert sandstorm. Even in the sand dune areas it takes years for the sand to cover a dead camel. You won't have to sleep out a storm more than a few days at worst. Remember sandstorms are not blizzards. Sand doesn't accumulate as fast as snow. Your real danger is getting lost by traveling in zero visibility.

SUNGLARE AND DARK GLASSES

The color of the ground varies a great deal in different deserts. In areas where there is light sand as much as 80 per cent of the light that falls on it is reflected back, close to the amount of reflection from snow.

"Snow blindness" (photophthalmia) is due to the reflection of ultraviolet light. Since there is a little higher percentage of ultraviolet light in equatorial regions, there is probably a damaging concentration of these light rays at eye level from the reflected light in some desert regions.

Solar retinitis produced by the short infrared and visible light rays can also occur in deserts. You won't be bothered by this, however, unless you look at the sun or are scanning the sky in the area immediately adjacent to the sun.

All of which means that sunglasses of some sort are needed. Even though the glare does not seem painful to you, the very high intensities of the desert light will cause a decrease in your night vision.

Standard flying sunglasses in large frames are the easy and satisfactory solution to the problem of sunglare. Lenses should be preferably of neutral density with 12-16 per cent transmission, large enough to prevent light from the sides from striking the eye. Such glasses will provide partial protection against dust.

If you do not have flying sunglasses, the next best help is to make a cloth mask with narrow eye slits. Other helps are to shade the eyes from above with a hat or a turban which has cloth down the sides of your face. If other shading material is lacking, you get some relief from glare by blackening the area around your eyes with soot or a burnt stick.

7

Water: The Key to Desert Survival

MAINTENANCE OF BODY TEMPERATURE

The normal human body temperature is 98.6° F. Any variation, even as little as one or two degrees, from that normal temperature, reduces efficiency and is a symptom of illness or disorder of the body mechanism.

Patients have survived after a few minutes of body temperature as low as 20 degrees below normal (78.8° and 75.2°). In contrast, an increase in body temperature of six to eight degrees above normal for any extended period causes death.

Body temperature in a healthy person also can be raised to the danger point either by absorbing heat or by generating heat too fast. The body absorbs heat from air that is above 92° F, or from direct sunlight or radiant heat, even if the air is relatively cool. It can absorb heat reflected from the ground or direct from the ground by contact, as when lying down. Any kind of work or exercise, of course, produces body heat.

Regardless of where the heat comes from, the body must get rid of the excess and keep body temperature at the normal 98.6. This is done through the mechanism of perspiration and evaporation on the skin surface—a very effective and efficient process.

You can see how effective evaporation is in cooling if you fill a desert water bag and a canteen with water and hang them both in the sun. When the water in the canteen is 110° F, the water in the sweating desert bag will be only 70° F. Evaporation of sweat on the desert bag keeps it 40 degrees cooler. Evaporation of sweat on your skin keeps your body temperature normal.

DEHYDRATION

When you sweat, however, your body loses water, the loss being called dehydration. It is true that two-thirds of the human body is water, but every drop of body water is needed for circulation! Therefore when you lose body water by sweating you must replace that loss by drinking water. Otherwise the body pays for

201

the loss in reduced efficiency. Scientifically controlled experiments on men working in hot deserts have given us some figures on loss of efficiency compared to the per cent of dehydration or loss of body water.

For instance, a man who has lost 2½ per cent of his body weight by sweating (about 1¾ to 2 quarts of water) loses 25 per cent of his efficiency. Also it has been found that working in air temperatures of 110° F cuts down a man's normal ability about 25 per cent. That means that if your body lacks two quarts of water and the air around you is 110° F, you can do only about half as much work as you normally do. You can walk only half as far as you could with plenty of water in normal temperatures.

Your body must have water to form sweat and supply liquid for circulation. When the body dehydrates, the blood loses more than its share of water, becoming thicker and reduced in volume. The result is more work for the heart and less efficiency in circulation.

Efficiency lost by dehydration is quickly restored by drinking water. Replacing water lost by sweating will in a few minutes restore a man who has collapsed from dehydration. That means you can keep your efficiency in summer desert weather by drinking plenty of water. Without water in hot deserts you will not travel far, and the product of your labor will be small.

It is important to remember that there is no permanent harm done to a man who dehydrates even up to 10 per cent of his weight. If you weigh 150 pounds, you can sweat off 15 pounds *if* you drink enough water to gain it back later. You probably would not be able to walk to a nearby drinking fountain if you dehydrated that much. Yet if you could struggle over to it and drink a quart or two of cool water, you would be back on your feet in a few minutes as soon as you had replaced all the lost water. Ice cold water may cause stomach distress if drunk too rapidly, but warm or cool water may be swallowed as fast as you like.

There is no evidence that anyone can acclimatize to dehydration.

Here's how you feel when you dehydrate. First you are thirsty and uncomfortable. Then you start taking it easy, in slow-motion fashion, and have no appetite. As you lose more water, you get sleepy, your temperature goes up, and by the time you are dehydrated to 5 per cent of your body weight, you get sick at your stomach.

From six to 10 per cent dehydration, the symptoms follow in this order:

You experience dizziness, headache, difficulty in breathing, tingling in arms and legs, and a dry mouth; your body gets bluish, your speech is indistinct, and finally you can't walk. From there on you need help. The full range of symptoms are given in Table 7-1 below. They range from dizziness and delirium to cyanosis.

TABLE 7-1

SIGNS AND SYMPTOMS OF DEHYDRATION IN MAN*

Body-Water Deficits, per cent of Body Weight		
1-5%	*6-10%*	*11-20%*
Thirst	Dizziness	Delirium
Vague discomfort	Headache	Spasticity
Economy of movement	Dyspnea (labored breath-	Swollen tongue
Anorexia (no appetite)	ing)	Inability to swallow
Flushed skin	Tingling in limbs	Deafness
Impatience	Decreased blood volume	Dim vision
Sleepiness	Increased blood concen-	Shriveled skin
Increased pulse rate	tration	Painful micturition
Increased rectal temp.	Absence of salivation	Numb skin
Nausea	Cyanosis (body blue)	Anuria (defective mic-
	Indistinct speech	turition or none)
	Inability to walk	

* From *Physiology of Man in the Desert*, by E. F. Adolph and Associates, New York: Interscience Publishers, 1947. Items arranged in approximate order of first appearance as dehydration in the heat progresses to exhaustion and beyond.

It is probable that man can survive 25 per cent dehydration in air temperature of 85° F or cooler. At temperatures of 90° and higher, 15 per cent dehydration is probably fatal.

In summer desert heat, thirst is not a strong enough sensation to indicate the amount of water you need. If you drink only enough to satisfy your thirst, it will still be possible to dehydrate slowly. The best plan is to drink plenty of water any time it is available and particularly at mealtime.

WATER SUBSTITUTES

There is no substitute for water to prevent dehydration and keep the body at normal efficiency, unless you consider milk, soft drinks, tea and coffee as substitutes. These are mostly water and will prevent dehydration. Alcohol, salt water, gasoline, blood, or urine—any of those liquids which desert and sea castaway romances say men have tried as substitutes for water—*only increase dehydration,* because all contain waste products which the body must get rid of through the kidneys. More water is required to carry off the waste through the body than is contained in the liquids mentioned. For example, sea water is more salty than urine; therefore when sea water is drunk, the body must add more water to carry away the extra salt.

You can drink brackish water—water with half as much salt as sea water—and get a net gain of moisture for the body. Any liquid containing a higher percentage of waste than urine can do only harm to your cooling system.

Do not adulterate fresh water. However, if your fresh water accidentally gets mixed with salt, don't waste it. Drink it and get all the possible good from it.

Chewing gum or pebbles carried in the mouth may be a pleasant form of masking the symptoms of thirst. They do *no harm* but are not a substitute for water, nor will they aid in keeping your body temperature normal. Only water, sweated out and evaporated on your skin surface, can do that job. You may smoke, too, if you like. It will not change your need for water.

SALT IN HOT WEATHER

Recent studies on salt needs of the body indicate that a little extra salt on your food at mealtimes may be necessary for the first few days you are living in hot climates. When you have adjusted to living in the heat, food salted to your taste will supply all your body needs. Unless plenty of water is available, salt will definitely be harmful.

Sweat does contain salt, but the body is able to regulate the amount of salt in sweat and so conserve what is needed. In other words, don't worry about your salt but do keep up your water supply.

RATION YOUR SWEAT, NOT YOUR WATER

Your body produces so much heat every hour while at rest that unless that heat is lost, you will have two degrees of fever in one hour. Evaporating sweat takes care of that heat just as fast as it is formed. In order to keep your body temperature normal, every 100 calories of heat generated by your body and absorbed from air, sun, or ground, must be balanced by the evaporation of 173 grams of sweat.

In hot deserts you need about a gallon of water per day. If you follow the rules and walk in the "cool" desert night, you can get about 20 miles for that daily gallon. If you do your walking in daytime heat, you'll be lucky to get 10 miles to the gallon. Whether you sit out your desert survival or walk out, you'll need water, at least three to four quarts a day.

The only way to conserve your water is to ration your sweat. Drink your water as you need it, but keep heat out of your body. That can be done if you wear a shirt or similar light garment, white or light-colored if at all possible, in addition to the usual trousers, hat, and shoes. Clothing helps ration your sweat by not letting it evaporate so fast that you get only part of its cooling effect. Light-colored clothing also reflects or turns away the heat of the sun and keeps out the hot desert air.

Stay in the shade as much as possible during the day. Desert natives have tents open on all sides to allow free circulation of air during the daytime. If possible, sit up a few inches off the ground, rather than lying down. It is 30 to 45 degrees cooler a foot above the ground than on the ground itself. That difference can save you a lot of sweat.

Slow motion is better than speed in hot deserts. Slow and steady, slow and easy are desert working rhythms. If you must move about in the heat, you'll last longer on less water if you take it easy. Remember the Arab. He is not merely surviving in the desert; he *lives* there—and apparently likes it. He isn't lazy; he's just living in slow motion, the way the desert makes him live.

If you have plenty of water—two or three gallons per day— you can work as hard as you like, so long as you can drink as often as you like. In fact you had better drink more and oftener than you think your thirst requires if you want to stay healthy and keep efficient.

DESERTS ARE ALSO COLD

Heat is certainly a desert characteristic in summer daytime— from May to October in the Sahara, July and August in the Gobi, and summer in southwest U.S.A. During the rest of the year, however, you'll need winter clothing in the Sahara and arctic winter clothing in the Gobi.

Even if the thermometer falls the distance between wells does not change. You can dehydrate when the temperature is 65° in the shade, but it will take days instead of hours.

Winter or summer, afoot, on horseback, in a jeep, or aloft in a four-engined aircraft, travel in sight of the trails if not actually on the caravan paths. Plan your flight with trails in mind, for they will lead you to water.

Evidence left by those who have died from lack of water indicates that in temperatures over 100° F you may live a couple of days without water. Some have lasted only 18 hours in Arabia without water. Less than three quarts of water will not increase your survival time. If you conserve your energy and keep in the shade to avoid absorbing heat, every gallon of water you have is equal to another day of life. Rationing yourself to one or two quarts of water per day is actually inviting disaster (at high temperatures), because such small amounts will not prevent your dehydration. Loss of efficiency and resulting collapse follow dehydration, as surely as night follows day. *Ration your sweat but not your water.*

SUMMARY

There is no substitute for water. Pebbles in the mouth, chewing gum, or smoking may make you *feel* better but they will have no effect on your body's need for water. Alcohol, salt water, urine, or any liquid containing quantities of waste material which must be eliminated from the body through the kidneys will *increase* dehydration. Only the water in your stomach will keep you on your feet in hot summer deserts.

Arabs and Berbers, Mongols and American Indians live and travel in deserts. There are many plants and animals that survive under desert conditions. If you profit by the lessons these desert dwellers have given—if you understand the limitations under which you must walk or wait in the desert—if you practice what we've been preaching, you'll live to know the value of these desert lessons.

In summer desert temperatures you can conserve body water by keeping fully clothed and sitting in the shade during the day. Necessary work or walking should be done at night. Under such conditions in summer a man should be able to travel about 20 miles on a gallon of water. If you work or travel in the heat of daytime deserts, twice or three times as much water is essential to your body.

If you are flying in desert areas, plan to study your maps. Keep in mind the general locations and directions of the trails. Plan now to learn about deserts and desert people. Plan for your water if you are in desert areas. Your water needs are great even if you are riding across the desert in a jeep.

8

Desert People and You

People who inhabit the great deserts are conservative and
well adjusted. In general they have come to terms with nature's
elements; they have learned to endure extreme heat in summer
and cold in winter. They expect long periods of dryness, and
know how to conserve water. They get along with little food, but
know how to enjoy a banquet on occasions. They know the limits
of the land that can be grazed or used by their family and their
tribe. They know their friends and their enemies, and understand
what to expect from both. They know the rules of the desert and
abide by them.

DESERT CUSTOMS

When an American or other foreign traveler steps into the land
of desert people his adjustment is thrown off balance. The
desert native does not know where you fit into his scheme of
things. You make confusion in his world. He has no clear idea
what to do about you.

What he actually does will depend on several things, but above
all else it will depend on You. If his group has had previous contact with white-skinned, hat-wearing, trouser-legged individuals
like you, he'll treat you according to the pattern his people have
decided upon.

GETTING INTO TROUBLE

If the last white traveler he has met or heard about was a
troublemaker, the desert man will be expecting more of the same.
Don't give it to him. On the other hand, if the previous friend
of democracy the desert people knew was honest, friendly and
courteous, then you will have a minimum of difficulty, providing
you can be equally decent.

You may find books and magazine articles written by desert
travelers which call the natives treacherous, vicious, sly, hostile,
and dangerous. Most of those authors had already formed their

opinion before they reached the desert. Some of them wanted to prove how brave they were in going in "a land of terror." Some newcomers got into trouble and never knew why. Often it was because they had rudely violated some simple custom like putting out the wrong hand in greeting. Others boast of how they cheated the natives. Many were looking for trouble "with a gun on each hip and chip on each shoulder." Naturally the desert people were on guard against such unfriendly or arrogant intruders.

MORE BLESSED TO GIVE

Arabs are exchangers of gifts. Gifts represent friendship. If you learn what simple presents you can give in your particular section of the Sahara or Arabia you can get more cooperation than money can buy.

One of the authors once gave a 50-cent Swiss jackknife to a Tuareg noble in the Sahara. Later he received courtesies out of all proportion to the demands of hospitality. Finally the noble explained. "When you first came here you gave me a knife that closes. All my life I have wanted a knife that closes. You are my friend. Anything I have is yours."

The Bedouin you are likely to meet on the Sahara and Arabian deserts have a really hard life. They have little food and few clothes in a rugged climate. Cash money is hard to come by, and it is usable in many ways.

THE ARAB CODE

A Bedouin will do a great many things for money, but money will not tempt him to sacrifice his honor. He sticks rigidly to his six-point code. His allegiances may be summed up as follows: His first duty is toward God. His second duty is the protection of his tent neighbor. Third, he must give due attention to the laws of hospitality. Fourth is his duty to a traveler under his "safe conduct." Fifth comes attention to the laws of personal protection and sanctuary. Sixth is his duty to himself; to raid when he can and to keep what he has captured.

Raiding is no sin but a virtue—payment, you might say, for the five good deeds above. To kill your enemy is a greater virtue. To steal your enemy's cattle is not morally wrong, but something to be proud of, since your enemy will do the same to you if you give him a chance.

Some Americans and other foreigners have lived among the

desert people as friends and equals. Those who have treated the desert people as decently and honestly as they would treat their friends at home all agree that desert people are hospitable, dignified and friendly.

HOW TO BEHAVE LIKE A FOREIGNER

Experienced desert travelers have found that an honest effort to understand the desert people pays off. A sincere respect for their customs, no matter how different from yours they may be, will result in satisfactory relations all around. That applies even in the exceptional regions where groups or individuals may be hostile or trigger-happy.

Remember when you enter the land of desert people *you* are the foreigner in *another's* home town. It is up to you to act in accordance with local customs. When you are the foreigner, act with the decency you'd expect of a foreigner in your home.

Among desert people, if you give your word you must keep it. In Saudi Arabia, the courts will see that you do keep your verbal agreements. For example, if you say you will pay a certain price for a rug and later see another which you like better you can't back out of your first verbal deal even though you have not paid anything down nor taken delivery. The people of Saudi Arabia can't understand our custom of signing a written agreement and having witnesses sign. They give their word and keep their verbal promises.

Desert people are not fist-fighters. They don't lay violent hands on each other in anger or in horseplay as youthful Americans sometimes do. To inflict physical injury on an Arab, for example, is a very serious offense. You may find yourself legally obliged to support the injured and his family.

Article 39 of the Saudi Arabian laws prohibits you from striking a person, using abusive speech or treating him with scorn or contempt.

There are many very interesting angles of the customs of desert people, and in well-organized Saudi Arabia many of those old customs are written into law.

DO'S AND DON'TS FOR THE TRAVELER IN ARABIAN DESERTS

Here are a few of the most important *don'ts*. In general they apply to the deserts everywhere.

Don't reprimand an offender in front of other people.
Don't draw sand pictures or maps with your foot—stoop down and draw with your right hand.

Don't swear at a native.

Don't expose the soles of your feet to others. Sit tailor fashion or on your heels.

Don't ask about a man's wife.

Don't throw a coin at a man's feet. That is insulting.

Don't try to gamble. It is forbidden.

And here are a couple of DO's worth remembering.

DO HAVE PATIENCE when dealing with desert people.

DO ACT FRIENDLY.

VARIETY OF CUSTOMS

Customs differ in different desert regions. They differ sometimes between tribes of the same region. For instance, some natives we have met in the Gobi stuck out their tongues as a "hello" type of greeting. Later we learned it was more characteristic of Tibet than Mongolia. Others in Mongolia extended the right hand as a fist but with the thumb up. The same sign was used to ask the expedition physician if the patient would get well. In the Algerian Sahara Berber Tribesmen extended the right hand to touch ours, almost like a simple handshake. There was no firm grip and shake but just a touch of the right palms. Then each man put the back of his hand to his lips. These are just a few of the greeting customs of desert people. This book cannot give the customs of all groups; its purpose is to give you general ideas of what customs to look for. With this background you should quickly begin to learn the local etiquette in any desert, and the customs for your region. When a man shakes his fist at you, he may actually be saying, "Hello, Friend."

HOW TO ENTER TENTS

In some parts of the Gobi you should only approach a yurt or a tent from the east, which is the front where the only door is located. If you happen to come from some other direction, you should circle the yurt at a reasonable distance. Give the Mongols a chance to see you before you get close to their dwellings.

You enter the yurt through the left side of the door. You leave your whip or club outside, above the door. There are rules regarding what part of the yurt is reserved for each member of the family and for guests. Good nature and friendliness, however, will help you until you know the rules.

Some Mongols are extremely informal and enter without knocking. In Arabia the guest must also approach the tent from the front. Front will be in the lee of the wind. If the wind changes, the back will be raised and become the front. Stop some distance away to give the girls time to get their veils in place. During summer heat all sides of the tent will be raised so you better observe the people from a distance to be sure which is front.

WELCOME, STRANGER

Don't surprise desert people if you want their help or hospitality. Their reaction to surprise may be a disappearing act, or a hostile reception if you are in bandit country.

In some sections of the Arabian Desert and in some parts of the Sahara a guest will be welcomed with a bowl of milk. In Arabia, it will be buttermilk. In the Algerian Sahara one is usually offered sheep or goats' milk and a tray of dates; in the Gobi, a piece of stone-hard cheese. In parts of the Arabian Desert, when the man of the tent is away, his wife will welcome a passing group. If she has reason to believe that the approaching group is led by the Sheik or other important personage, she hangs out her best dress as a banner on a pole by the tent.

Set phrases of welcome and greeting are repeated and answered in all regions. Learn those used in your region. Even if you pronounce the phrases badly your effort will be appreciated, and it may even cause some merriment among your hosts, which always increases friendliness.

SOUTHERN (ARABIA) HOSPITALITY

The adherents of Islam in North Africa, Arabia, and the deserts of Central Asia consider hospitality an important duty. The traveler in those regions accepts that hospitality naturally. Gentlemanly instincts are highly developed even among the poorer desert men. They approach a tent "modestly and with becoming diffidence" and call out a friendly greeting like "salaam aleikum" (peace be upon you). A guest would never dream of offering payment for his accommodations and such an offer, if made, would not be accepted. Neither would the guest think of imposing on the hospitality of a neighbor if he could reach his own tent.

Three days is the limit of one's stay as a guest, to remain longer is not only bad manners but obliges your host to urge you to continue your journey.

The rule of hospitality is so rigid that it could easily be the ruin of a poor man whose tent is located on a main trail. Accordingly, the poor often hide their camp in a hollow or behind a hill away from traveled routes, since they dare not refuse hospitality to a stranger although feeding him may mean going without food themselves. Your best bet therefore is to look for a side trail branching off behind a hill, as it may lead to hospitality.

DESERT RELIGIONS

Religion among desert people ranges from fanatical ritualism to the most casual lip service. Among Gobi Mongols two-thirds of the male population before the Communist era were lamas or priests of Lamaism. Most Westerners consider Lamaism a decadent form of Buddhism. Certainly it has absorbed a great many local spirits, and the common people were imposed upon by the lamas through serious superstitions which they kept alive. The largest collections of permanent buildings in Mongolia were the lamaseries. Since the region has been controlled by the Soviets the number of lamas has been greatly reduced. It is thought that they now include only three per cent of the male population instead of the former 60 per cent. Probably the average Mongol should be considered more superstitious than religious. The Soviets have reduced the power of the lamas, but it is doubtful if they have eliminated superstition.

Among the Arabs of Arabia and the Sahara many of the tribes are deeply religious. They truly believe in one God. They do not need priests or saints to intercede for them, each man praying direct to his God. This he does with dignity, secure in the knowledge that before God he stands on an equal footing with every other man.

The true believer in the Moslem religion knows that there is no God but God (Allah), and Mohammed is his Prophet.

He says his prayers five times each day. He gives alms to the poor and needy. During the month of Ramadhan he does not eat, drink, nor have sexual intercourse between sunrise and sunset, but he can and does indulge during the night. If his means permit, he will make the journey to Mecca at least once in his lifetime. This is becoming easier to do now that airlines in the Near East can fly the pilgrim as far as Jidda.

The believer in Islam prefers to be called a Moslem rather than a "Mohammedan," because while he accepts Mohammed as the true Prophet, he does not worship Mohammed, but Allah.

A Moslem can and does worship wherever he is—in the desert or in the lobby of an office building in the city. When prayer times comes, he will stop whatever he is doing, face Mecca and go through the seven positions of prayer while he repeats set phrases and suras from the Koran.

In cities and in oases there are mosques where Moslems go to pray and to meditate. In the courtyard or somewhere near the entrance is a place for the believer to wash his hands and feet before entering the religious sanctuary. He always removes his shoes or sandals before entering the mosque. You will show the same courtesy and remove your shoes. In tourist cities extra sandals are sometimes provided for non-Moslems who are visiting the holy places. Put these on over your shoes. In the desert you may not be allowed inside the mosque at all but don't defile the holy place with your shoes if you are allowed to enter; the offense is serious.

SUPERSTITIONS AND TABOOS

Many desert people are superstitious about photographs. They rationalize their fear by saying that the Koran forbids pictures. Actually there is no such ban on pictures in the Moslem religious book, but it will do you no good to try to argue the matter.

You will have to learn the "temper" of the desert people you encounter and follow their taboos. Respect their prejudices. Don't ridicule or make fun of desert people. They are proud people, following customs that have proved satisfactory to them for more centuries than your ways have decades.

THE DISTAFF SIDE

Women among desert people have varied positions. Except among the very wealthy families, all desert women do their share of work about the camp. In Mongolia there is no double standard of morals. Among the Arabs most tribes do not allow their women to show their faces to any man except the closest members of the family. In contrast to this strict seclusion, the women of tribes just north of Yemen on the Arabian Peninsula "expose more of their bodies than would be tolerated in other parts of Arabia." They have greater freedom and freer intercourse with men than in the more puritanical districts of Arabia proper.

Most Arab and Berber peoples of Arabia or the Great Sahara tolerate no nonsense between their women and men to whom they are not married. Violations of the code brings swift, sure punishment, sometimes including the death of the woman.

In contrast the Tuaregs of Sahara pride themselves on the complete absence of jealousy. The women go unveiled (Fig. 8-1) before all men while the men never show their faces even in all

Fig. 8.1. Tuareg women in the Sahara do not hide their faces as other Moslem women do. Their flowing garments are efficient protection against summer desert heat. (*Photo by Alonzo W. Pond.*)

male gatherings (Fig. 8-2). Their Ahal gatherings include young married and unmarried men and women. They play the imzad (one stringed violin) and sing during the early part of the evening, then return to their tents, milk the camels and eat supper. After supper the second session of the Ahal continues far into the night. Although a man will show no sign of annoyance when a fellow Tuareg steals his girl, there is no assurance that his tolerance will extend to you.

As far as desert women are concerned, there are three factors which should hold you in check: swift, sure trouble from most tribes for violations of the codes; the certainty of VD where the women are given liberty; and your sense of sight and smell.

Fig. 8.2. Tuareg men of the Sahara Desert hide their faces from the world from the age of 12 or 13. Only their eyes are seen by friends or strangers. Their robes like their veils are made from cotton cloth woven in two inch strips and sewed together. The cloth is dyed blue-black with indigo, a powder which the ladies also use as eyebrow paint and lipstick. (*Photo by Alonzo W. Pond.*)

NEXT TO GODLINESS

Cleanliness among desert people varies as much as the observance of religion. If you compare a poor shepherd with an American businessman, the desert shepherd is definitely dirty. However, some wealthy Arabs wear spotlessly white garments and bathe regularly. The Moslem religion prescribes that one must wash before prayers; you will see men doing so in the entrances to mosques, although in the desert where water is scarce they may go through the motions with sand. Religion also prescribes that both men and women must have a complete bath after sexual intercourse, even though only a small bowl of water is available. Nevertheless, many of the desert people you meet will certainly seem very dirty. Unless you have contacts, you are not likely to meet many of the wealthy class who can afford the luxuries of regular baths and clean clothes.

In the deserts of Mongolia where people wipe their fingers on their garments you can smell the rancid mutton-fat almost as far as you can see the man. Even there, cleanliness varies with individuals.

Toilet habits also vary. Among most desert people their voluminous flowing robes permit them to squat and relieve themselves wherever nature calls. In oases and towns of Sahara or Arabia there are pit latrines, while in some desert camps each individual will dig a small hole and cover his feces. In contrast when prickly pears are ripe in North Africa you need to watch your step anywhere near a patch of that cactus. In Mongolia promiscuous defecation is practiced but the dogs consider human feces a delicacy. The final result is no worse than one finds in dog-infested residential districts of American cities.

TABLE MANNERS

If you are invited to eat with desert people watch their etiquette, and follow your host's lead. Among the Mongols of the Gobi, individuals carry their own food bowl and chopsticks. In Arabia and the Sahara a central dish heaped high is placed in front of the diners, each serving himself from the section directly in front of him. You use your right hand and make an excavation in the mound of food before you. Do not encroach on the excavation of your neighbor. Each mouthful is a small "bite size" ball formed with your fingers and plopped into your mouth. In some regions on the north edge of the Sahara spoons may be provided. If meat is served you tear it off with your right hand.

Your host may or may not appear while you are served in Arab desert regions. His women certainly will not eat until after you have been served, and you probably will not even see them. They will watch you through tiny openings in tent curtains, and will hear your conversation.

In some tribes of Arabia all diners must stop eating when one guest indicates he has finished. That means you gobble your food or leave the banquet still hungry. Among many tribes it is most courteous to belch loudly after a meal. That shows your appreciation of good cooking and bountiful food. To break wind, however, is a very serious breach of manners.

Cooking in desert regions is all done over open fires. In Africa and Arabia you will probably find the food palatable. In some cases wood ashes will flavor the roast and sand and ashes may cling to the bread. The cooked food will be safe to eat.

You may not be enthusiastic about the tea of Mongolian deserts. Often it is thickened with flour and butter is added. Dates are good in Arabia and Africa. They vary from soft, delicious, honey delicacies to hard, dry fodder resembling peanut shucks. All are nourishing, however.

Eat the dates with your right hand and watch your companions. In some Sahara regions it is insultingly bad form to throw the date stones over your shoulder. Remove the stone from your mouth with your right hand and place it on the edge of the serving tray. Date pits are collected and crushed between rocks for camel food. Don't waste them.

When you sit in the company of desert people, sit cross-legged, tailor fashion or on your heels, depending on how the people of the region sit. Generally, it is bad form, even insulting to show the soles of your feet when sitting in company.

SUMMARY

Desert people have customs and forms of etiquette which are important for you to know.

It is important to know how to approach a desert camp and what forms are used in greeting strangers. The rules of hospitality apply to both the host and the guest. Religion is truly sacred among most desert people. It must not be ridiculed nor its sacred places desecrated.

It is always safe to leave women alone in deserts. They may offer you food and water if their menfolks are not around. Protect your future—*don't make passes at desert lasses.*

Desert standards of cleanliness and sanitation are not those of modern American apartment houses. "Table" manners exist among desert people and courtesy requires that you follow them as you would expect a stranger to do in your home. Food, when cooked, is safe and often palatable. Dates can be eaten raw.

Learn all you can about the people in your area *before* **you** find yourself afoot in the desert.

9

Tropical Rain Forest: Environmental Considerations

A man can live on his own in any part of the tropics if he follows certain simple rules and uses his head. The requirements are proper preparation, a general understanding of the nature of the area, a knowledge of how to find food and water, how to maintain health, and reach safety. A working knowledge of survival techniques and procedures will reduce the chances of your becoming panicky and making dangerous errors.

Few people in the United States and other temperate-zone countries have seen or had first-hand experience with the tropics. The majority of people derive their conceptions from adventure stories, movies, and TV productions. These media are often guilty of gross exaggerations and inaccuracies. The impressions usually gained are that all tropic areas have hothouse climates, consist of impenetrable masses of jungle growth, abound with poisonous snakes, alligators, and other reptilian forms, and are the habitats of primitive and hostile tribes. Nothing could be farther from the truth. There are vast tropical areas, such as those of Mexico, Ecuador, and Madagascar, which have temperate climates, open savanna and steppe areas, a meagre reptilian population, and are settled by millions of people of advanced economic and cultural development. True, some low areas near the equator are hot, humid, and steamy and have a luxuriant vegetation that in places is almost impenetrable. And others, like Venezuela and Ecuador, have tribes that are hostile toward white people. But these are the exception rather than the rule.

The tropics comprise a zone roughly 2,500 miles wide which circles the earth at the equator. Its northern limit is the Tropic of Cancer, 23° 27′ N latitude, and its southern limit is the Tropic of Capricorn, 23° 27′ S latitude. The tropical zone has a broad variety of climate, vegetation, and terrain. Here are found tropical rain forests, commonly called "jungle"; mountainous rain forests, commonly called "cloud forests"; mangrove and other swamps; open grassy plains called savannas or llanos; and semi-arid coastal areas (Fig. 9-1). Each has its distinctive plants, animals, and climate and each, too, has its own distinctive problems relating to emergency survival.

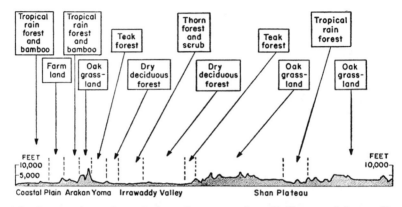

Fig. 9.1. Variety of tropical environments is well illustrated in profile of Burma at latitude 21° N. They range from rain forest, scrub forest, and dry deciduous forest to grass land and cleared farm land.

For those who have to face the tropics on its own terms, a knowledge of these different tropic environments is essential.

TROPIC ENVIRONMENT I—THE RAIN FOREST

The tropical rain forest, geographically the most extensive of the tropic environments, is the vegetation characteristic of the areas which lie between 10° S latitude and 10° N latitude. It is a dense, high forest consisting of evergreen trees more than 100 feet high and a rich undergrowth of herbaceous and woody vines, saplings, shrubs, bromeliads, orchids, and other flowering plants. Rainfall is abundant and regular throughout the greater part of the year.

Distribution.—The earth has three great tropical rain forest areas: America, Oceania, and Africa (Fig. 11-1). The largest, and in many respects the most luxuriant, is the American tropical rain forest. It covers more than one million square miles of the land areas of Middle America, Central America, and South America. In South America it extends along the equatorial zone from the eastern slopes of the Andes to the shores of the

Guianas, and includes all the territory of the vast Amazon basin and much of the upper Orinoco river drainage. In Central America the rain forest extends beyond the normal 10° N latitude geographical limits northward into the Peten area of Guatemala. A similar northward arm extends into the states of Chiapas, Tobasco, and Vera Cruz in southern Mexico.

Oceania has, in terms of land area, the smallest of the three great rain forests. This is to be expected, considering that the area embraced is one of small land masses and vast expanses of ocean. What it lacks in size it makes up in grandeur, for next to the American rain forest it is the most impressive in the equatorial zone. Except for occasional gaps, the Oceania rain forest extends from India and Ceylon eastward and northward to include Java, Borneo, Sumatra, Thailand, Malaya, New Guinea, the Philippines, and the hundreds of islands in the south and west Pacific known collectively as Melanesia, Polynesia, and Micronesia. As in the American rain forest, there are extensions beyond the equatorial zone, examples of which are Southeast China and Assam.

The African rain forest covers an area of approximately 1½ million square miles. It extends, with minor breaks, along a 7°-wide equatorial belt from Liberia and the Gold Coast on the west to the borders of Uganda and Tanganyika on the east. The western segment of this vast forest is commonly referred to as the Guinea rain forest or jungle, and the large central and eastern mass is known as the Congo rain forest.

Although the American, Oceania, and African rain forests have the same general characteristics, differences occur in the number and types of plant communities, in the animal and human life, in the composition of the soil, and in the climate. But most of the general rules of survival apply equally well to all jungles regardless of location.

Climate.—Whether it be America, Oceania, or Africa, the climate of the lowland rain forest is humid and hot. The amount of rainfall varies greatly, but in all parts there is 80 inches or more of precipitation spread over the entire year or concentrated into 8 to 10 months. To a large degree the climate is distinguished by the amount of rain and how it is distributed over the year rather than by differences in temperature. The temperature remains relatively uniform regardless of month and geographical location. The usual range in the equatorial zone is 76 to 86° F.

In the higher altitudes (up to 10,000 feet) the temperature and rainfall are vastly different from those of the lowlands. Rainfall, cloud cover, and humidity increase with altitude, while the temperature decreases. In general, there is a drop of about one degree F in temperature for every 300 feet of elevation. Both Bogota, Colombia, and Quito, Ecuador are on the equator, yet they have mean monthly temperatures of 58° F because of their high (9,000 feet) elevation. Actually climbing to a point 300 feet higher brings the same temperature relief as moving 90 miles north of the equator. Bogota at 9,000 feet is climatically equivalent to moving 2,400 miles north of the equator. In Bogota and Quito, one speaks of "going down into the tropics."

In general, the most abundant and regular rainfall is at the equator and it diminishes progressively as one moves either north or south. Some sections of Venezuela and Brazil have a rainfall exceeding 95 inches. Singapore in Malaya has a mean annual rainfall of 96 inches, while Dutch Borneo has 130 inches and Victoria and Debundja in the Cameroons have from 165 to 400 inches.

Heavy rainfall coupled with low elevation produces a hot, humid, oppressive climate. At the equator rain falls at all seasons and the climate of each month is identical to that of the preceding month. This sameness, without the seasonal breaks that mark the temperate zone, makes the temperature appear hotter than it actually is. However, equatorial temperatures rarely reach the 105-110° F maximums that are experienced in the south and central parts of the United States, nor does the record equatorial rainfall come even close to matching the 550 inches recorded for midlatitude Assam.

In the zone from 3°-10° N or S, rainfall is not uniform throughout the year but is confined to two seasons each of which is followed by a dry season, one short and one long. There are heavy rains during the four months of February, March, April and May and again during the period July to November. The first is followed by a short dry season in June and the second by a long, dry season lasting from November until February. These double wet and dry seasons are typical of the rain forest areas in the Guianas, Panama, Liberia, Ceylon, Java, and parts of the Amazon.

Farther from the equator, and extending to the limits of the intertropical zone, the year has but two seasons—one wet and one dry. A long wet season of seven months begins in April and continues into late October. It is followed by a five-months' dry season beginning in November and terminating in April. Southern Mexico, the Peten of Guatemala, the Matto Grasso of Brazil, the Gold Coast of West Africa, and the Philippines are examples of rain forest areas having two distinct seasons.

Throughout the intertropical zone the relative humidity is always high. At night it ranges from 85 per cent to the saturation point and during the day it rarely drops below 60 per cent. This high relative humidity is a characteristic feature of all rain forest areas. Days and nights are of approximately the same duration (12 hours) at or near the equator, but the days become shorter as one progresses north or south, although nowhere within the intertropical zone is the day less than 10 hours.

Contrary to popular belief, the tropics do not have cloudless skies. There is far less cloud cover by far in the midlatitudes than in the tropics. Those areas close to the equator are in more or less of a permanent cloud belt and cloudless days are rare. Although the amount of cloud cover decreases with distance from the equator, it still is better than 50 per cent at latitudes 10° north and south, and better than 30 per cent at latitudes 20° north and south. Cloudiness also increases with elevation, being greater by far at 4,000 feet than at sea level. Anyone who has attempted color photography in the tropics is aware of the limited amount of bright sunshine.

Plant Life. Perhaps the most outstanding feature of the tropical rain forest environment is the richness and great variety of plant forms, both woody and nonwoody (herbaceous) (Fig. 9-2). The woody or tree forms predominate over the herbaceous plants by a ratio of about five to one. Both are evergreen and almost all species are unique to the tropic zone. There are giant hardwood and softwood trees such as mahogany and balsa; bamboos; climbing lianas (vines) of all sizes, lengths and shapes; and hundreds of species of palms, shrubs, and ground herbs. Growing on the trunks and branches of trees is a luxuriant and unbelievably rich vegetation of orchids, bromeliads, ferns, mosses, lichens, and flowering plants.

If you were to stand in the center of a rain forest and look skyward you would see that the vegetation is arranged in layers or tiers—sometimes two, more often three, and occasionally four. The upper layer consists of very tall trees ranging 130 to 160 feet in height. The trunks of these trees are straight and without branches for the first 80 to 100 feet. Above this point the branches arch upward and outward to form an umbrella or canopy. These

Fig. 9.2. Mountain or Cloud Forest between Mt. Duida and Mt. Marahuaca, Venezuela. (*Photo by Paul H. Nesbitt.*)

giant trees are the "emergents" of the rain forest. Below them is
the middle layer made up of trees 100 to 125 feet high and so
numerous and evenly distributed that their crowns or umbrella-
like tops form a continuous vault or canopy over the entire forest.
Underneath this canopy is a third layer of vegetation, the young
seedlings, palms, and shrubs. Lastly there is the herbaceous
ground layer consisting of ferns, mosses, and flowering plants.

The rain forest then, is a series of three "vertical" forests one
above the other. Because little sunlight can penetrate the multi-
layered green roof, the forest interior is dark, damp, and gloomy.
The amount of light is one-tenth to one-fiftieth of that received
outside the forest—an important factor in travel, procurement of
food and water, effectiveness of signal equipment, and in mental
and physical health.

Many of the giant trees are reinforced with powerful flying buttresses in the form of great roots that extend over the ground to distances of 30 feet or more. Some of the smaller trees are equipped with "stilt" aerial roots.

To the above picture of the rain forest interior must be added the lianas, or vines, which are found everywhere from ground level to the tops of the tallest trees. In places they form an inextricable entanglement. They are of all shapes—round, flat, twisted, straight—and of all sizes from pencil thickness to three or four inches in diameter. Lianas grow from the soil and anchor themselves to trees or to each other by twining or by means of hooks and tendrils. Thus supported they climb like taut cables skyward to the upper level of the forest. They continue to grow, but for want of support can rise no higher. So down they come to eventually reach the ground where they trail along to a new support and again head upward.

Fig. 9.3. Rain forest interior, South America. Giant palm in foreground. (*Photo by Paul H. Nesbitt.*)

Hollywood movies invariably symbolize the tropics by stands of palm trees, and to a certain extent the palm is an accurate symbol. Although found in such varied environments as savannas, islands, and steppes, the favorite habitat of the palm is the forest. More than one thousand different species grow in the world's tropical forests (Fig. 9-3). Oceania and America are exceedingly rich in palms; Africa, on the other hand, has relatively few species.

Undoubtedly the species that holds the place of honor is the coconut palm. It is found throughout the tropics mainly because it has been widely dispersed by ocean currents. The sago palm, raffia palm and oil palm also have wide distribution throughout the equatorial zone. Many other palms have considerable economic value and are of paramount importance to the survivor as a source of food, liquid, shelter materials, and fibers.

There are large areas of the rain forest that have been destroyed by tropical storms and hurricanes as well as by the agricultural and mining pursuits of man. Perhaps the most important cause of destruction has been that system of shifting cultivation known as "slash-and-burn" (Fig. 9-4). A patch of forest is felled,

Fig. 9.4. Man-made clearing in South American rain forest. Thatch house is that of the Motilone Indians, one of the most hostile tribes in South America.

the fallen trees burned and crops of corn, rice or manioc planted. After one or more crops have been harvested, the plot is abandoned because all the nourishment is gone from the soil and it is simply too poor to produce another crop. A new patch of forest is then felled and burned, and the process repeated. Shifting agriculture of this type has been practiced for some two thousand years by the primitive food-gatherers and agriculturists of the rain forests of America, Oceania, and Africa. Thousands of square miles of virgin forest have been thus destroyed, being replaced by secondary forests. In a few years' time these widely dispersed secondary forests become a chaotic wilderness of trees, shrubs, lianas, bamboo, and herbaceous plants, so dense and tangled that they cannot be penetrated without a knife or machete.

The secondary forest does not have the multitiered roof of the virgin rain forest. At best it has a fragmentary canopy through which light and sunshine, of almost full intensity, reach the forest floor. This light, plus moisture, pushes the development of rapid-growing climbers, perennial plants, softwood trees, and shrubs. Provided that repeated cuttings have not destroyed the vegetation completely, the forest will eventually regenerate. The process is, however, exceedingly slow, and it is estimated that more than one hundred years would be required for the forest to regain its former appearance. There are vast expanses of secondary forests in Central and South America, in the Belgian Congo, Philippines, Malaya, and in many of the large islands of Oceania. They present a number of survival problems not encountered in rain forests.

Animal Life. The animal population of the rain forest is equally as abundant and diversified as the vegetation. Tropic animals are more striking looking than their northern relatives. Some are remarkable for their size, such as the 30-foot long pythons and anacondas, the quarter-ton land tortoises, the giant gorillas, and the crocodiles. Even some of the insects are of the heavyweight class—7-inch-long scorpions and moths, giant beetles, ants, and spiders. Many are distinguished by their showy or gaudy coloring and strange shapes. Among these the birds of paradise, the macaws, the toucans, and the golden frogs of Panama stand out.

The population of ants, leeches, spiders, mosquitoes, and other insects is infinite and ranges the rain forest from ground level to the tops of the tallest trees.

Animal life is most abundant at the forest roof and decreases progressively in both species and individuals to the forest floor. Such birds as the parakeet, fruit pigeons, birds of paradise, toucans, and trogans are in full possession of the tree crowns. The forest roof is also the habitat of monkeys, apes, sloths, iguanas, marsupials, squirrels, and a rich insect and reptilian life of snakes, spiders, centipedes, and ants.

The rain forest floor has the least amount of animal life. The reason for this is lack of cover. In open areas and in secondary forests, where there is good shrub and bush cover, large animals such as deer, tapirs, wild pigs, okapis, lions, tigers, and anteaters may be found. But on the dark, bare floor of the rain forest there is only a fauna of lizards, landcrabs, grubs, termites, and ants.

Another dweller of the luxuriant rain forest is man. From the Amazon to Malaya and thence to the Belgian Congo, millions of people have lived their entire lives in the jungle. Some live by primitive agriculture, others by foraging, hunting, and fishing. The total native population numbers several million people; those in Africa are predominately Negroid, those in Southeast Asia and Oceania are a mixture of blacks, whites, and yellows, while in America the dwellers of the rain forest are predominately Indian. All are masters of their forest environment and with few exceptions all are kind, amiable, and peaceful.

10

Tropical Rain Forest: Survival Considerations

Jungle or tropical knowledge is almost a requirement of this air age, where commercial airlines and military aircraft regularly fly established air routes that cross and recross rain forest areas. From the air bases and terminals of America, Euorpe and Asia, there are daily scores of mission flights, training flights, and cargo and passenger flights to various parts of the world. More than 40 of these air routes involve flying over tropical forests.

NATURE OF THE EMERGENCY

When the rain forest is viewed from an aircraft the crowns of the tallest trees look like cauliflowers floating erect in a sea of multishaded greenery. Rivers appear as narrow, black ribbons interwoven into an endless mosaic. The bottom of this billowy mass is not apparent from the air.

What can you do when a real emergency takes place above the jungle or rain forest? On planes that do not carry parachutes there is little or no chance of survival for the crew and passengers in a direct crash landing in a tropical rain forest. If the plane is at high altitude and the pilot has good visibility of the country below, it may be possible for him to glide the plane to a successful landing in a clearing, or ditch it into a stream, lake, or coastal waters. But if a crash into the rain forest is inevitable the occupants will need parachutes. Bail-out is the only chance of reaching the ground alive.

A survival experience begins with the aircraft emergency and bail-out and ends with the successful recovery of the personnel by Air Rescue Service or other means. The duration of the survival period is variable, extending from a few hours to several weeks. An analysis of several thousand tropical survival incidents endured by U.S. Air Force personnel during and since World War

II revealed the average time to be about three days. The longest survival incident recorded was 23 days.

The problems encountered in tropic survival are, in general, of three kinds. First, those pertaining to injury, food, water, shelter, travel, and hazards. Second, those pertaining to survival equipment. Lastly, those related to mental attitude and will-to-live.

IMMEDIATE ACTION

If you have bailed out over a rain forest, the chances are about 100 to 1 that your fall will not carry you through the double forest roof or canopy. You will be suspended by chute and shroud lines well above the forest floor. The distance above ground will depend upon the height of the trees and the density of the overhead forest canopy. You will have to free yourself from the chute and improvise some means of getting down. You might descend hand-over-hand on a large liana, or pull yourself to the trunk of a tree and slide down. The large rain forest trees have few or no branches except at the crowns.

Injuries are especially likely to occur in crash landing or in bail-out. Once on the ground, check for injuries, bruises, and cuts and apply first aid as required. It is very unlikely that you will have a companion with you, for in bail-outs the crew and passengers will be scattered far and wide over the rain forest. You will have to be your own doctor. When the first-aid job is done sit down, relax, and calmly take stock of your situation.

It may seem urgent to you to get out of the jungle as quickly as you can, but this desire is really a result of fear of the unknown. Do not make the mistake of running off in panic; the men who become rattled are the ones who do not make it back. After the shock of landing has worn off, you can begin to plan a sensible course of action. Get all of your signaling devices together and ready for immediate use. Make an inventory of everything you have that will help you to survive.

The first few hours are hours of decision. Should you improvise a camp and stay put until a rescue party finds you? Should you go in search of the others who bailed out? Are you physically able to endure travel? You are a prisoner of the rain forest; above you is a solid roof of vegetation and 20 to 50 feet on all sides are trees that blend into a solid wall. You cannot be seen from a rescue aircraft even if the pilot is flying at tree-top level. And the pilot cannot read you on the radio, for your small set is not effective when used under the thick canopy roof.

If you want your survival experience to be of short duration you must start walking. The chances of finding or encountering one of your fellow survivors is slim indeed unless on the way down you saw him land close by. Your radio will not reach him nor will shouts and gunshots be of much aid to establishing contact; sound has very limited range in the rain forest.

TRAVEL

It is to be hoped that you landed with at least part of your emergency kit. Give careful thought to the selection of equipment you will carry on the walkout. A 50-pound pack is a heavy load; 20 to 30 pounds is much more reasonable. The four most important equipment items for jungle travel and living off the land are the machete, the compass, the first-aid kit, and the parachute.

The stories of men who have walked out of the jungle show clearly that the big problems are medical first aid, food and water, protection from insects, and finding the way. The machete will not only help you to get through dense undergrowth but will serve a dozen useful purposes; the compass will help you maintain direction; the first-aid kit will keep you going in the face of fever and risk of infection; the parachute will protect you against insects and provide you with a comfortable and effective shelter.

Be sure to retain sufficient clothing to protect you against sunburn in the open country and against mosquitoes. Long-sleeved shirts and long pants worn loosely give you the best protection. If your shoes were lost bailing out, or if they wear out on the trail, you can improvise footgear out of your parachute harness and parachute cloth.

Once the equipment is selected, the next problem is to design a pack. The only comfortable way to carry equipment on a long jungle trek is on your back. You can make a good durable pack from the parachute harness and the parachute cloth. A good pack lets the weight fall on the shoulders without swinging or bouncing. Pad the straps so that they do not cut into the muscles under the armpits or on the neck and arrange the load so that it will not bang or slap the hips or kidneys at every step. Do not carry anything in your hands except a machete or a stout wood stick—get as much of the weight on your back as possible.

Determining your starting position is a most important factor in undertaking travel. Think back over the flight and bail-out and try to remember what your position was in relation to coast-lines, rivers, mountains, open areas, and other landmarks. However, even if you are lost when you land, it is still possible for you to determine in a general way where you are. Your compass will give directions at any time of day quicker and more accurately than any other method. Even if you lack a compass you can still determine direction from the sun, stars, or the prevailing winds.

The simplest way is by observation of the sun. For all practical purposes, the sun in the tropics rises approximately due east and sets due west, the maximum possible error being about 25 degrees, depending on the time of the year. The Southern Cross may also be used to determine which direction is south. However, under the canopy of the rain forest neither of these methods is effective. The sun itself is not visible, only its filtered rays, and the Southern Cross is completely shut off from view. You will need to observe the sky from a clearing to determine direction by these means.

In selecting direction of travel and destination, choose a river, a coastline, a savanna, or a village that you have a chance of reaching. Your main objective is to get out from under the canopied rain forest and into a clearing where your signal equipment will be effective and your supply of food and water more plentiful.

In making your way out of the rain forest follow this cardinal rule: ALWAYS FOLLOW THE EASIEST WAY. Don't spend an hour fighting your way through a patch of brush which you can walk around in ten minutes. Never go through a thicket or tackle a swamp if you can walk around them. Don't try to crash through thick secondary growth; push it aside and choose your steps carefully. In this way you will avoid sprained ankles, broken legs, bruises and scratches, and also conserve your energy. *Take the easiest way,* regardless of time. Follow trails whenever possible even though they may meander. By keeping to trails that move in the general direction you wish to go, you will cover ground faster and with much less effort than by cutting your own trail.

Start early in the morning and put in a long marching day, broken by frequent 10- to 15-minute rest periods. Drink plenty of water to make up for heavy sweating. It is important to keep alert, to study your surroundings, and to select your route with care. It's not easy when you are tired—you must force yourself to do it.

If you reach a high point in the jungle, look for rivers, lakes or clearings in the distance. If you see something you want to head for, such as a large clearing, use your compass to get its direction. Distances in the jungle are very deceiving—a clearing may appear close at hand but may take a day or two to reach. Ordinarily, a compass route to your destination will not be a straight line. Dense secondary vegetation, swamps, fallen trees, rivers, and other natural obstacles will require that you make frequent detours. All changes from the direction in which you are marching should be noted, preferably on a sketch of your route, so that you can correct for them later. Use your compass frequently, once every hundred yards or so, to maintain a straight course. This will keep you from circling, and will help to make you more alert to your surroundings.

JUNGLE HIGHWAYS

The highways of the jungle are the trails and the streams; use them if you have to do any extended traveling. The beds of small streams are usually used as trails by the natives, because it is easier to wade in shallow water than to push through thick undergrowth. Trails are rarely found along the banks of large rivers such as the Chagres, Amazon, Orinoco, and Congo, for the undergrowth here is almost impossible to penetrate; trails in these areas are more often found on the crests of adjacent ridges.

Traveling downstream is most often the best method in the tropics. If your emergency survival equipment includes a rubber raft your job is made easy; if not, you will have to build a raft, which should be made of light wood. Many jungle trees are of very hard, heavy woods which will not float. There are two other essentials: Make the raft large enough and bind it tightly enough so that the logs cannot work loose. This can be done by using small, pliable vines or the nylon shroud lines from your parachute.

Use a long pole, preferably with a fork or knob at the end, to push a raft or boat in shallow water. In deeper water, use a paddle hewn out of a young tree.

The greatest hazards of river travel are rapids and falls, especially in such West African rivers as the Congo and Zambezi. Pole along the edge of the bank and whenever possible avoid getting into deep water. If you hear a roar ahead, land and reconnoiter. In many places, it will be necessary to carry your gear around the rapids, and to carry your craft around or build another one below. In such places, always look for a portage trail before you start off blindly through the brush.

Whether you are traveling by foot through the rain forest or downstream on a raft, travel only during the daylight hours. The days are approximately 12 hours long in the tropics and there is little or no twilight. You should stop at least two hours before sundown and prepare camp or erect your shelter. Even at midday the interior of a forest can be surprisingly gloomy; the overhead canopy, as we have seen, shuts out better than 80 per cent of the light.

It may seem most urgent to you to get out of the jungle as quickly as you can. Actually if you know how to obtain food and water, how to construct a shelter, and how to avoid some of the hazards, there should be no great haste. It is better to take it slowly and conserve your strength, rather than wear yourself out in the first few days. Coming safely and soundly out of a tropical rain forest is pretty much a matter of keeping a clear head, thinking things out, and applying your knowledge of survival.

SHELTER

Shelter from rain is essential in the jungle. The easiest shelter to make is a tent of parachute cloth, propped up with poles or slung with rope. It may be your only available shelter in the rain forest where ground vegetation is either absent or meager. In clearings and in secondary forests an adequate rain shelter can be made of a framework of small poles covered with a thatch of palm or other broad leaves.

If near a stream, build your shelter well above the high-water level on high ground. If the campsite is open enough to get a breeze, mosquitoes will be less troublesome.

Don't sleep on the wet ground. In the rain forest, as in other parts of the tropics, the best bed is a hammock. It's cool, keeps you off the wet ground, and is difficult for ants, spiders, leeches, scorpions, and other pests to reach. A hammock can be improvised from the parachute. If you prefer a bed, a simple one can be made by driving four forked sticks into the ground and placing poles covered with branches or palm fronds across them. To make the bed comfortable, use long-leaf palm; split the leaves down the stem and lay the stems to the outside edge of the bed and pile several layers deep.

In mountainous areas the nights will be cold and you may have to construct a windbreak to stay comfortable, or make a mat of grass and leaves.

FIRE-MAKING

You should have a fire for signals, cooking and as a means to dry wet clothes. Even if you have matches, it may not be easy to build a fire in the rain forest. The ground cover of leaves, sticks, logs, and assorted small plants is constantly damp. Your

Fig. 10.1. Termite nests are often fifteen feet in diameter. The nest makes excellent fuel.

best bet for kindling is dead standing trees, or the insides of dry termite nests (Fig. 10-1). In areas where palm is found you can get excellent tinder by using the fibers at the bases of palm leaves. Don't use bamboo for fuel if you can possibly avoid it—it burns too quickly, and frequently explodes because steam pressure builds up in the hollow shaft. Keep spare kindling and wood dry by stowing it under your shelter and the next day take along what you can conveniently carry for future use.

WATER

A plentiful supply of good water is most important in hot jungle country. There is little air movement and you sweat profusely, especially if you are traveling. So drink several quarts every day to keep up your efficiency. You can get along for days without food, but you cannot live for long without water. Even if you have a full canteen, look for more. When you find a good source, drink plenty and carry as much as you can with you.

In the rain forests of America, Oceania, and Africa you will find adequate water in streams, springs, and pools. The main problem is one of purity. No surface water should be drunk without being boiled or chemically treated. Don't try any short cuts; the few minutes you spend purifying your water (boil for two minutes at sea level plus one minute for each additional 1,000 feet of altitude) may save you weeks of illness, or even save your life. Rainwater is always safe to drink and can be conveniently caught in a parachute cloth stretched between trees or in containers made from bamboo. The taste of rainwater can be improved by aeration—simply pour the water from one container to another.

Where no surface water is available, you have to investigate other possible water sources. Getting water from plants is one of the easiest ways. In the rain forest the big ropelike vines or lianas that hang down from the trees are full of water. To get at the water, select a good-sized vine and cut off a section five to six feet long, making the top cut first. Then hold at head-height and let the water drain into your mouth. A six-foot section will contain about half a glass of cool water. Be sure you cut through the top end of the vine first before you sever it lower down. Grapevine also contains pure water and may be extracted the same way. Bamboo, too, is a source of water, the hollow stem serving as a reservoir.

Observe one important rule always: NEVER DRINK FROM A VINE THAT HAS A MILKY SAP.

In the American rain forest the branches and trunks of trees support many air plants which give water. The rainwater collects in the cuplike hollows at the base of the leaves and remains there for a long time. The water is safe to drink without purifying, although you may have to strain out a few ants and bugs. Unfortunately most of these rain-catchers are high in the trees and out of reach.

In Oceania and some sections of the American tropics the coconut is a bountiful source of liquid. The green, unripe nuts contain nearly a pint of water.

ANIMAL FOOD

In any survival episode the matter of food is one that will be extremely important. It may not be pleasant to contemplate, but in an emergency you will find that many unconventional creatures are edible, and are eaten by the local inhabitants or natives, who are experts in knowing how to live off the land. When faced with an emergency in the jungle you can do no better than copy their ways, but in doing so you will have to forget many of your civilized prejudices.

There is plenty of good food in the tropics, enough to keep you going almost indefinitely. There is food from plants and trees and there are animals and birds of many kinds, and fish, snakes, and lizards. All of them are good to eat. The meat from the hindquarters and the tail of the lizard makes a delicious meal. The iguana, a giant lizard of Central and South America, is also a delicacy much sought after by both Indians and whites. All jungle animals should be cooked in order to kill the parasites and improve the taste.

All snakes are edible but they are not found as frequently as is commonly thought. They taste much like the white meat of chicken although the flesh is a bit stringy and slightly salty. In preparing snakes and lizards, skin, remove the viscera, and cook as you would any other meat.

In the dense rain forest most of the animals are high in the trees, out of sight and reach. There are few animals on the forest floor. In some places there may be considerable variety but usually it will be limited to land crabs, land turtles, lizards, and snakes. The larger animals and birds of the rain forest make the best eating, but they are difficult to catch. Most people will walk through a tropical forest without ever seeing game of any kind even though it may be there in considerable abundance. Too much reliance should not be placed on the larger animals as a source of food.

In the clearings and areas of secondary growth where there is good cover, animals like the agouti, coati, squirrel, deer, wild pig, tapir, anteater, sloth, and monkey may be found. The basic principle in hunting these animals is to look for "sign." Keep an eye open for tracks, trails, disturbed leaves, fresh droppings, partly eaten food, or other evidence that animals have been in the vicinity.

Iguanas, found mostly in Central and South America, are ugly-looking lizards from one to five feet in length. You may find them in trees or in the open. They are very good to eat and taste like chicken. The iguana has sharp biting teeth and can give you a nasty wound if you are careless in handling them.

Traps and Snares.—There are several types of traps and snares that will catch animals. The simplest type of snare is a loop of wire or cord spread across a trail in such a way that the animal puts its head in it, as described earlier on page 51. Other snares for small game (Figs. 2-13 and 2-14) may be set with a trigger and tied to a bent sapling so that when the trigger is released the animal is jerked off the ground. "Figure 4" box traps and deadfall traps may also be used successfully. They should be baited and placed along a trail which animals travel, or near places where they feed. For bait use fruits, nuts, berries, or meat.

The chief objection to such devices is that it may be necessary to wait hours or even days to catch your quarry. This would be poor survival procedure because your primary objective is to get out of the rain forest as soon as possible—to reach a large clearing or a river where signaling will be effective. Also, plant food is more abundant and easier to find than animal food. You will make better time and your survival experience will be of shorter duration if your hunting of wild animals is postponed until after you have reached a good signaling location and established your permanent camp.

The rain forests of all tropic areas are crisscrossed by rivers, streams, brooks, and caños. In South America the Amazon, the Orinoco, the Parana, the Cunucunuma, and many others, have many tributaries. Africa has the Congo, the Niger and the Zambezi, each with a network of smaller streams that drain the vast rain forest areas. From these streams you can satisfy most of your food wants. Fish are often abundant and can be caught easily with a hook and line. Use the shroud line to make a fish line and if you don't have a fishhook, you can make one from a piece of wire, from a pin, or whittle one out of wood or bone. For bait use worms, insects, snails, small pieces of meat, or a lure made from metal or bone. Fish can also be obtained through spearing and trapping.

In addition to fish, you can find many other types of food in these tropical fresh waters, such as shrimps, clams, snails, and turtles. All of these animals are good to eat and none is poisonous, but all food taken from fresh water should be cooked to avoid parasites. In addition to the animals in the water there are many frogs along the banks of streams. Some, like the golden frog of Panama, are of brilliant color. Both frogs and toads should be skinned before eating for some have poison glands in the dorsal skin layer.

Along the banks of streams there may be snakes, crocodiles, and alligators; these make delicious survival dinners and should not be passed by if you are hungry.

PLANT FOOD

There are hundreds of different plants in the tropics that can be eaten. Many of them are unknown to white men but are the main source of food to natives. This, however, does not mean that plant food is abundant or easy to find. There may be plenty of food in some places at certain seasons, and practically no food at others. Many kinds of plants produce fruit only at certain seasons, while others bear more or less continuously. Greens and roots are present the year around, and in general there is always some food available but you have to search long and hard for it.

Plant food of one kind or another may be found almost everywhere—in the tall trees, on the ground, on low bushes, or underground. At first sight a tropical forest may seem to contain several dozen kinds of plants scattered at random, but if you observe carefully you will see that certain kinds of plants grow in certain places. Some grow best only along streams, some in deep shade, others in open clearings. It all depends on altitude, soil, water, light, and neighboring vegetation. You can use this knowledge to find food plants when alone in the jungle. If you are in a rain forest and find nothing, look in a clearing, thicket, swamp, or along a stream. If the fruit is not quite ripe high on a mountain slope, go downhill 1,000 feet; it may be in prime condition there. When you find food, notice not only the plant on which it grows, but also the kind of surroundings. When you see the same surroundings elsewhere, the chances are that you will find the same kind of food again.

Seashores, abandoned clearings, and margins of streams and

swamps are the most likely places to find food. The least productive are the rain forest interiors and the montane or cloud forests. The best places to find food are, of course, those places where men have been growing it. In many abandoned clearings you may find foods such as coconuts, yams, and sugar cane, not in large quantity perhaps, but in *sufficient amount to satisfy your appetite.*

Once you find a plant food that looks edible, you have to determine whether it is safe to eat. Most fruits, berries, nuts, roots, and succulent stems are edible, but unfortunately there are a few poisonous kinds. Only an expert botanist can tell the difference from appearance alone, but if you use your head and follow a few simple rules you can eat in safety. One way is to experiment by trying a small quantity of food; if it tastes all right, and there is no burning sensation, eat a spoonful and wait for six to eight hours. If there are no ill effects, try a larger helping and wait again. If you are still well, you can eat reasonable quantities safely. Remember that an unpleasant taste does not always mean that the plant is poisonous or even unpalatable; olives, for example, are bitter and grapefruit is sour.

To help you further, keep in mind the following general rules. All berries that closely resemble cultivated strawberries, blackberries, or raspberries are safe to eat. All wild figs (Fig. 10-4) are safe; the fruits may be small and almost any color—red, black, yellow, or greenish. One common variety of fig found in the American tropics is known as the "strangler" because it grows around another tree, eventually completely enclosing and killing the support on which it started its vine. Fig fruits can be easily recognized by their structure—a small sack filled with seeds borne on fleshy strings.

A safe rule to follow, and one that has been previously stated in earlier chapters, is to avoid plants having a milky sap unless you can definitely identify them. There are, as you perhaps know, several exceptions to the milky-sap rule. Breadfruit, wild figs, papaya, and mangoes all have a milky sap and yet are quite harmless and nonpoisonous, cooked or uncooked.

The pulp of many fruits is edible but the seeds may be poisonous; for example, the glycoside in the kernel of a peach contains hydrocyanic acid, although enzymes in the fruit dissolve the glycoside and render it harmless. This "safety feature" may not be present in the unknown fruit you sample, so it is wise to spit out the seeds.

It is often said that anything animals and birds eat is all right for man. This is largely true, yet monkeys will eat the fruit of the strychnine tree, which contains poisonous seeds. Pigs can tolerate certain poisons and birds often eat fruits with poisonous seeds which they do not digest. The same is probably true of monkeys when they swallow the seeds whole.

Nothing would be gained by naming and describing all of the plant forms suitable for emergency and general use. It is almost impossible to recognize them from taxonomic descriptions and drawings. Yet there are a few common and obvious ones, which are widespread throughout the American, African, and Oceania tropics, and are readily identified. These plants that you would be most concerned with are discussed in the following pages.

The Coconut. The coconut palm (see also page 226) grows throughout much of the moist tropics, especially on the east coast of Africa, tropical America, Asia, and the islands of the South Pacific. It grows mainly near the seashore, but sometimes is found some distance inland.

Where there are coconuts your survival problem is quite simple. The nuts will supply you with food and drink, the trunks and branches of the palm can be used for shelter, the fiber around the base of the leaves can be used for clothing or cordage, and the heart of the palm is a very succulent vegetable. The great importance of the coconut justifies a brief description of its qualities together with directions as to how the nut can be collected, husked, and opened.

The coconut grows in clusters on a tall palm. The first problem in the use of a coconut is to get it down from the tree. Some coconut palms are very difficult to climb unless you have had considerable practice, but there is a simple device known as "the climbing loop or bandage" which you can make out of a belt or rope. Put the belt or rope around the trunk of the palm tying it to leave enough room for your feet, and step on it with both feet; the loop will catch on the other side of the tree and support your weight. Reach up and grasp the trunk with both hands; pull up the bandage with your feet, and repeat the process until you reach the fruit. To get down, reverse the process, using normal precautions.

Coconuts are covered with a very tough husk, about two inches thick, which can be removed with a machete, or by the South Sea Island method of sharpening a stake set firmly in the ground and striking it sharply with the nut. Then give the coconut a twisting motion to pry off a small portion of the husk. By repeating this process, you can entirely remove the husk from the nut. Both green and mature coconuts can be husked in the same manner.

Once the nut has been removed from the husk, your problem is to break through its hard shell. To open a young nut, strike it with a stone just below the two "eyes" at the stem end. This will crack the shell and the top of the nut can then be picked off. To break open a mature nut, revolve it by quarter turns, at the same time strike the middle of it sharply with a stone. Continue to turn the nut, striking it each time until the nut cracks in half.

Coconut oil, a good preventive for sunburn and a repellent of insects, can be rendered by exposing the meat of the coconut to heat over a slow fire. Another method for extracting the oil is to boil the coconut meat in a container of water or section of bamboo. When the mixture cools, the oil will rise to the top.

The natives of the South Pacific Islands have found that coconut oil is an excellent preventive of salt-water sores and bloating. Prior to going fishing they smear their legs and feet with this oil, which keeps their skin in good condition despite the fact that they often have to stand in salt water for many hours at a time.

Other Palms. Although the coconut is the best known of the palms there are many other species widely distributed throughout the tropics. Among them are the sugar palm of India and Oceania, the fishtail palm of Southeast Asia, the buri palm of Malaya and Indonesia, the screw palm of Africa and Asia, and the sago and nipa palms of Oceania. In addition there are literally hundreds of small palms to be found scattered about such tropic countryside as swamps, brushland, open woodland, in the high, dense forest, or along streams.

Any part of any palm is safe to eat. Some of the above palms, such as the nipa, bear juicy fruits and a sweet-tasting sap. On others, the fleshy part may be skimpy or absent, but there is a nut with a kernel which can be eaten raw, ripe or green. It may not taste good but it is safe and nourishing.

In addition to the fruits and nuts, palms also provide another source of vegetable food (Fig. 10-2). The flower stalks and flowers can be eaten, if sufficiently tender, and the "cabbage," in most kinds, is delicious. The "cabbage" is the tender point growing at the tip of the trunk beneath the base of the leaves. It can be eaten raw or cooked. Palms are also a source of drink and edible starch, particularly the sugar palm, the fishtail palm and the sago palm.

The sago palm, in particular, would be of immense value in a survival situation. It is a low tree, rarely over 30 feet in height, with a stout spiny trunk. The outer bark or rind incloses a spongy inner pith of high starch content. The extraction and processing is, however, an involved and laborious process. The

Fig. 10.2. Edible palm shoot. White part is tender and succulent; stringy part is bitter and should be cooked. (*Photo by H. Morgan Smith.*)

soft, white pith must be pounded or ground as fine as possible, kneaded in water, and strained through a fine cloth. The fine, white sago will soon settle out. Pour off the water after one or two more washings. Knead the remaining water from the sago and roll the moist meal or flour into balls and dry in the sun or over a low fire. After this it may be wrapped in palm leaves and kept indefinitely.

Sago meal, nutritious and easy to digest, may be prepared

either as a gruel or as pancakes. The gruel is made by adding boiling water to a lump of sago flour. Pancakes are made by frying the gruel or by spreading it out on leaves and allowing it to cool. Natives usually carry these cakes with them when they go on trips.

The sago and other palms having a pithy center which contains starch are found only in the Old World tropics. None of the American palms provides this starch.

Papaya. The papaya is a treelike plant growing up to 20 feet in height, with a single stem and a tuft of long-stalked leaves at the top. On the stem, below or among the leaves, grow large melonlike fruits resembling squash or elongated muskmelons. They grow in all humid tropical countries, around clearings and former habitations, and also in open sunny places in the uninhabited tropic forests.

The fruits are green in color before ripening, and yellow or yellowish-green when mature. Green fruit may be placed in the sun where it will ripen in a very short time. The ripe fruit is high in vitamin C, and the flesh is pepsin-flavored and truly delicious. If milky juice oozes from the rind when it is cut, the fruit is not ripe enough to eat. Be careful not to allow the milky juice to remain on your skin because it will cause irritation. If the juice gets into the eyes it will result in intense pain and perhaps temporary blindness.

The flower, leaf stems, and young leaves may be eaten cooked as greens provided several changes of water are used to remove the bitter and harmful substances from the sap.

Bananas and Plantains. From a nutritional point of view, the most important tropical fruit is the banana. It grows mostly in the humid rain forest areas at elevations of from 3,000 to 4,000 feet. It is abundant in America, in Africa, and in southeast Asia.

The best known commercial variety of banana is the "Big Mike," grown in the American tropics. Other varieties are the distinctly flavored red banana; the smaller, creamy-tasting Manzano or apple banana; and the little, sweet-tasting finger banana. Although found in abundance in almost all tropical countries they are seldom seen in northern commercial markets because they are too perishable to be shipped abroad.

Plantains look like bananas but are larger; they never soften even when ripe. The starchy plantains should not be eaten raw, but always boiled, fried, roasted or baked and eaten as a vegetable rather than as a fruit. The plantain is of African origin. The famous Swedish botanist Linnaeus called it *Musa paradisiaca* or "paradise fruit" because of a legend that it, and not the apple, was the forbidden fruit of paradise.

Horseradish Tree. The horseradish tree is a tropical plant, native to India, but now widespread in many tropical regions throughout southeastern Asia, Africa, and America. It has pungent roots similar to the horseradish plant.

In appearance it is a small tree, rarely more than 20 feet in height, with fernlike leaves. At the ends of the branches are produced the flowers and the long pendulous fruits, which are similar in appearance to a giant bean pod. The pods are triangular in cross section and are from 10 to 25 inches long.

The pod and the seeds within make an excellent vegetable. Cut the pod into short lengths and cook in the fashion of string beans, or fry in oil, if it is available. Very young seed pods can be chewed when fresh, in which case the inner pulpy part and soft seeds are eaten. The flowers may also be eaten as an ingredient in a salad.

Breadfruit. The breadfruit grows in most tropical countries, but is especially common in the East Indies, the Pacific Islands and in some parts of tropical America. The tree is 30 to 40 feet high with large, leathery, ornamental leaves.

The fruit hangs at the ends of the branches, is about six inches thick, and is rough-surfaced and yellowish-green. The ripe fruit can be eaten raw, after it is scraped to remove the skin. Pick off the pithy center with your fingers, separating the seeds. When a sufficient quantity has been thus prepared, squeeze the flesh into a container to form a mash. It is now ready for eating, and though it may have a greenish, unappetizing appearance, it actually is quite delicious.

Breadfruit is more often eaten cooked than raw. After light scraping and removal of the stalk it may be grilled, baked, or boiled like potatoes. There are many other ways of preparing and cooking breadfruit but they are involved and time-consuming—leave them to the natives who prefer their survival situation to recovery.

Sugar Cane. As survival food, the sugar cane and its wild relatives, deserve an honorable mention for the sweet juice which may be chewed out of the ripe cane. For best results peel off the outer layer of the stem. Sugar cane grows throughout the tropics as both a cultivated and a wild plant. You are more likely to find the wild variety if you are down in an uninhabited jungle, although you would probably not be able to tell it from the cultivated form. Both look like cornstalks eight to 20 feet high, the only difference being that wild sugar cane contains less sugar.

Fig. 10.3. Wild sugar cane at border of jungle and savanna. (*Photo by Paul H. Nesbitt.*)

Bamboo. Bamboo thickets form one of the densest kinds of jungle growth and are likely to be found almost anywhere in the warm, humid parts of Asia, Oceania, Africa and America.

Growing bamboo looks like the familiar cane or rake pole at the corner hardware store except that it is green in color. The young sprouts, those up to 12 inches high, are very tender and succulent and you need look no further for a good survival food. Sometimes bamboo grows in stands covering a thousand acres or more. The young shoots which appear in quantity during and immediately following the rains, grow very rapidly, sometimes as much as 12 inches a day.

Bamboo shoots should be prepared in much the same way as asparagus. Although you can eat them raw, they are better boiled.

The stems of the bamboo become very hard and woody when they mature. They can be put to a great number of survival uses such as fishing poles, containers for cooking, knives, and mats.

A very effective weapon, the blowgun, is made from a species of bamboo (cerbatana) found at elevations of from 4,000 to 6,000 feet in the Mt. Marahuaca region of southeast Venezuela. The distinctive feature of this bamboo is the great length of the sections or joints (internodal distance), which, unlike that of other varieties may be as much as 18 feet. The length of the sections decrease from the base upward. The first section will be 15-18 feet long, the second section 8-12 feet, the third section, 5-7 feet, etc. The most desirable section for making a blowgun is usually

Fig. 10.4. Arrowroot.

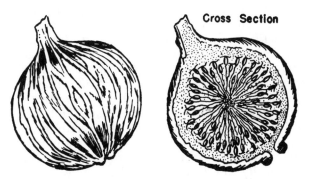

Fig. 10.5. Wild fig.

the one closest to the ground, since it is longer and more cylindrical.

When dry, the cerbatana bamboo is light, thin, and fragile. To protect against breakage and warping, a palm-wood tube of somewhat larger size is hollowed out and slipped over the bamboo. The darts, usually about eight inches long, are made from reed, split palm wood, and bamboo. A wad of wild kapok or cotton is tied around the base of the dart to furnish compression when placed in the blowgun tube or barrel. A quick explosive puff of air into the mouthpiece propels the dart effectively and accurately up to 30 yards. Some South American Indians dip the point of the dart in curare, a strychnine-base poison. Birds and game animals struck by the poison-darts die quickly from asphyxiation. The poison is equally deadly to man.

Arrowroot. The arrowroot is found as a wild plant in nearly all jungle areas of the world. It is a typical rain forest plant and thrives best in forested areas having a high rainfall. Because the arrowroot has been cultivated by man, the plants are frequently found in abandoned fields and gardens.

The arrowroot is a large, coarse herb with tremendous leaves (three feet in diameter) and green and purple flowers. Although the plant is rarely more than three feet tall, the edible underground tubers are sometimes nearly 12 inches across, and weigh two pounds or more.

The tuber has about a 22 per cent starch content and is very bitter when eaten raw. When boiled, or roasted, it becomes sweet and very palatable.

TROPICAL HAZARDS

The popular notion that a man landing in a tropical rain forest is at the mercy of snakes, man-eating animals, and hostile, primitive natives, is not borne out by fact. Actually, the deep jungles are comparatively safe places in which to live—safer perhaps from injury or sudden death than most big city streets. Some dangers do exist but they are not of the sensational variety.

Dangerous Animals. You will probably never see a poisonous snake, or a large cat. The ocelot, the puma, and the jaguar are comparatively rare and timid; they will usually hear and smell you long before you can see them. All large animals, of course, can be dangerous if cornered, or if surprised at close quarters. This is especially true of females with young.

Crocodiles, alligators, and caymans are numerous in the larger streams of Africa and tropical America but cases of their attacking humans are rare. In water, as in crossing rivers, you can avoid them by using rafts, or scare them away by splashing the water.

Snakes. Although there are numerous poisonous snakes in the tropics, they are seldom seen; if you wear shoes and heed a few precautions there is little danger of being bitten. First, so far as precautions go, you should assume that all snakes are poisonous. In moving about at night inspect the ground carefully with a flashlight or torch. Sleep off the ground if possible and examine your bed before you turn in. Don't put your hands on trees, into the bush, or into the grass without first looking. Consider yourself lucky, however, if you should spot a large boa constrictor or anaconda and have a good chance to kill it. Neither are poisonous and there is a great deal of edible meat in one of these huge snakes.

Dangerous Fish. All fish caught in fresh water are safe to eat, but some kinds found in salt water have poisonous flesh. All of the more common poisonous fish belong to a single group and are fairly easy to recognize. Throw away any salt water fish you catch that does not have regular fish scales, that has a body covered with spines or bristles, that has a turtlelike beak, a peculiar body shape, or that puffs itself up with air. Certain fishes have poisonous spines capable of inflicting painful wounds. The most common poisonous fish are the puffers or globe fish, trunk or box fish, horn fish, file and trigger fish.

The barracuda, the moray eel, and various sharks living in the tropical oceans are always a serious hazard. So, too, are the sting rays which occur in salt water and in most rivers of northern South America.

Electric eels are found in nearly all tropical rivers, though more commonly in the American tropics than elsewhere. In Venezuela, they are found in the Orinoco River and its tributaries. The electric organs, which are modified muscles, are columnar structures located on each side of the tail. A sluggish creature usually found in shallow water, the electric eel reaches a length of eight feet and a thickness of 12 to 18 inches. It produces an electric shock powerful enough to knock down a horse.

The Dreaded Piranha Fish. The most feared fresh water fish in the American tropics is the caribe or piranha. It prefers clear, backwater bayous and eddies rather than swift, muddy streams. Although the largest is only about 20 inches long, they are fearless and voracious, having jaws armed with sharp, sawlike teeth.

Although normally feeding on other fish, they quickly cut to pieces any animal unlucky enough to fall into a stream which they inhabit. Blood attracts them by the thousands and the victim's flesh is torn from the bones in a matter of minutes. In some places fishing by rod and line is almost impossible, for the caribes quickly devour any hooked fish, including those of their own kind.

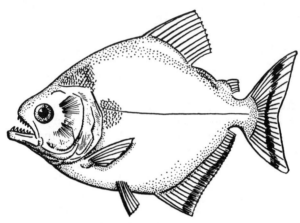

Fig. 10.6. The piranha, a ferocious and much feared fish found in the fresh waters of South America.

Insect Pests. The greatest hazard of the tropics is the flies, ticks, mosquitoes, and other pests that carry and spread diseases. This means taking precautions at all times. If you are particularly careful about water, food, personal cleanliness, and keeping the body well covered, you are pretty sure to stay in good shape. The malaria mosquito must always be considered one of your real dangers, for there is no inoculation against it. However, if you haven't got malaria when you hit the jungle, you can't possibly get sick from it for another seven or eight days. Even if the first mosquito that bites you drops the germs, it will take at least a week for malaria to show up. By that time, with any luck at all and intelligent planning on your part, you should be back at your home base bragging about your jungle episode.

Leeches. Blood-sucking leeches are common in the damp forests of southeast Asia, the Philippines, and certain islands of Oceania. They cling to low-lying brush and attach themselves to you as you pass. They look like thick short worms and, unless removed, cause painful ulcers. Since the bite of the leech is painless you get them on your body without knowing it. It's a good idea to stop and de-leech yourself every few hours. Don't pull them off roughly but use a drop of iodine, a bit of tobacco juice or put a hot cigarette on them and they will come off. They sometimes enter the bowel or crawl up inside the penis but are usually expelled when nature's functions are performed. The best protection against leeches is a strong insect repellent and clothing that fits tight at the ankles, wrists, and the neck.

So far as possible, stay out of fresh water in areas you know are close to human habitations, for the swamps, ponds, ditches, and canals may contain the larval forms of such human parasites as blood worms, flat worms, or flukes. They get into your body through the skin or from drinking water that has not been purified. The danger areas for these flukes are the Belgian Congo, all of equatorial Africa, Madagascar, China, southeast Asia, equatorial South America, and Puerto Rico.

Sleeping Sickness. African sleeping sickness is restricted to equatorial Africa, being found especially in the Congo Basin and Tanganyika. The tsetse fly, carrier of sleeping sickness, bites only in the daytime. If you should be on your own in these areas, avoid the heavy growth near water courses and wear a headnet and gloves at all times.

Poisonous Plants. These are a definite hazard if you go about blindly touching and eating everything you see. If you follow the "edibility" rules mentioned earlier (page 54) you should have no more trouble than you would in the woods and fields of your home state. Actually you probably have as good a chance of getting your skin poisoned by contact with poison oak or poison ivy on your home grounds as you do in the deepest jungle.

The number of different poisonous plants found throughout the world would make a list many pages in length. It would not be practicable to list them here nor would it aid you in recognizing them. But there is nothing to prevent you from extending your knowledge, as much as you have time to, by reading booklets and other descriptive material on the subject. And whenever possible get into the forest and bush country for a little first-hand experience with the plants.

FEAR AND PANIC

What you don't know may constitute one of your greatest dangers. You are likely to feel terribly frightened or even become panicky through *lack of knowledge* of the new strange world around you. You have heard that there are certain dangers and these loom foremost in your mind—you begin to worry and get a panicky feeling that you must move and move fast. The best way to overcome this threat to successful survival is to learn, in advance, all you can about the animals, plants, natives, and other things you are likely to find in jungles. This will cut down the chances of your getting panicky, especially over dangers that are not there. Knowing what to expect in the jungle makes the adjustments to the emergency easier; your worries and fears are reduced, and you know there is something you can do about the predicament you are in. The more you learn about the jungle from books, natives, explorers, and other sources, the easier your mind will be when you are in the jungle, whether lost or not.

SIGNALING

If you think rescue or help from the air is probable, you will have to make signals; otherwise you can't be located. But signals can neither be seen nor heard from under dense jungle growth. If a smoke grenade or flare is set off, the smoke is not likely to get through the overhead canopy, or if it does, it will dissipate too rapidly to be seen by a search aircraft. Obviously a signal mirror is of no use in the rain forest. Noises such as shots, whistles or shouts are, as we have seen, ineffective in the deep forests; the dense, high growth restricts even loud sounds to short distances. Nor will your emergency radio be effective in penetrating the overhead forest roof.

A wide stream bed is a good place from which to signal, especially where there are sand bars out in the stream. Several smoke fires should be prepared and ready to set off the moment you hear or see a plane. Your parachute spread across the stream also makes a good signal. And, most important, with an open sky overhead your emergency radio will effectively transmit and receive voice or cw signals for a 20-mile line-of-sight range. Also, on a sunny day you may be able to use your signal mirror—depending on the height of the surrounding trees and the position of the sun.

One man, a group of men, or even an aircraft is not easy to

spot from the air, especially when visibility is limited. Your emergency signaling devices should be directed at making you bigger and easier to find.

For information on emergency signaling from open areas, see Chapter 8, pages 269-70.

11

Savannas: Environmental and Survival Considerations

SAVANNA ENVIRONMENT

As one moves away from the equator the rain forests are frequently replaced by relatively flat, open regions called savannas. The vegetation is entirely different from that of the rain forest, consisting for the most part of vast areas of grass, shrubs, and isolated trees. Savannas range in size from small pocketlike areas of a few acres to vast regions encompassing several thousand square miles.

For the survivor the savanna environment presents a situation quite different from that encountered in the rain forest. In many ways survival is made easier and the chances of early rescue are infinitely better.

DISTRIBUTION

The large savannas are very unequally distributed throughout the tropics (Fig. 11-1). Much of equatorial Africa consists of savanna; the entire area extending from the Sudan to the Ivory and Gold Coasts is, with few interruptions, a grassland characterized by scattered trees and shrubs.

Oceania and Malaya have, compared to Africa, relatively small savanna areas. The same holds true for Mexico and Central America. There are, however, hundreds of small open areas which form pockets in the luxuriant rain forests and areas of secondary growth. Many of these are the result of man's handiwork and economic enterprises such as agriculture, stock raising and lumbering. Although less significant in a geographical sense than the vast savanna areas, they are of equal importance in the effective and expeditious recovery of personnel facing an emergency survival situation.

South America, like Africa, is characterized by vast savanna areas. The llanos of the Orinoco River basin—a huge geographic

254

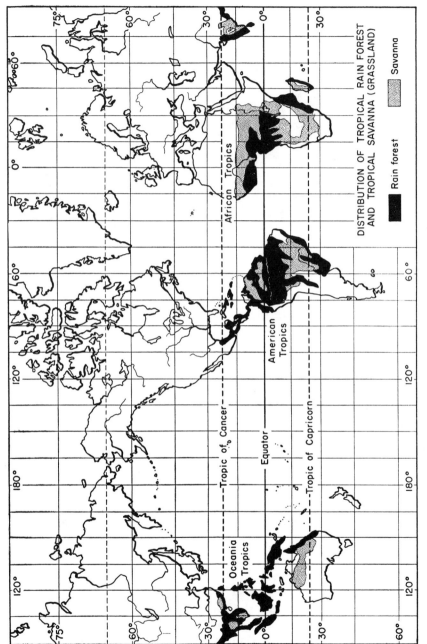

Fig. 11.1. Distribution of Tropic Vegetation.

DISTRIBUTION OF TROPICAL RAIN FOREST
AND TROPICAL SAVANNA (GRASSLAND)

Rain forest

Savanna

255

Fig. 11.2. Mountain savanna and rain forest. Territory de Amazonas, Venezuela. (*Photo by Paul H. Nesbitt.*)

region partly in Venezuela and partly in Colombia—occupy some 130,000 square miles. Savanna is also the typical landform of central and southwest Brazil. In addition, there are countless numbers of small, grassy, treeless areas distributed irregularly throughout the rain forests of the Guianas and the Amazon Basin.

CLIMATE

Because many of the vast savannas are located some distance from the equator, they fall into the zone characterized by seasonal rains. Rainfall is less than in the forest, normally ranging from 40 to 60 inches per year. The rains are concentrated into a four- to five-month season which is followed by a long dry season of seven to eight months. During the season of heavy rainfall the rivers swell, overflow their banks, and inundate extensive areas. At times more than a third of the llano areas of South America are inundated. During the dry season the heat becomes suffocating, frequently exceeding 100° F, and the savanna takes on a withered appearance. Thus, the llanos are alternately rain-drenched and sun-baked.

VEGETATION

The vegetation of the savanna is vastly different from that of the rain forest. Absent are the giant trees, the hanging vines, the bromeliads, the ferns, and a vast array of other plant forms. The vegetation is composed mainly of grasses, ranging from one to more than 12 feet in height, and a few scattered trees and shrubs. The grasses grow in separate clumps set very close together, between which there is usually a small area of bare soil. Some savannas, including a large area of the llanos of the Orinoco basin and the campos of Brazil, are composed of grass only, but the more common type is that sparsely sprinkled with trees and related woody forms.

The trees are of different species from those found in the rain forest. They range from 10 to 40 feet in height, have twisted or gnarled trunks and branches, and deeply scored bark. Certain of the plants and trees are adapted to resist the action of fire and, along with the grasses, quickly become green with the first rains. Savannas of this type are the dominant type in the Sudan, in British East Africa, Madagascar, southern Brazil, and in certain parts of Oceania and Malaya.

Vast areas, however, are flammable and are destroyed or denuded by fires during the dry season, some started by man, others ignited by natural causes. It is these fires that produce the gray, smoky haze that characterizes so many tropical regions during the dry season. The resultant poor visibility is a serious handicap to effective signaling by survivors on the ground as well as hindrance to spotters in search aircraft.

ANIMAL LIFE

The animal life of the savanna is abundant and varied, and tends to be more uniform than that of the rain forest. In the main this uniformity is due to the fact that we are dealing with forms restricted to ground-level habitat.

The larger animals are of two general types, the "vegetable eaters" or herbivores, and the "meat eaters" or carnivores. Among the herbivores are animals such as the gazelle, antelope, elephant, and numerous birds and rodents. Of these the elephant is to be found only in the savannas of Africa and southeast Asia; the gazelle is confined, in its tropical distribution, to Africa. Because the herbivores have both a good food supply and excellent cover, they are the foremost dwellers of the savannas. The carnivores, however, are also well represented in the form of lions, tigers, pumas, and vultures which prey on the herbivores. Their number is closely correlated with the herbivore population; when herbivores are scarce there is a corresponding scarcity of the carnivores that feed upon them. Likewise when the herbivores are plentiful, so are the carnivores. Most of the large animals, regardless of class, are exceedingly swift of foot; among the fastest is the gazelle.

Although any one of the large animals mentioned above would provide a survivor with food for a long period of time, they are not often observed because of the thick and dense grass cover.

The small animal life is diverse and highly specialized. It includes spiders, ants, termites, crickets, beetles, locusts, grasshoppers, snakes and birds, the population of each varying according to whether the season is wet or dry. The large numbers of seeds and insects on the floor of the savanna attract birds of many kinds, including a variety of game birds such as the bustard.

The highest concentration of human population in the savanna areas is found in Africa and Malaya, the least in the llanos and campos of Venezuela and Brazil. Those in Africa are predominately of the Negroid race, those in South America are Indian, and those in Malaya and Oceania are a mixture of Mongoloid, Negro and Caucasian. With the exception of a few small groups occupying pocket-size savanna areas in the upper Orinoco basin and the Amazon basin of South America, all are peaceful and friendly.

SURVIVAL CONSIDERATIONS

It was pointed out earlier that you must have tropic "know-how" in order to cope successfully with the rain forest under emergency survival conditions. The same holds true for survival in the savanna areas. As in the rain forest, you will be faced with the problems of procuring food and water, erecting a shelter, protection from natural hazards, and devising means to effect your early rescue. The survival pattern is the same but the environmental situation is different; it calls for techniques and procedures different from those you would use in the rain forest.

Let us begin with the in-flight emergency. Here the pilot or the aircraft commander and passengers have a choice denied them when over the rain forest. An emergency landing can, in most cases, be made in the level grassland. The savannas of Venezuela, Brazil, and equatorial Africa, over which commercial and military air traffic is heavy, contain vast areas in which an emergency landing can be successfully made (Fig. 11-3). Whereas over the rain forest your only chance of reaching the ground alive is to bail out, over a savanna you have two chances—bail-out and crash-land.

Fig. 11.3. Many aircraft have landed successfully in savanna areas and jungle clearings. Here a successful crash-landing was made in the llanos of Colombia.

CRASH LANDING ON THE SAVANNA

A successful crash landing sets up a chain reaction which permeates and effects subsequent decisions, mental attitudes, food- and water-supply problems, and early recovery by search aircraft or ground parties. The aircraft can be used as a shelter; it should contain water, food, and equipment which would not be available to you in case of bail-out. It is possible that the aircraft's radio will still function, but even if it doesn't the plane is a large signpost for searching aircraft. While in bail-out you are very likely to face a survival ordeal alone, in crash-landing you will be one of a group. The panic associated with being alone in a trying and complex situation will be replaced by a feeling of confidence and willingness to assume your share of the job ahead.

Emergency survival in a savanna area presents few problems. It is pretty much a question of how long it will be before a search aircraft or ground party locates you. You can expedite recovery by intelligent use of your communication aids, signaling equipment, and advance preparation of a landing strip for the search aircraft. Your survival experience may last but a few hours or it may last for several days, depending to a great degree upon your cooperation.

BAILOUT

Conditions or circumstances may be such that a forced landing in the savanna cannot be made and your only alternative is to bail out. This will result in a multitude of survival problems not inherent in a crash-landing. You will have less food, less water, less equipment, no ready-made shelter, and last but not least, you will probably have to face the survival ordeal alone. How far and wide the survivors will be scattered depends on the altitude and wind conditions at time of bail-out. Personnel may be separated by many miles. Should the savanna grass be more than head-high, as is so frequently the case in South America and Africa, your chances of sighting a fellow passenger are practically nil. Your best bet in locating other passengers is through the use of the emergency radio or signaling devices such as flares, smoke signals, and firearms.

NATURE OF THE SURVIVAL PROBLEM

If you were to study a vegetation map of Africa or of South America you would find that practically the entire hearts of those two continents consist of rain forests and savannas. You would also note that in these vast areas there are, with the exception of jungle streams, few if any highways. Next consult an airways map of the same continents; you will see a maze of routes operated by a score or more airlines. Air traffic over these vast wildernesses is heavy because it is the only transportation available. Flight emergencies are rare indeed, but they do occur. Whether a passenger on an aircraft in distress, a member of an ill-fated expeditionary party, or simply a born adventurer, it is good insurance to be prepared for a few days on your own.

Savanna survival problems, like those of the rain forest, are threefold. First are those that pertain to first aid, water, shelter, travel, and hazards. Second are those pertaining to the effective use of survival equipment. Third are those related to mental attitude and will-to-live.

IMMEDIATE ACTION

Whether you crash land or bail out, your first concern is to check for injuries, cuts, and bruises and to render first aid as required. When the job is done sit down, relax, and calmly plan your course of action. Your objectives should be twofold: first, do everything possible that will assist in effecting your rescue, and second, draw upon your tropical knowledge to make yourself comfortable and to preserve your strength.

If the weather is severe, construct a temporary shelter using the parachute canopy or parts of the aircraft. If the plane's radio or the emergency radio is available and operative, get on the air as soon as possible. Be careful to conserve your electrical power by using the equipment according to procedures given in your training. If the radios are not operative, gather all available signaling equipment such as signal mirrors and flares and have them readily available for use.

Determine your position by the best means available and include this position in any radio messages you may transmit. If the position is based on celestial observations, transmit the observation also.

Organization and planning are as important in themselves as they are in the actions that result from them. The case histories of many men who failed to survive reveal that the main pitfall has been the blind and almost hysterical actions of the persons involved.

TRAVEL

In a savanna situation your chances of being located and rescued are greatly increased if you stay with your aircraft and await rescue. A downed aircraft or aircraft wreckage is much easier for your rescuers to sight, and it also provides many items for your survival and comfort. However, let us assume that you bailed out and that no aircraft wreckage or passengers are in sight. What then should be your decision? You should travel only far enough to select a good camp site in the open and on relatively high ground. This may mean not having to move from where you landed, or it may, during the rainy period, mean a walk of many miles to escape from inundated areas. Obviously if you can see or know the location of aid and are physically capable of navigating and surviving until that location is reached, you should set out for it. Leave a message giving the date and the hour of departure and the direction of travel. If possible, mark your trail at regular intervals.

Should you come down in the sparsely populated llanos of South America or the campos of Brazil, your chances of finding aid close by are exceedingly slim. Unless the grass has been burned by the natives, the savannas become almost impenetrable, for they are dominated by very tall, coarse grasses that grow from five to 12 feet high. Natives who dwell in the area occupy only those lowlands where moisture is sufficient to grow crops and where the permanent rivers supply fish. Your immediate job will be to select and make temporary camp.

If there are any trees at all in the area, locate your camp near them so they can serve as supports for your hammock. The trees will also be about your only supply of firewood. Savanna grasses are often several feet high and you should tramp down or cut down the area where you decide to make your camp. You will be less troubled by insects, have a better view of the landscape about you, and can be more easily spotted from the air.

SHELTER

During the dry period the best shelter is your parachute, a few panels of which can be used to improvise a hammock and the remainder used to form an open shelter for protection against the hot sun. The floor of the shelter can be padded with bunched grass to any height desired and the chute can then be draped over it as a protection against insects. Such a floor or bench can readily serve as a bed should you be in a treeless area where it is impossible to sling a hammock.

The rains are torrential and of long duration during the rainy season; your parachute alone will not keep you dry. If you have access to trees, cut poles to form an "A" type framework or a simple lean-to and shingle it with several layers of bunch grass. Over this place two thicknesses of parachute and secure it with pieces of shroud line. Above all, do not sleep on the ground in either the wet or dry season where you would be made miserable by dampness and by countless ants, termites, locusts, beetles, and other pests.

FIRE-MAKING

Prepare the location of your fire carefully. Clear away leaves, twigs and dry grass, so that you don't start a grass fire. If the ground is dry, scrape well down to the bare soil. The bunch grass of the savanna provides you with all the flammable kindling you will need to get the fire going. Fuel may present a problem, however, unless you are in an area where trees, dead wood, and dead branches are to be found. In treeless areas the picking will be very poor, but with diligent search and ingenuity natural fuels can be found. The coarse dry grass can be twisted into compact bunches and used as a fuel; animal dung also makes a good fuel.

If you are with the aircraft you can burn gasoline and lubricating oil or a mixture of both.

WATER

Water will be one of your first and most important requirements and you should start looking for it immediately. Unlike rain forests, savannas do not have plants and vines that provide a ready supply of palatable water. You will have to get your water from surface sources such as streams, pools, marshes, and springs. The water may be discolored or turbid, in which case it should be cleared by filtering through parachute or other finely woven cloth. Water from surface sources is safe to drink only after it has been purified. Boiling is the surest and best purification method.

During the rainy season all your water needs can be satisfied by collecting rain water. In a savanna the best procedure is to dig a hole and line it with a tarpaulin or a piece of canvas. Rain water collected in a clean container is safe to drink without purifying. If it has a flat taste it can be improved by aeration—simply pour the water, several times, from one container to another.

ANIMAL FOOD

More than one man who has walked out of an uninhabited South American or African savanna has had difficulty finding food; some survivors came close to starvation. But a good woodsman, or one who knows how to use his survival training, can find enough palatable food in almost any wilderness. The important thing is to forget your civilized prejudices; there is plenty of good food in tropical savannas; if you are not finicky, there is no reason for going hungry. Regardless of your prejudices, do not pass up any food once you know it is safe to eat. As stated elsewhere, lizards, snakes, grubs, locusts, and grasshoppers are perfectly good food and are commonly a regular part of the diet of primitive peoples.

The larger animals of the savanna such as the deer, antelope, and gazelle make the best eating, but unfortunately they are the most difficult to catch. If your survival equipment includes a rifle your hunting efforts may prove successful. Animals are most likely to be found near water holes where they come for water; hunting in the open is difficult, especially since the animals have keen eyes and are very wary. The best method of hunting is to lie in wait near the water in the early morning or about dusk in the evening.

The smaller animals, such as rodents and birds, live concealed in the grass or bushes, or in holes in the ground. Animals that dive into a hole at your approach will usually pop up again in a few minutes. These can be snared by means of a noose placed over the hole. In Venezuela, the Piaroa Indians often burn off a patch of grass and pick up the small animals killed by the fire.

There is an astounding variety and abundance of fish in the rivers flowing through the llanos or grasslands of South America. One species, the pavon cebu, will take almost any conceivable bait. Its average weight is seven to 16 pounds.

The banks and islands of the lower Orinoco River are vast hatcheries for turtles, a highly prized food. Also edible are their eggs, covered by a tough membranous shell, which are buried in the sand or loose earth.

A typical reptile of the savannas is the tortoise or land turtle. This animal, often cited for its slow movements, is valuable for its delicious meat. It should be cooked by roasting or baking. Tortoises are notoriously rough in courtship, which is to your advantage when hunting them; when armored male caresses armored female by bumping shells, the noise is audible for considerable distances.

Birds are the easiest animals to see but the hardest to bring down unless you are equipped with a shotgun or firearm that will accommodate scatter-type ammunition. Select a spot near a tree or water hole and sit quietly until an easy shot presents itself. The important thing is to remain perfectly still; small birds will often come within a few feet. If you are without a gun, use a throwing stick or stone, or make a slingshot from the webbing and shroud lines of the parachute.

Birds' eggs and fledglings are another possible source of animal food. If you see a bird leave a clump of grass, look there for a nest. Nests may be found on the ground, in bushes or in trees.

If you are lucky enough to kill a large animal, preserve the excess by drying and smoking. This is a common trick in the tropics where food spoils quickly because of the high temperature and high humidity. Clean the meat carefully, cut it into strips, and dry it over a smoky fire in the sun. When dried, wrap the strips in chute cloth. Dried meat should be cooked before eating as the parasites are not killed by the drying and smoking process.

PLANT FOOD

There is little variety to the wild plant food. It consists mostly of grass or grasslike plants, and possibly nuts and fruits from a few scattered trees. Since there are no poisonous grasses, any that are found may be eaten without danger. True grasses can be recognized by their jointed stems and by their characteristic flowers, which are never conspicuously colored. Because their seeds fall off readily after ripening they are generally difficult to gather. Also the seeds usually have to be ground into some kind of flour and cooked before being eaten.

Grasses. During the long dry season the grasses become so woody in fiber that they are unpalatable and have little food

Fig. 11.4. Manioc or cassava growing on edge of savanna. (*Photo by Paul H. Nesbitt.*)

value. Even animals die from sheer hunger and thirst at this time. The poor quality of the grass is also a reason why the natives have burned it for centuries, for almost immediately thereafter the tender green shoots start to emerge.

If you find grass with a growing head, grab the head and jerk it; where it breaks loose from the stalk you will find a soft edible stem. Some grasses have swollen roots or small bulbs which may be eaten. An example of this is Nut Grass or Chufa, which is widespread in many parts of tropics. It has a thick underground tuber about one-half inch to an inch in diameter, which

Fig. 11.5. Roots of the bitter cassava. Root looks like potato but is much larger. (*Photo by Paul H. Nesbitt.*)

contains starch. It tastes slightly sweetish and nutty, and the tough, dry rind makes good, though hard, chewing. The tubers can be boiled, peeled, and ground into a palatable and wholesome flour, which may be brewed as a coffee substitute.

Cassava. All other roots and tubers should be regarded with caution. Some are poisonous, particularly if eaten raw. *Cassava,* also known as *manioc* or *yucca,* is a staple food over much of the tropics of South America and Africa and is widely cultivated. It may possibly be found growing wild in the savanna. The raw roots of the so-called "bitter cassava" contain so much hydrocyanic acid that they are exceedingly poisonous. The natives remove the harmful acid by squeezing out the juice, washing the pulp in water, and cooking. While "sweet cassava" can be eaten raw, there is little or no difference in taste between the bitter and the sweet, and it is advisable to mash the roots of any cassava plant to a pulp (**Fig. 11-6**), squeeze out the juice, and then cook or bake the remaining pulp. Cassava as a food is as important in the tropics as potatoes are in temperate regions.

Fig. 11.6. Grating cassava into pulp is first step in extracting the bitter hydrocyanic acid. (*Photo by Paul H. Nesbitt.*)

Monkeybread or Baobab. The African savanna possesses both dwarf and large trees, even gigantic ones such as the monkeybread or baobab. The latter can be distinguished from all other trees by the enormous girth and swollen appearance of the trunk in comparison with the low height of the tree. A tree 60 feet high may have a trunk 30 feet in diameter. The mature fruit hangs loosely from the tree and is filled with mealy pulp and numerous seeds. Both the pulp and the seeds are edible. The tender root of the young baobab tree is also edible.

No attempt has been made to describe cultivated plants, for obviously where you find cultivated plants the chances are that you will find inhabitants and safety.

Cooking Methods. Perhaps the most satisfactory way of cooking food in a savanna is the ground oven method. Scrape out a shallow hole in the ground and build a fire in it. When it burns down bury the meat or vegetables, wrapped in mud, in the embers and cover the fire with earth. The size of the oven and the cooking time required vary with the type of food.

HAZARDS

Insect Pests. As has been noted elsewhere in this book, the popular notion that a man landing in a tropical savanna is at the mercy of wild tribes of man-eating animals is false. You will probably never see a poisonous snake, an elephant or a large cat. The most dangerous creatures are the small and inconspicuous insects, many of which are hosts for diseases or parasites. You don't have to worry about yellow fever, as you will have been given inoculation against it, but, as we have seen, there is no such protection against malaria. Hence, you should guard yourself against mosquito bites as much as possible. Since malaria-bearing mosquitoes fly only in the evening, the best way to escape infection is to get under a net as soon as possible after sunset. If you have no net, improvise one from your parachute cloth and cover all exposed parts of the body as far as possible. A smudge fire will help to drive off the mosquitoes and other insects.

Mites and Chiggers. Seldom seen but often felt are the mites, commonly called red bugs, bêtes rouges, bicha colorada, and chiggers. Always abundant in grassy places, you will find them the worst pest of the savanna. Their bites do not start to itch for several hours, but once they begin the itching lasts for several days. The only sure protection against mites is to avoid going into the long grass, a practical impossibility in foraging for food and water in the savanna. It will help to tramp down or remove the ground cover about your temporary camp site.

In the grasslands of Venezuela, Brazil, and West Africa there is a small flea which has a great affinity for both men and animals. It is the true chigger and bites like other fleas, but the female has the further unpleasant habit of burrowing into the skin, usually under the toenails, where in the course of a few days a swelling the size of a small pea appears, recognizable as a whitish area with a dark brown spot in the center. The chigger should be removed as soon as possible with a sterile needle or knife point, and the affected area painted with iodine. The best protection against chiggers and mites, in the absence of chemical repellents, is to keep your trouser bottoms tucked into your socks and your sleeves and collar buttoned. *Never go about barefoot.*

Wasps, Spiders, Scorpions. There are many types of wasps, spiders, centipedes, and scorpions in practically all tropical grassland areas, some of them very large. Most are poisonous, but while their bite is extremely painful and may cause temporary swelling and illness, it is not likely to be fatal. Two exceptions are the black widow and her cousin, the veinte-cuatro, which are black, gray, or spotted spiders with a body about the size of an aspirin tablet, and with long legs that are hairless or slightly hairy. Both have a red or yellowish spot shaped like an hourglass on the under side of the abdomen. The veinte-cuatro, found commonly in the Guianas and in the Duida region of southern Venezuela, is believed by the local Indians to produce a fever that will kill the victim in 24 hours, hence the name, veinte-cuatro, Spanish for twenty-four. Although this belief exaggerates the toxic effect, case records of Maquiratare Indians bitten by the veinte-cuatro show that the bite of this spider causes extremely severe muscular cramping and illness, and often severe dizziness. The administration of any drug that will relieve pain and the application of moist heat to the cramping muscles is an effective first aid.

Ants. These are always a nuisance, particularly the army or driver ants which move along the ground in vast swarms, devouring vegetation and most everything else in their way. The best way to avoid them is to move your camp a few yards away from their direct line of advance.

Grass Fires. During the long, dry season the possibility of a grass fire is always a serious threat to your safety. The tall grass is highly flammable, so that in addition to the precautionary measures you should follow in building a fire you will also have to be on guard against being trapped in fires started by natives or ignited by natural causes.

SIGNALING

The length of time before you are rescued will depend to some degree on the effectiveness of your signals and the speed with which you can have them ready for use. Whether you reach the ground through bail-out or crash landing you should have a radio, smoke flares, signal mirror and flashlight. If operative, all of this equipment will prove effective in the open savanna. Select the most prominent elevation in your immediate vicinity for your signal operations.

Radio. Your aircraft radio or emergency radio is your best rescue aid and you should attempt to establish radio contact at once. The effective range, in the open savanna, of small, light weight, emergency transceivers is about 20 miles. You would do well to conserve the power supply as much as possible, using it only to sweep the horizon at regular intervals and when you hear the motors of the search aircraft.

Smoke Signals are almost always effective in open country unless strong winds disperse the smoke. Keep the smoke flares dry and ready for instant use but do not waste them; use only when an airplane is heard or help is sighted. Practice the use of your signaling mirror during the day, and be prepared to signal with the flashlight at night. Sound travels considerable distances in the open savanna; a shot from a gun, the sound of a whistle, or a shout may attract the attention of distant natives.

An effective signal is a fire built to keep a smoke column rising all day and a bright flame going at night, but this may be difficult to accomplish, since many savanna areas have a very limited amount of fuel. The bunch grass when twisted tightly and secured with string (from the parachute shroud line) will make an excellent torch for either daytime or nighttime use.

Markers. Cut giant-sized markers or designs in the vegetation and otherwise disturb the natural grassland as extensively as you can. Place the yellow-and-blue cloth signal panel and panels from your parachute on clumps of grass, or suspend them from the branches of isolated trees.

TRAVELING

In a savanna area your chances of rescue are better than in almost any other type of tropic terrain. Normally all you have to do is make yourself comfortable, have your signaling equipment ready for use, and wait for the rescue aircraft to show up. But if you have come down a considerable distance off course and are unable to transmit your location at the time of emergency— and if in addition the weather is foul, you may be in for a rough time and forced to make a major decision. That decision is— should I stay put or should I travel? The best advice is to stay where you are and await rescue. Most rescues have been made when downed crews remained with the aircraft or when crew members, on bailing out, landed in savanna or open areas. You should travel or leave the site only if you are certain of your position and know that you can reach water, shelter, food, and help —or, if after waiting several days, you are convinced that rescue is not coming.

12

Seashores and Coasts: Environmental and Survival Considerations

SEASHORE AND COASTAL AREAS

How much of the land area of the tropical belt is coastline or seashore is not accurately known. If we include all of the islands and atolls of the Atlantic and the Pacific, an estimate of the total shoreline would be several hundred thousand miles. Africa alone has more than 6,000 miles of coastline; Central and South America has considerably more.

MANGROVE SWAMPS

Many tropical coastlines are studded with swamp forests of mangrove trees, which can give all sorts of trouble in an emergency landing. Mangrove swamps are found in West Africa, Madagascar, Malaya, numerous Pacific Islands, and in Central and South America. A rather sparse mangrove vegetation is found on the west coast of Florida.

Mangrove swamps are confined to areas in ,which the water is salty or brackish. Except along rivers and estuaries that are fed by high tides, mangroves do not extend inland. Mangrove vegetation consists of a dense forest of trees and shrubs, from 10 to 30 feet high, supported on tall, stiltlike roots that arch outward in clumsy fashion to anchor in the murky water and mud. They are so well secured that only a violent gale can dislodge them. The trees are as close together as the slats of a picket fence and the arched roots of one interlock with those of others. The result is an impenetrable mass of twisted trunks, branches, and roots. Countless numbers of air roots project above the mud and water, adding to the tangled maze. All of this maze is flooded at each high tide, and when the water recedes it exposes roots slimy with mud and colonized by oysters, crabs, and various other marine life.

In some cases a few screw pines and nipa palms may be found

272

growing in the swamp, but aside from these the mangrove swamp offers little in the way of food-producing plants.

CLIMATE

Coastal areas and islands have a uniform temperature with an annual mean of 75-85° F. The prevailing winds south of the equator are the southeast trades, which are interrupted by winds from the north or northeast during the storms. North of the equator the northeast trade winds prevail. Along the equator are the doldrums, a narrow shifting zone of equatorial calm. Rainfall is the most changeable factor in the climate, the amount varying from island to island and from coast to coast. Rainfall averages from 70 to 200 inches per year, the area of the doldrums being the wettest.

SURVIVAL CONSIDERATIONS

In an emergency the chances of your landing on a sandy beach or near the coastline are far greater than your landing in a tropical rain forest. There are several reasons for this. First, there is more coastal area than there is rain forest area; second, more than 50 per cent of the principal air routes are over water areas

Fig. 12.1. Coastal beach, Gulf of Mexico. No trees and no surface water. Parachute shelters in left foreground.

dotted by islands and atolls and outlined by continental coasts; lastly, the aircraft commander, when given a choice, will beach or ditch the aircraft in preference to making an emergency landing inland.

Assume you are flying over a rain forest at 30,000 feet and your engines fail you. You can still glide a considerable distance, perhaps far enough to make a successful beach or water landing. (In 1954 this actually happened near the east coast of Venezuela. A United States Navy pilot, faced with an emergency over the Guiana rain forest, glided the aircraft some 40 miles to the mouth of the Orinoco river where a successful landing was made in the mud flats of the Orinoco delta.)

If you should have the misfortune to land near a mangrove swamp, don't waste your time trying to fight your way through it, or searching for food. Some mangrove belts along the coasts of Sumatra, Malaya, and Gambia, West Africa are more than a mile wide; to go through them would require days and nights of the roughest and most exhausting traveling. First attempt to work your way along the coast to a point where there is a break in the vegetation and an open beach.

Upon reaching the shore you will have to decide whether to stay at your landing point or leave it. If it seems probable that help will reach you where you came ashore, sit tight. If you decide to travel, it is often better to move along the coast than to go inland. Don't leave the coast except for such obstacles as swamps and cliffs unless you find a trail that leads to human habitation.

If you find that you are on an uninhabited island or coast you will face a survival situation greatly different from that encountered in a rain forest or a savanna. If you like to hunt or fish and know the ABC's of survival procedures and techniques, you will fare beautifully—in fact, with a few breaks, it will be like a weekend vacation at the beach. Your main needs will be water, food, and shelter and in almost all places these are readily available.

SEA FOOD

If stranded on a beach you should have no difficulty keeping alive indefinitely on fish, shellfish, or mollusks. A simple and easy way of finding sea food is to work along the beach when the tide is out. There will be no difficulty in finding an ample supply. All shellfish like oysters and mussels can be eaten raw, but it's best to cook them.

Crabs and lobsters may be trapped or caught by hand most easily at night, the time when they generally move about. A simple device is to use a throwline baited with dead fish or spoiled meat—the riper the better. No hook is needed but you should add a sinker of some kind and tie the bait on just above it. From time to time pull the line in slowly to see if you have attracted something; if you have, be prepared to stun it with a club or dip it up with a net made from your parachute. Tropical lobsters or sea crayfish do not have large pincers on their front legs but they do have sharp spines on their backs which can produce severe lacerations; accordingly, wear gloves when seizing or handling them.

All crabs and lobsters are safe to eat provided they are fresh. Salt-water forms can be eaten raw, but all land varieties and those found in fresh water should be thoroughly cooked, since they may be infected with lung parasites that can. prove fatal to humans if the meat is consumed raw. The easiest way to cook crabs and lobsters is to drop them into boiling water when still alive and keep them boiling for 20 to 30 minutes. The shells and pulpy gills are easily removed after cooking.

Turtles and turtle eggs are good food. Turtles frequently come ashore at night, dig a hole in the sand, and lay their eggs. Look for small parallel tracks along the shore. Follow the tracks, and where they end, dig for turtle eggs. All turtles are good to eat. Should you see one on the beach, rush it, turn it over on its back and kill it with a stone or club. Practically everything on a turtle can be eaten, except the shell, the kidneys, and the stomach. The meat should be cooked by boiling or baking, preferably the latter.

Another good shore food is the sea cucumber, usually found on tropical reefs and rocky shores. As the name implies, it is shaped like a cucumber and has a grooved and warty skin. The sea cucumber can expand and contract its body from a maximum of 12 to 18 inches, to about half that length. The edible portion consists of five long white muscles on the inside of the body. These can be stripped off and boiled, fried, or eaten raw.

Still another source of sea food are sea urchins or sea eggs. They can be found on all tropical reefs and along all rocky shores. In some parts of South America, the West Indies, and the Southwest Pacific they form an important source of food for the local inhabitants. Sea urchins are globular in shape, somewhat flattened, from two to six inches in diameter, and are covered with spines, looking like a pincushion full of long needles. The edible portion is the mass of eggs, usually five rows of them, on

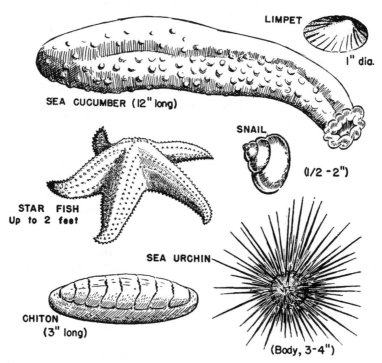

Fig. 12.2. Common marine forms found on the beach or in shallow water. All are edible.

top of the body inside the shell. These may be eaten either raw or boiled.

There are two forms of urchins that should be avoided—the needle urchin and the soft-bodied urchin. The needle urchin is black and reddish in color, and has needle-pointed spines 15 inches long. These spines have tiny barbs and are very brittle, breaking off after penetrating the skin. The soft-bodied urchin lives throughout the Southwest Pacific and can be readily identified by its flexible, parchmentlike shell. It varies in color from dark purple or green to white, and has short, needlelike spines rather widely scattered. Some of these are very poisonous and should never be touched with bare hands.

Fish of many kinds are usually plentiful on reefs, in lagoons, along the shore, and just off the shore. It is possible to catch them in large numbers by using various traps or by using nets. However, you need nothing elaborate and can catch all you need by simple hook-and-line fishing. If you do not have an emergency fishing kit with you, try making your own. Parachute shroud lines make excellent fish line; fishhooks can be made from safety pins, hard wood, and the spines of the sea urchin. For bait use small pieces of crab, crayfish, mollusk or even the flesh of another fish.

Fish caught in tropical waters spoil quickly. Immediately after catching a fish it should be bled by cutting out the gills and large blood vessels that supply them, and then it should be gutted. The fish must be washed in clear water and cooked within a few hours. Good fish flesh is firm. If, on pressing the thumb against the fish it feels soft or flabby, the fish is probably decaying. Discard it.

POISONOUS FISH

Most fish are palatable and safe to eat but there are species that have very toxic flesh, and it is important that you be able to recognize these. They are the one big hazard in water and seashore survival. Toxins are found in all parts of poisonous fish, especially in the liver, intestines, and eggs. A small amount of the flesh of one species, the puffer fish, will prove fatal in a matter of a few hours. The toxins produce a numbness of the lips, tongue, tips of the fingers and toes. They also produce severe itching and sudden changes in body temperatures. These sensations are accompanied by nausea, vomiting, dizziness, loss of speech, and a paralysis which in the final stage may result in death.

Even broth or chowder containing parts of poisonous fish will be harmful, for no amount of cooking will destroy the poison. Nor is freshness any guarantee of safety, since fish toxins are not the result of fish spoilage. There are so many poisonous fish, many only seasonally toxic, that it's almost impossible to distinguish the poisonous from the nonpoisonous. A good example of this is the red snapper, a well-known table delicacy in many parts of the world, but which in the tropics accounts for many fatal cases of fish poisoning.

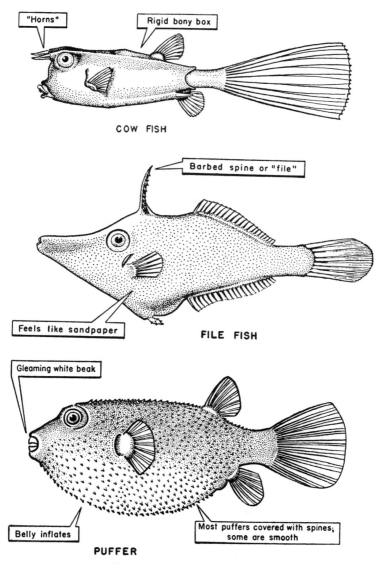

COW FISH

FILE FISH

PUFFER

Fig. 12.3. Poisonous fish are found in all tropical waters. Those above are among the most common and widely distributed.

In general, the severity of illness from eating the poisonous flesh of fish is dependent upon the amount eaten. It will be more severe if the liver or intestines are eaten. To date there is no known successful antidote; induced vomiting and bowel movements should be attempted.

Poisonous fish are widely distributed in the warm, shallow waters of the tropics. They are especially numerous in the Caribbean and in the Central and South Pacific. In the area about the Phoenix, Canton, Midway, Line, and Johnston Islands, it is estimated that there are some 300 species of poisonous reef fishes. Although there are no simple rules to tell the desirable fish from the undesirable ones, the worst offenders (see page 278) have round or boxlike bodies with hard, shell-like skins covered with bony plates or spines. They have small parrotlike mouths, small gill openings, and the belly fins are small or absent. Their names suggest their shape: puffer fish, file fish, globe fish, trigger fish, porcupine fish, moon fish and the like.

Certain other fish should be avoided for a different reason. They are the venomous fish which produce injurious effects by means of spines and stingers located on their heads and in their fins. These spines cause a burning and agonizing pain that is out of all proportion to the severity of the wound.

VENOMOUS FISH

The worst of the venomous fish are the *Scorpaenidae*. They are known by the following common names: scorpion fish, stonefish, zebra fish, and stinging fish (see page 44). The almost invisible stonefish will not move from your path. When wading on a reef you should keep a sharp eye out for it. A full charge of venom from the 13 spines on its dorsal fin will cause agony and serious illness.

Sharp-spined animals, such as the sting rays, are also very dangerous. They, too, are found in shallow water where they lie on the bottom concealed in the mud or sand. Sting rays, because of their distinctive appearance, are easily recognized. They have a flat, globular body and a long tail armed with one or two serrated, needlelike spines. When stepped upon, the ray repeatedly whips its tail upward with great force and fury, and can drive the spine through a leg or foot. The pain is severe and nauseating and infection usually results. When wading in turbid or muddy water poke ahead of you with a stick. Should your feet just touch a hidden sting ray it will dart away quickly, but if you set your foot squarely on one, your weight will anchor it down and provide the leverage needed to put the tail spines into lashing action.

Some catfish have poison glands at the base of the spines on the breast fins. This poison causes sharp pain but it is usually

Fig. 12.4. Handle the sting ray with extreme care. The spiny tail is capable of puncturing your skin several times in a single whip-like stroke. (*Photo by USAF.*)

of short duration. Some of the larger catfish have barbed spines which can make a deep puncture wound if you are careless in handling them.

In crossing deeper portions of a reef, be on the lookout for moray eels, sharks, and barracudas, all of them very ferocious. Moray eels, which hide in dark holes among the reefs, are angry, vicious and aggressive when disturbed. In estuaries, bays or lagoons, man-eating sharks may come in very close to shore. Many shark attacks have been recorded on bathing beaches in the tropic seas. Barracudas have also made such attacks.

PLANT FOOD

Seashores and coastal areas are, as a rule, much more likely places to find survival food than deep tropical jungles or mountain tops. Many of the sandy, tropical shores have plants which are found all over the world.

The best all-around source of plant food in an emergency situation is the coconut palm; it characteristically lines many tropical coasts. The many uses of the coconut have already been described in the section on jungle food (page 241). Where you have coconuts your survival problems are greatly lessened.

Another tree that is commonly found is the screw pine or pandanus. It is easily recognized by its stiltlike roots and by the spiral arrangement of its long leaves. The fruits are large, roughened balls covered with a hard husk that encloses the

Fig. 12.5. Pandanus.   Fig. 12.6. Nipa palm.

fleshy, edible pulp and the seeds. The pulp may be boiled or baked and the seeds roasted.

The breadfruit tree (page 245), commonly planted by the peoples of the Pacific Islands, may also be found along or near the shore.

A medium-sized tree called the Polynesian chestnut is found throughout much of Oceania. It grows abundantly along the shores and bears pods containing a single large seed that provides excellent food when boiled or roasted. Cooking is necessary to remove the bitter tannin which the nuts contain.

Another plant found on or near the shore is the arrowroot (page 247), which has an underground tuber that can be eaten after it has been boiled or roasted.

WATER

Many islands and coastal areas have a good supply of fresh water, while others do not. In the Pacific the larger volcanic islands have a plentiful supply, but on coral islands and on many of the smaller volcanic islands drinking water is scarce. In a good many cases you will have to use a substitute. It is interesting to note that some natives live permanently on islands that lack streams; they obtain water in a number of other ways—for example, from holes and hollows in the rocks that collect rainwater. Shallow pits or holes are also dug to catch rain or the seepage of water after rains.

On seashore beaches fresh water can frequently be found behind the first line of sand dunes. Use a scallop or other shell for digging. Stop digging as soon as you strike water. You may only have to dig 18 inches, or you may have to dig much deeper. The first water you strike will be fresh or nearly fresh and potable. Don't make the mistake of digging deeper in hope of increasing your water supply—you will only succeed in tapping salt water. The best way to increase the supply of potable water is to dig several shallow wells. The shell you used for digging can also be used to ladle out the water.

Upon atolls or coral islands which do not have enough rainwater to support trees, there is usually found a plant known as pigweed, or purselane, a rather short (eight inches), nondescript-looking plant that covers the ground in patches in both tropic and temperate zones. It has a reddish hue, and the stems are quite fleshy. All parts of the plant, except the roots, may be chewed for their moisture content and food value. The tips of the aerial roots of the screw pine or pandanus may also be chewed for their moisture content.

Where there are coconuts available, your water problem is much simpler. The husk of the half-grown coconut is green or light yellow and it is at this stage that the water or milk is best for drinking. It rates next to water and is better than beer as a thirst quencher. Over two pints of cool fluid may be found in one young nut. Do not drink the fluid in mature nuts as it contains oil which acts as a purgative and may cause abdominal pains.

SHELTER

You must build an effective shelter if you are to enjoy good sleep and avoid getting damp and chilled. If you are staying with your plane, use it for shelter and try to make it mosquito-proof with netting or parachute cloth. If you are on the move, stop early enough in the afternoon to build yourself a shelter.

Choose the best campsite you can from the standpoint of health and comfort. High, open areas above the beach which have an inshore breeze will have fewer mosquitoes. If possible camp within easy reach of your source of drinking water, provided it has not attracted swarms of mosquitoes.

You can put up a temporary shelter very quickly by draping your parachute over a rope or vine tied between two trees.

Fig. 12.7. "A" frame covered with chute cloth makes satisfactory sea shore shelter. Frame is made of driftwood. (*Photo by Paul H. Nesbitt.*)

During heavy rains this will not give you full protection, so if the weather is wet and miserable you will be more comfortable in something more sturdy and waterproof. A good rain shelter can be made by covering an "A" type framework with a good thickness of palm or other broad leaves. Lay the thatch shingle-fashion, with the tips of the leaves pointing downward, starting from the bottom and working up.

As stated frequently in preceding chapters, *don't sleep on the ground;* it will be damp and chilly. Make a hammock from your parachute. It will keep you off the ground and will discourage insects and other pests. Or, if you prefer, you can make a comfortable bed by building a four-poster framework of poles, and adding bamboo or wood slats to support a mattress of palm leaves or grass. Cut the corner poles long enough to support a mosquito net or parachute fabric cover. This type of bed is especially good if you have to camp in one spot for an extended period.

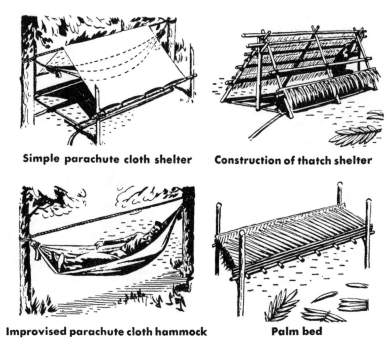

Simple parachute cloth shelter   **Construction of thatch shelter**

Improvised parachute cloth hammock   **Palm bed**

Fig. 12.8. Types of shelters that are effective and easy to make. They are suitable to all tropic environments.

In New Guinea, because of the occurrence of mite-borne typhus, camps should be built on high ground, avoiding sago palm and water bamboo swamps, grassland along river banks, and low scrub jungle along mountain streams. (See pages 31 and 234 for additional information on shelters.)

HAZARDS

Much of the material in the section on hazards in forest and jungle areas (pages 248-51) is also applicable to tropical coasts and seashores.

There are two major coastal and shore hazards. First, the insects, many of which are hosts for diseases or parasites. Second, there are the poisonous and venomous fish which cannot be readily distinguished from those which are safe to eat. These fish have been described above and the information need not be repeated here.

On the west coast of Malaya, especially in mangrove swamps near the mouths of large rivers, there are many crocodiles which have been known to attack man.

On most islands and coasts some protection from the sun is necessary to prevent sunstroke and severe sunburn. There are several things you can do to minimize these dangers. Keep out of the sun as much as possible during the middle of the day; make a head covering from the chute cloth and wear it; smear coconut oil over the exposed parts of the body.

SIGNALING

The general instructions for use of radio and ground signals given on pages 27-31 apply equally well to coastal areas. The signal mirror is especially effective along coasts and sandy beaches. Even though no aircraft or ships are in sight, continue sweeping the horizon; on a clear day the flash from the mirror is visible as far as 15 miles, somewhat less in hazy weather. A mirror can be improvised from a ration tin by punching a hole in the center of the lid. In a recent incident along the Gulf of Mexico the flashes from two such makeshift signal mirrors were picked up by the pilot of a Navy search plane several minutes before the three signal fires were seen.

13

Dwellers of the Tropics

WESTERN HEMISPHERE

The tropical inhabitants of the Western Hemisphere may be classified into a number of well-defined races—Indians, Negroes, whites, and mixed races. The most widely distributed race is the Indian, members of which inhabit the interior regions of Mexico, Central America, and South America. The Negro is the dominant race in the Caribbean Islands and in the interior of Dutch Guiana. The white race is confined almost entirely to the coastal belts although there are a few camps of oil and rubber workers in the interior of the Guianas, Brazil, and Venezuela. The mixed race, composed of Indian, Negro, and white elements, is well represented in Mexico, Central America, South America and parts of the Caribbean.

English and Spanish are spoken in the Caribbean Islands, Venezuela, parts of Brazil, and the coastal zones of Mexico and Central America. Elsewhere Indian dialects are employed, there being more than fifty in the hinterland areas. The Bush Negroes of Dutch Guiana speak "talkee-talkee," a language made up of African, English, Dutch, and Indian elements.

Population density is greatest in the Caribbean Islands, southern Mexico, and Central America. Elsewhere the jungle area is sparsely inhabited or uninhabited. Indian and Negro villages in South America are small, often many miles apart, and are located on or near streams or in forest clearings. In general the areas between rivers is uninhabited. This is particularly true of the many tributaries of the Orinoco and Amazon rivers. In southern Mexico and Central America there are vast stretches of jungle area entirely without inhabitants.

Agriculture is the pivot of economic life for all tropical peoples, with the exception of the Ges Tribes in the interior of Brazil, the Guaharibo of the Upper Orinoco drainage, and a few scattered tribes in the area extending from the Amazon to Central America. The chief food products of the Caribbean Islands

286

are sugar, coffee, cocoa, and bananas. The Indians and Negroes raise corn, manioc, and sweet potatoes. They are also expert hunters, familiar with the jungle trails, and good river navigators. Indians of tropical South America invented the hammock which Europeans now so widely employ at sea and in tropical areas. The Indians use it as a bed and make a daytime lounge of it. In the jungle areas of Yucatan, Honduras, and Guatemala are the remains of many ruined cities, built by the Maya Indians centuries ago. The Maya, a highly civilized Indian tribe whose em-

Fig. 13.1. Many persons have been rescued by friendly natives. This South American Indian, an expert on jungle living, served as guide to a scientific party studying the region. (*Photo by Paul H. Nesbitt.*)

pire once extended over all of southern Mexico, are now confined to Yucatan and Guatemala.

In general the tropical people of the Western Hemisphere are cheerful and intelligent, but inclined to be reticent. Judged by modern standards, of course, many of them are exceedingly primitive.

Most of the people are well disposed and friendly toward whites. The outstanding exceptions are the Motilone Indians of eastern Colombia and adjoining Venezuela and the Auca of Ecuador, who are hostile and should be avoided; for example, the Motilone shoot barbed unpoisoned arrows from ambush. In 1956 five evangelical missionaries, on a peaceful mission to the Cururay River, Ecuador, were ambushed and murdered by the Auca. Other tribes that might prove unfriendly, but not hostile, are the Guaharibo Indians of Southeast Venezuela, the Guahivo Indians of eastern Colombia, the Jivaro of Ecuador, the Diau and Trio of Dutch Guiana, the Carayas of Brazil, and the Guariba Maku of the middle Amazon. They should be approached with special tact.

OCEANIA

The inhabitants of Oceania cannot be considered a single homogeneous ethnic group. On the contrary, they represent a number of entirely different racial elements. The long distances between islands, intermixture between races, and environment, have in the course of time produced differences in race, culture, and language. Today, four provinces may be said to exist.

1. MELANESIA

Melanesia is the great archipelago beginning in the west with New Guinea, and extending eastward to New Caledonia and Fiji. It is inhabited exclusively by Negro and Negrito peoples, principally the former. The majority of the people speak the Melanesian language but in parts of New Guinea the language is Papuan, an unrelated tongue.

The people are good agriculturists and stock breeders of pigs, dogs, and poultry. Taro, yams, and cocoa are the principal foods. Melanesians are expert sailors, good workers, and are of friendly nature. However the natives of the interior of the larger islands may or may not be friendly. This is particularly true of New Hebrides, the Trobriand Islands, and New Guinea, where head-hunting and cannibalism have not yet been completely stamped out.

2. POLYNESIA

Polynesia is the name given to the islands of the middle Pacific which are located east of the Fiji Isles. The inhabitants constitute one of the tallest and handsomest races of the world. They are a composite of whites and Mongolians with a slight admixture of Negro blood.

The Polynesians live by tillage, fishing, and some stock raising. Taro, breadfruit, coconuts, bananas, and yams are the chief crops. There is practically no hunting.

The people are excellent wood carvers, skilled navigators, expert at making bark cloth, and are fond of all kinds of competitive games such as wrestling, boxing, and foot racing. The Polynesians are a friendly, likable, industrious people, and lead a serene and peaceful existence.

3. MICRONESIA

Micronesia includes the island groups known as the Marianas, Pelews, Carolines, Marshalls, and Gilberts. The inhabitants are a mixture of different racial elements which include Mongolian, Negro, and white. In appearance they are a cross between Melanesians and Polynesians.

The economic life centers in fishing, although taro is grown wherever possible. There is little hunting as no large game exists.

The Micronesians are expert navigators of rafts and outrigger canoes, and until Japanese intervention were on friendly terms with Europeans.

4. AUSTRALIA

The native inhabitants are a mixture of ancient strains of Negro and white. They are dark-skinned, have enormous brow ridges, hairy bodies, and skinny legs. The language, of which there are many dialects, is not related to that of the surrounding areas.

The Australian native is exceedingly primitive and leads a simple and crude life. There is no agriculture and he is restricted to the vegetable and animal food he can procure by gathering, hunting, and fishing. Great dependence is placed on wild fruits, lichens, larvae, beetles, ants, and worms. They have an astounding knowledge of the animal and plant life of the bush country and know when and where to find it.

Australian tools are made of stone and wood, houses are mere windbreaks, and as a rule the natives go completely naked. In spite of their material simplicity, the natives have evolved such a complex social and religious system that, like Einstein's theory of relativity, it is beyond comprehension of the ordinary man.

Throughout all four areas of the Pacific the native villages are usually situated near shore and in the jungle-cleared areas of the interior. In general the interior of the islands, and Australia, are sparsely inhabited.

SOUTHEAST ASIA

The inhabitants of this area belong to several different races as follows: (a) *Dravidian*. A race in which the features are a mixture of white and Negro. The Dravidians inhabit the west coast of India and are represented in Ceylon, parts of Borneo, and the Celebes. (b) *Mongolian*. Found in Assam, Burma, Indochina and parts of the Malay Peninsula. The people resemble the Chinese in appearance. (c) *Malay*. This race has yellowish-brown skin, is slight of frame, and shows relationship to the Mongolians. People of this type are widespread throughout the area extending from the Malay Peninsula to the Philippines. (d) *Negrito*. This is a dwarflike Negro race and is sporadically distributed throughout the area being present in the Andaman Islands, Malay Peninsula, Palawan, and the Philippines.

Burmese, Dravidian, Malay, and Tai are the most widespread languages but there are scores of native dialects whose affiliations are with the Malayo-Polynesian language family. Pidgin English and Pidgin Malay are used to a limited extent.

Population density is greatest in southwestern India, northeastern India, and the islands of Java, Borneo, and Sumatra. Villages, except in rare instances are but a few miles apart.

The people are agriculturists except for the Negritos, who depend on hunting for their livelihood. Rice is the staple crop but yams, millet, beans, breadfruit and coconuts are also important foods. The Malay are skilled wood and iron workers, good navigators, and construct excellent houses. In spite of strict governmental supervision, headhunting persists in parts of Borneo and the Philippines. It is not a symptom of senseless bloodthirstiness but rather a deep-rooted aspect of their religious views.

The natives are dignified, quiet-spoken, and calm. They are normally well poised, polite, and friendly. Some interior tribes of the Malay Peninsula, Sumatra, and the Philippines, however, are still suspicious of whites, and are likely to be unfriendly.

AFRICA

The people of Africa are predominatenly negroid with three types represented: (a) The "Forest Negro" in the Niger Basin and in the vast area drained by the Congo and its tributaries. (b) The pygmies, dwarflike Negroes, scattered in small groups through the Congo forests. (c) The Bantu, a Negro-white mixed type, in southeast Africa.

Madagascar has two races: (a) A negroid people in the western half of the island and (b) a Malay people, mongolian in appearance, in the eastern half. The population of the jungle area is estimated at fifty million people, of whom less than one per cent are white.

The Forest Negroes speak a non-Bantu language in which Tshi, Ewe, and Yoruba dialects predominate. The Pygmy and Bantu peoples speak various dialects of the Bantu language which is so widely distributed throughout south Africa. The inhabitants of Madagascar speak a Malayo-Polynesian language which affiliates them with southeastern Asia and not Africa. European languages are practically nonexistent.

Except for the Pygmies who live solely by hunting, the people are agriculturists. Yams, corn, pumpkins, cassava, and bananas are the chief foods. The Bantu and Forest Negroes have large herds of cattle which play an important economic and cultural role in the lives of the people. Cattle cannot be raised in the Congo basin because of the tsetse fly. The economic life of Madagascar does not conform to the African pattern but is similar to that of southeastern Asia from whence the Malay came several centuries ago. The Malays are stock farmers with a highly developed rice culture.

The African Negroes have great talents for iron working, metal casting, carving in wood and ivory, and are expert carpenters and canoe builders. They are gifted in music and dance and have evolved despotic governments and highly dramatic religions. Marriage is by "bride purchase" in which the monetary unit is cattle. As many people are poor, brothers frequently pool their cattle to purchase a common wife. Marriage of this type, called fraternal polyandry, is widespread.

The people are friendly toward whites and no known hostile tribes exist. Many have had considerable contact with Europeans and have adopted a monetary exchange and other customs. Pygmies may run and hide when approached, but friendship and trust among them and other hinterland tribes may be fostered by gifts of cowrie shells, olivella shells, and knives, all of which are highly prized.

14

Oceans and Seas: Survival Considerations

WATER SURVIVAL

DITCHING PROCEDURES

The majority of fatalities in water crashes and ditchings are caused by the failure of the aircraft crew and passengers to get into rafts soon enough after the aircraft is on the water. Studies of water survival incidents by both the Coast Guard and the Air Force indicate that survival after ditching can be increased considerably if passengers and crew are well briefed on the proper procedures in getting out of the aircraft and in launching the life rafts. The crew should have practiced evacuation of the aircraft in detail, including the actual inflation of rafts, so that they will know automatically, without stopping to read an instruction booklet, the location of rafts and life-vests in the aircraft, and how to get the rafts into the water with the minimum of delay. Such preparations and practice are time-consuming and often boring, but they are better life insurance than money can buy.

Stowage of flotation gear will depend on the aircraft used and the cargo carried. However, a few dry runs will show you the feasible locations for stowage. After the possible locations have been determined, don't put the rafts in any other locations. You probably won't have time to shift cargo or pull a heavy raft through a small opening after you have ditched.

When launching a raft don't throw it into the water without securing the retaining line to the aircraft. A raft drifts rapidly even in moderate winds and can easily be carried out of reach. Keep the raft attached to the aircraft until the last person has boarded or until the aircraft starts to sink. One crew member should keep a knife ready to cut the retaining line when necessary.

Rafts will take almost one minute to become rigid enough to

support passengers. Therefore, if you are using more than one raft inflate them simultaneously, otherwise you may run out of time before all rafts are inflated.

Whenever possible, enter the raft directly from the aircraft without going into the water. In cold water, prolonged immersion will cause suffering and possible death. Even warm-water immersion contributes to suffering from exposure. More important, boarding the raft from the water is difficult for even a healthy person under most conditions and can be almost impossible for an injured person without considerable help. Also, once in the water the survivor stands a chance of being separated from the raft. If the raft is floating free, a moderate wind will move it much faster than a man can swim.

If it is necessary to inflate the raft in the water, the person inflating it should crawl into the raft before it is completely inflated and avoid the expenditure of energy needed to board a raft from the water unaided. The first person in the raft should see that the others in the water have good handholds on the life line circling the raft. Then they should be pulled aboard one at a time. As survivors enter the raft they should be placed so as to balance the load instead of congregating on one side.

Survivors upwind of a drifting raft may have to be rescued by throwing them a line. Multipassenger aircraft should carry one or more heaving lines in the raft kits and crew members should be trained in their use.

What of the survivor who finds himself adrift on the open sea, wearing a life vest, but without a raft? His chances are not as good as that of a man in a raft, but he is not without hope. In the fall of 1956 one crew was rescued from the mid-Pacific after floating in life vests for more than two days. Many military pilots have had similar experiences. The main disadvantage of the life vest is that it presents such a small visual target for search. Therefore all life vests should be equipped with sea-marker dye and signal mirror.

FLOTATION GEAR

Flotation, by life raft or by life vest, is obviously the key to water survival. The ideal piece of flotation gear would be light in weight, occupy little space when stowed, and require no maintenance. Unfortunately, no such ideal equipment is available at the present writing (1959).

All flotation gear requires frequent checking to insure serviceability. This statement applies to the newest item as well as to war-weary surplus. When buying military surplus items, demand an inflation check and a check for leaks. Much of this gear has been in storage so long that the fabric may have cracked or rotted and will thus not maintain inflation. Such a piece of equipment may satisfy safety regulations but it won't save your life.

When buying new equipment, get a written guarantee from the dealer but in addition make an inflation check before taking any overwater flights. Check the equipment periodically according to the manufacturer's recommendations, or oftener if you are operating in a very hot or very cold climate which would tend to accelerate deterioration.

Some life vests will not support a heavy man in a safe position, with his face out of the water, especially in heavy seas. Check your vest while wearing full flight gear or equivalent clothing in a swimming pool or calm water. A satisfactory vest should support you with your head out of water (in salt water) with only one side inflated.

These statements should not be regarded as derogatory of the manufacturers of any specific flotation equipment. The sad truth is that no foolproof flotation gear has as yet been put on the market.

SHARKS

Prior to World War II there was considerable controversy among ichthyologists, fishermen, and others authorized either by education or experience to express opinions on the subject publicly, as to whether a shark would attack an uninjured man swimming in the water or afloat on a raft. Some survival manuals used during World War II stated flatly that sharks were cowards and would not attack an uninjured man. Authenticated observations during the war proved this statement to be wrong and established the fact that some sharks will attack. However, the question as to which shark will attack and which shark will swim by has not yet been answered.

Shark attacks are more likely in warmer waters both because of the presence of more sharks and because of more edible humans in swimming.

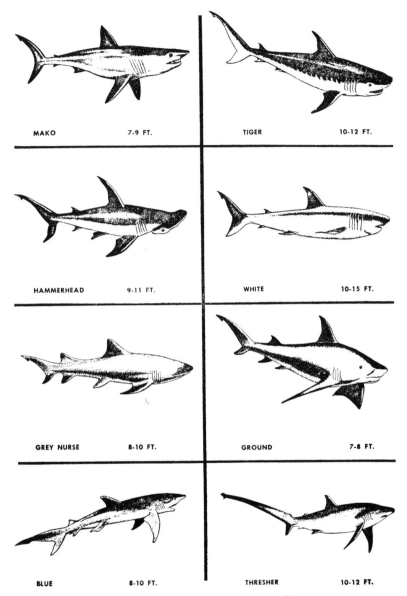

Fig. 14.1. Sharks known to have attacked humans.

The shark repellent developed by the U.S. Government during World War II has recently been subjected to extensive testing and found to be useless in discouraging a shark from attack. As noted above, not all sharks will attack. The most effective defense against feeding sharks appears to be the shark bag, essentially an inflated ring with an opaque pouch suspended beneath it.

PROTECTIVE MEASURES AGAINST SHARKS

In the Water.—Keep a sharp lookout for sharks. Keep your clothing and shoes on. If sharks have been noticed, be especially careful of the methods in which you eliminate body wastes. Urinate in short spurts and allow it to dissipate between spurts. Fecal matter should be passed in as small a quantity as possible into the hand and thrown as far away as possible. Vomiting, when it cannot be prevented by swallowing the regurgitation, should be done into the hand and thrown away as above.

If in a group threatened or attacked by a shark, bunch together and form a tight circle. Face outward so you can see an approaching shark. If the sea is rough, tie yourselves together. Ward off attack by kicking or stiff-arming the shark.

Stay as quiet as possible. Float to save energy. If necessary to swim, use strong regular strokes; don't make frantic irregular movements. When swimming alone stay away from schools of fish.

If a single shark threatens at close range:

1. Use strong regular swimming movements; try feinting toward the shark—it may be scared away.

2. Don't swim away directly in the shark's path; face the shark and swim quickly to one side; outmaneuver it.

3. Kick or stiff-arm a shark to push it away, or grasp a side fin and swim with shark until you can veer away from it.

4. Make loud sounds by slapping the surface of the water with cupped hands; use regular slaps. Or, put your head under water and shout; skin divers report that this will scare away most sharks.

5. Use a knife at close quarters in a showdown.

On a Raft.—Don't fish from raft when sharks are nearby. Abandon any hooked fish if a shark approaches. Don't clean fish into the water when sharks are sighted. Don't throw waste overboard if sharks are around.

If a shark threatens to attack or to damage the raft, discourage it by jabbing snout or gills with oar. Be careful not to break the oar, and don't take roundhouse swings that may upset you.

Fire a pistol above a shark—it will frighten him away.

Check for sharks around and under the raft before going into the water or in landing.

First Aid for Shark Victims.—The first and most important measure is to stop bleeding quickly. Help the victim into a raft or ashore as soon as possible. Stop bleeding and treat for shock.

If in the water in a group, form a circle around the victim and stop bleeding by using a tourniquet improvised from an article of clothing.

IMMEDIATE ACTION

Stay upwind and clear of the aircraft (out of gasoline-covered waters) but in the vicinity until the aircraft sinks.

Make a thorough search for missing men. Carefully patrol the entire area near the crash, especially in the direction toward which waves are moving. Look very carefully—some of the missing men may be unconscious and floating low in the water. If men are in the water and sharks are in the vicinity, use shark repellent.

Salvage floating equipment. Stow and secure all useful items by lashing them to the raft. Check rafts for inflation, leaks, and points of possible chafing. Bail out your raft, being careful not to snag it with shoes or sharp objects. Put out the sea anchor. In cold oceans, put on an antiexposure suit, if available. Rig a windbreak, spray shield, and canopy. If you are with others, huddle together. Exercise regularly within the limits of the available space.

Check the physical condition of all aboard. Give first aid if necessary. Take seasickness pills if available. Wash gasoline from skin and clothing.

If there is more than one raft, connect rafts with at least 25 feet of line. Connect rafts *only* at lifeline around outer periphery of raft. Unless the sea is very rough, shorten the line if you hear or see an aircraft. Two or more rafts tied close together are easier to spot than scattered rafts.

Get the emergency radio into operation—directions are on the equipment. Use emergency transceiver only when aircraft are likely to be in the area. Prepare other signaling devices for instant use.

Start a log, assuming you have logbook and pencil. Record the navigator's last fix, time of ditching, names and physical condition of personnel, ration schedule, winds, weather, direction of swells, times of sunrise and sunset, and other navigation data. Inventory all equipment.

Keep calm. Save water and food by saving energy. Start fishing as soon as possible. Don't shout unnecessarily, and don't move around unnecessarily. Keep your sense of humor active; use it often. Remember that rescue at sea is a cooperative project. Search aircraft contacts are limited by the visibility of survivors. Increase your visibility by using all possible signaling devices— keep your mirrors handy and use your radio whenever you can, as well as your signal panel and dye marker when you think an aircraft can see them.

Inspect all debris that comes from the aircraft. Salvage all rations, canteens, thermos jugs and other containers, parachutes, seat cushions, extra clothing, and maps. Beware of sharp metal objects.

Secure equipment by lashing it to raft and storing it in raft pockets and kit containers where provided. Keep these closed when not in use. Keep such items as flashlights, signal guns, flares, watches, sextants and the like in waterproof containers.

Exposure to cold, wind, and sun is an ever-present threat to the health, even the life, of the survivor adrift in a raft. In cold weather you must stay dry and keep warm. If you are wet, get down behind a wind-shield. Remove, wring out, and replace outer garments or, if possible, get into dry clothing. Dry your hat, socks, and gloves. (See *Shock*, pages 16 and 24.)

If you are dry, share clothes with those who are wet. Give them the most sheltered positions on the raft. Let them warm their hands and feet against your body.

Put on any extra clothing available. If you have no antiexposure suit, drape extra clothing around your shoulders and over your head. Keep your clothes loose and comfortable, and try to keep the floor of the raft dry. For insulation, cover the floor with canvas or cloth.

Huddle with the others on the floor of the raft. Spread extra tarpaulin, sail, or parachute over the group. If you are on a raft with a canopy, lower the canopy sides. Take mild exercise to restore circulation—repeatedly bend and open fingers and toes, exercise shoulders and buttock muscles, and warm hands under armpits. Periodically, raise your feet slightly and hold them up a minute or two. Move your face muscles frequently to detect frostbite. Shivering is normal—it's the body's way of quickly generating heat. However, persistent shivering may lead to uncontrollable muscle spasms—avoid this by exercising your muscles. Give extra rations to men suffering from exposure to cold.

In warm oceans, protection against the sun and obtaining drinking water will be the most important problems. Exposure to the sun increases thirst, thus wasting precious water and reducing the body's water content. The sun can also cause serious burns. Improvise a sunshade and get under it. If you are on a 20-man raft, erect the canopy and furl the sides. Use the tarpaulin, light side up, to attract attention—blue side up is for camouflage in unfriendly waters. In rigging your sunshade, leave space for ventilation. In a one-man raft, use the spray shield for a sunshade.

CARE OF RAFT

Be sure that your raft is properly inflated. If main buoyance chambers are not firm, top off with pump or mouth-inflation tube. See that valve is open before pumping (to open, turn to the *left*). Inflate cross seats where provided unless there are injured men who must lie down, but don't overinflate—air chambers should be well rounded but not drum tight. Regularly check inflation; hot air expands, so on hot days release some air, adding air when the weather cools.

Always throw out the sea anchor or improvise a drag from the raft case, bailing bucket, or roll of clothing. A sea anchor will help you stay close to your ditching site, and your searchers' problem will be easier. It will also help to keep the raft headed into the wind and waves. Wrap the sea-anchor rope with cloth so that it will not chafe the raft.

Be careful not to snag the raft. In good weather, take off your shoes; tie them to the raft. Don't let fishhooks, knives, ration tins, and other sharp objects cut. Keep them off the bottom.

In stormy weather, rig the spray and windshield at once. In a 20-man raft, keep the canopy erected at all times. Keep your raft as dry as possible, and keep it properly balanced. All men should stay seated, the heaviest men in the center.

Leaks are most likely to occur at valves, seams, and underwater surfaces. They can be repaired with the repair plugs provided. Most multiplace rafts have buoyancy tubes separated into two chambers. If one chamber is damaged, keep the other fully inflated.

SIGNALING

Remember that you are in a small raft on a very large ocean, so get your signals into operation immediately.

Transmit your radio distress signals at frequent intervals or otherwise follow briefing instructions. Send signals as indicated in the instructions packaged with transmitter; send steadily when using hand energized transmitters. Exercise discretion in using battery-operated transceivers, since the batteries have a limited life. If you have a "survival blanket" with an aluminized surface, spread it out but do not let it trail in the water since the reflective surface may attract sharks.

If you have a corner reflector or other radar signaling device, set it up and leave it up except during storms. Handle it carefully.

Practice signaling with the mirror in the raft kit. If you have no signal mirror, use an ordinary pocket mirror or any bright piece of metal. Punch a hole in the center of the metal piece for sighting. (See Chapter 2 for instructions on use of improvised signal mirrors.) On hazy days, aircraft can see the flash of the mirror before survivors can see aircraft, so flash the mirror in the direction of an aircraft when you hear it, even when you cannot see it. When the aircraft is sighted, keep signaling, but stop flashing if the aircraft is attempting a landing. Some raft paddles and oars are coated with material which will reflect the beam of a searchlight at night.

Use smoke signals in the daytime, and fire signals at night. Keep signal flares dry; don't waste them. *Be very careful of fire hazard when using flares.* Keep the flares dry at all times.

Use sea marker during daytime *only in friendly areas.* Except in a very rough sea, these spots of dye remain conspicuous for about three hours. Conserve the sea marker by rewrapping when not in use, and use the marker only when aircraft is heard or sighted.

At night, use flashlights, recognition light, or blinker signal light of the radio. Any light can be seen from the air over water for several miles. At night or in fog, use the whistle from the emergency kit to attract surface vessels or people on shore, or to locate another raft if it becomes separated.

RESCUE TIPS

Your rescue is not complete until you are safely on board the rescue aircraft or surface vessel. Do your best to assist your rescuers until you are aboard—or you may never get aboard.

Keep your signals in operation until you are positive the rescue craft can't lose sight of you. This means that they must be right on top of you, for a raft is quite low in the water and with any sea at all you may be hidden from view at times. However, *don't* flash your signal mirror in an aircraft pilot's eyes when he is coming in for a landing; in effect you are thus putting the sun directly in his eyes and he won't be able to see you or the water.

Do keep a smoke flare going when an aircraft is landing or approaching you. This is especially valuable for a helicopter because it will show the pilot the wind direction and make it easier for him to hover for a pickup.

A helicopter may make a pickup by either a sling or by a rescue basket lowered on a cable. In either case, stay in your raft (if you are in one). The sling, which resembles an oversize horse collar, should be pulled over your head and shoulders and your arms clasped in front of you before you can be hoisted. The rescue basket can either scoop a swimmer out of the water like a dip net, or it can be lowered to the water surface next to your raft so you can step into it.

An amphibian making a pickup will try to approach so that the survivor can be pulled into the aircraft through the hatch on the left-hand side of the aircraft. This means that the wing of the amphibian will pass over the raft. Some survivors have assumed that the aircraft is running them down and have tried to paddle clear, making rescue more difficult. Paddle toward the hatch and be ready to grab the line that will be thrown to you. The pilot usually wants to get off the water as soon as possible, so do your best to get into the aircraft with the minimum of delay.

If the rescue craft is a surface vessel, use the flare, and in addition yell or use the whistle you should have attached to your life vest. Small craft especially will have difficulty in seeing you if the sea is at all rough.

DISCOMFORTS AND ILLNESS ON RAFT

First Aid.—The best first aid in a life raft is preventive medicine.

Seasickness.—Use seasickness pills if available. Do not eat or drink if you are seasick. If you are not vomiting but feel nauseated, lie down. The pills may make you drowsy, so secure all equipment before dozing.

Salt-Water Sores.—Do not open or squeeze salt water sores; use antiseptic. Keep sores dry.

Immersion Foot.—Immersion foot is caused by exposure to cold, immersion in water, cramped quarters, and restricted circulation. The symptoms are tingling, numbness, redness, and swelling; blotchy red areas and blisters eventually appear. Immersion foot cannot be cured in a life raft, so try to prevent it. Keep your feet warm and as dry as possible; maintain circulation by exercising toes and feet; loosen footgear. Elevate feet and legs for 30-minute periods several times a day. If you cannot dry your socks, at least wring them out occasionally. If you are suffering from immersion foot, stay off your feet after landing.

Sore Eyes.—Glare from the sky and from the water may cause your eyes to become bloodshot, sore, and inflamed. Here, too, prevention is easier than cure. Wear aviator's sunglasses or improvise an eye cover from cloth or bandage. If your eyes hurt, bandage them lightly, and apply cold compresses if you can spare the fresh water.

Constipation.—Lack of bowel movement is normal on rafts. Don't be disturbed about it. *Don't* take laxatives even if available. Exercise as much as possible.

Difficulty in Urinating.—If there is a shortage of drinking water, or if you are sweating a lot, you may have some difficulty in urinating. The dark color of urine and difficulty in passing it are normal—don't get worried.

Mental Disturbances.—Fear is normal among men in dangerous situations. Admit your feeling to yourself but carry on in spite of it. Remember that other men have had the same fear, yet have come through similar experiences. Fatigue and exhaustion resulting from severe hardships often lead to mental disturbances, which may take the form of extreme nervousness, excessive and violent activity, or mental depression. The best prevention is to get as much sleep and rest as possible. When not resting, keep busy with routine raft duties. Seeing mirages is not a sign of mental unbalance. Cheerfulness is a tonic and will spread to others.

Frostbite.—Frostbite may occur when wet skin is exposed to wind during winter in northern oceans. Your face, ears, hands, and feet are most susceptible; try to keep them dry and covered. If your shoes are tight, take them off and wrap your feet in dry cloth.

Sunburn.—Keep your head and skin covered to avoid sunburn, and stay in the shade whenever possible. Use cream or chapstick from kit. Remember that reflection from water causes sunburn, too. Protect your neck with an improvised shield. You can be sunburned on cloudy days, so don't relax your precautions if the sun is not visible.

Water.—Water is your most important need. With water alone and no food you can live for 10 days or longer, depending on your will to live.

When your water supply is limited and cannot be replaced by chemical or mechanical means but only by chance rain, use it efficiently. Keep your body well shaded from overhead sun and from reflection off the sea surface. Allow ventilation of air. Dampen your clothes with sea water during the hottest part of the day. Do not exert yourself; relax and sleep when possible. Fix your daily water ration after considering the amount of water you have, the output of sun stills and desalting kit, and the number and physical condition of your party.

If you have no water, don't eat. If your water ration is two quarts or more a day, you may eat any part of your ration or any additional food that you may catch, such as birds, fish, shrimp, or crabs.

To cut down loss of water from sweating, soak your clothes in the sea and wring them out before putting them on again. Don't overdo this during hot days when no canopy or sunshade is available.

Watch the clouds and be ready for any chance shower; keep a tarpaulin handy for catching water. If your tarpaulin is encrusted with dried salt, wash it in sea water. Normally, a small amount of sea water mixed with rain will hardly be noticeable and will not give you any bad physiological reaction. In rough seas you cannot get uncontaminated fresh water. At night, secure your tarpaulin as for a sunshade and turn up its edges to collect dew.

When sun stills are available, read instructions and set them up immediately. Use as many stills as possible, depending on the number of men in your raft and the amount of sunlight available. Secure the sun still to raft with a stout line.

When desalting kits are available in addition to sun stills, use them only for immediate water needs or during long periods of overcast when sun stills cannot be used. In any event, retain desalting kits and emergency water stores for periods when you cannot use sun stills or catch rainwater.

Don't drink urine or sea water (see Chapter 15).

In arctic waters, use old sea ice (page 130) for water. This ice is bluish, has rounded corners, and splinters easily. It is nearly free from salt. By contrast, new ice is gray, milky, hard and salty. Water from icebergs is fresh, but icebergs, as previously noted are dangerous to approach and should be used as a source of water only in emergencies.

FISH AND FISHING

Most fish in the open sea are edible. However, jellyfish are messy, contain little if any nourishment, and can sting. If your fishing kit is lost, improvise hooks from pins, pencil clips, shoe nails, pocketknives, fish spines, bird bones, and pieces of wood. Make hooks small and use as light a line as possible. You can get cord from shoelaces, parachute shroud lines, or thread from clothes. Fish will generally be attracted to the shadow of your raft. First catch any small fish that usually gather underneath your raft or that you may shake out of clumps of seaweed, then use these for bait, with heavier hooks and lines. Use dip net to scoop up fish, crabs, and shrimp. If you have no net, make one from mosquito headnet, parachute cloth, or clothing fastened to a section of oar. In using either the dip net or an improvised net, hold it underwater and scoop upward.

Shine your flashlight on the water at night, or use a mirror to reflect moonlight onto the water. The light will attract fish. At night, don't be alarmed if some fish—especially flying fish—lands in your raft; use it for food. Rig your rubber sheeting in such a way that it will reflect moonlight—natives use this trick to snare leaping or flying fish.

When fishing, don't make lines fast to the raft or to your person; fish or bright objects dangling in water alongside of raft may attract large or dangerous fish which can pull you overboard or upset the raft. Land fish with net or harpoon. As previously noted, avoid spiny fish, and those with bony, irregular teeth. Kill fish with a blow on the head before you bring them into the raft. Don't molest large fish or sharks.

Clean and cut all fish immediately and eat them before they spoil. Preserve any meat left over by cutting it into thin strips and drying thoroughly in the sun. Don't eat eggs or liver of fish, nor fish with unpleasant odor, pale and slimy gills, sunken eyes, flabby skin, or flesh that stays dented when pressed, as outlined in Chapter 12.

Sea turtles, like the land variety described on page 264, are good eating too. Kill them by shooting them in the head or snag them with a hook and then kill with blows on the head. Avoid their beaks and claws. The liver and fat are edible. The muscle is tough but can be chewed for awhile, then thrown away.

BIRDS

All birds are potential food. They can be caught on baited hooks, triangular pieces of shiny metal with a noose, or a baited toggle of metal or wood. Many birds will be attracted to the raft as a possible perching place. Sit still in the raft, and they may settle on the raft or even on your head or shoulder. Seize them as soon as they have folded their wings, but don't grab until you are sure you can reach the bird.

PLANKTON

Plankton, the microscopic animals and plants that float in the sea and provide food for the baleen whale, have often been suggested as human food. In fact, some survival manuals give detailed instructions on the use of nets to gather plankton. The idea of an inexhaustible storehouse of food afloat in the sea, merely waiting to be scooped up and eaten by the hungry survivor, is an attractive one, but completely impractical at the present time. It is true that animal plankton can be processed into a food resembling shrimp paste which is fit for human consumption. But this processing requires cooking, as well as careful control and selection of ingredients. If he is a competent marine biologist, the survivor afloat in a raft may be able to seine plankton from the sea and select the nutritious varieties. But even this optimum selection will be high in salt content, requiring extra water intake for elimination, and will have a high percentage of chitin—the horny substances forming the animal shells—which might be mechanically irritating to stomach and intestines.

The real danger in eating plankton is the possibility of ingesting poisonous organisms. The most widespread of these, as well as the most deadly, are the dinoflagellates, the toxic agent responsible for the well-known paralytic shellfish poisoning. The symptoms, which occur within 10 minutes after ingestion, are gastrointestinal disturbances with vomiting in severe cases; numbness of lips, tongue, and finger tips, followed by ataxia and generalized muscular incoordination; ascending paralysis; death from respiratory failure in from two to 12 hours. Other toxic or irritating organisms which might be mixed in with the nutritious animal plankton are hydroids of all sorts, including jellyfish with stinging tentacles.

The authors have searched the available literature in biology and survival and have been unable to find any instance in which plankton was actually used as a survival food. Human test subjects used by the Air Force in attempts to determine the edibility of plankton under life-raft conditions became violently ill. In the same investigation, rats fed on plankton died, apparently through not being able to utilize more than a small fraction of the energy contained in the food. When reports of the use of plankton as food for voyagers on rafts and small boats were tracked down, it usually turned out that the persons who supposedly had eaten plankton as a part of their diet had merely *sampled* it, proclaiming it to be a satisfactory survival food. But none had eaten substantial quantities of plankton nor had used it as a principal item of diet.

For all practical purposes raw plankton is an unsatisfactory and potentially poisonous food. Don't eat it unless you have enough biological training to pick out the nutritious organisms from the slimy mess that will accumulate in the net, and unless you are certain dinoflagellates and other poisonous organisms are not present in the area.

SURVIVAL SWIMMING

When entering the water from the aircraft or in your parachute, discharge only one of your CO_2 cartridges. One cartridge will usually keep you afloat, but two may hamper your activity.

A man who knows how to relax in the water is in very little

danger of drowning, especially in salt water where the body is of lower density than the water. Trapping air in your clothes will help to buoy you up in the water and give you a rest. If you are in the water for long periods, you will have to rest from treading water. If you are an experienced swimmer and able to float on your back, do so if the sea conditions permit. Always float on your back if possible. If you can't float on your back or if the sea is too rough, practice the following technique:

Resting erect in the water, inhale. Put your head face down in the water and stroke with your arms. Then rest in this face-down position until you feel the need to breathe again. Raise your head, exhale, support yourself by kicking arms and legs, inhale, and then repeat the cycle.

SEAMANSHIP

Put out your sea anchor immediately. Do not attempt to navigate your raft unless within sight of shore or if you know that land is near. Remember that the great majority of ·successful rescues are made within seven days of ditching. You can't go very far on a raft in seven days.

Assign watches; they should not exceed two hours. All men should serve except those who are badly injured or completely exhausted. Keep at least one lookout posted at all times, who should watch for signs of land, passing vessels or aircraft, wreckage, seaweed, schools of fish, birds, and signs of chafing or leaking of raft. He should be tied to the raft with at least a 10-foot line.

If you are within sight of land or know that land is near, *use* currents and wind—don't *fight* them.

When ocean currents are moving toward your destination, but winds are unfavorable, put out a sea anchor. Huddle low in the raft to offer as little wind resistance as possible. In the open ocean, currents seldom move more than six to eight miles a day.

Rafts are not equipped with keels, so they can't be sailed into the wind, even if you are an experienced sailor. However, anyone can sail a raft downwind. But don't try to sail your raft unless you know that land is near.

When the wind is blowing directly toward your destination, inflate the raft fully, sit high, take in the sea anchor, rig a sail, and use an oar as a rudder. Don't secure the corners of the *lower edge* of the sail. Hold the lines attached to the corners in your hands so that a sudden storm or gust of wind will not rip the sail, break the mast, or capsize the raft.

Take every precaution to prevent your raft from turning over. In rough weather, keep the sea anchor out from the bow. Sit low in the raft, with the passengers' weight distributed to hold the weather side down. Don't sit on the sides or stand up. Never make sudden movements without warning the other men. Don't tie a fishline to yourself or the raft; a large fish may capsize the raft.

In rough seas, tie the stern of the first raft to the bow of second and rig the sea anchor to the stern of the second raft. Use approximately a 25-foot line between rafts; adjust the length of the line to suit the sea. Keep the sea anchor line long; adjust its length so that when the raft is at the crest of a wave, the sea anchor will stay in a trough. In very rough weather, keep a spare sea anchor rigged and ready for instant use in case the one that is out breaks loose.

When the sea anchor is not in use, tie it to the raft and stow it so that it will hold immediately if the raft capsizes.

To right multiplace (except 20-man) rafts, toss the righting rope over the bottom, move around to the other side, place one foot on flotation tube, and pull on the righting rope. If you have no righting rope—if you can't improvise one from the sea anchor line, a belt, or a shirt—slide up on the bottom, reach across, grab the lifeline on the far side, and then slide back into the water, pulling the raft back over. Most rafts are equipped with righting handles on the bottom. Circular 20-man rafts are identical on both sides and therefore require no righting.

If several men are in the water, one man should hold down the far side of the multiplace (4-6 man) raft while the rest climb in singly from the other side. Grasp the seat to haul yourself in, or use the boarding ladder provided on the newest types of raft. Without help, the best place to board the raft is over the end. If the wind is blowing, board the raft with the wind at your back. The 20-man raft is provided with a deflated boarding station, which is hand-inflated after occupants are aboard. To board the one-man raft, climb in from the narrow end; slide up as nearly horizontal as possible.

MAKING A LANDFALL

The lookout should watch carefully for signs of land. A fixed cumulus cloud in a clear sky or in a sky where all other clouds are moving often hovers over or slightly downwind from an island. In the tropics, a greenish tint in the sky is often caused by the reflection of sunlight from the shallow lagoons or shelves of coral reefs. In the arctic, ice fields or snow-covered land are often indicated by light-colored reflections on clouds, quite different from the darkish gray caused by open water. Deep water is dark green or dark blue. Lighter color indicates shallow water, which may mean land is near.

In fog, mist, rain, or at night when drifting past a nearby shore, you may sometimes detect land by characteristic odors and sounds. The musty odor of mangrove swamps and mud flats or the smell of burning wood will carry a long way. The roar of surf is heard long before the surf is seen.

Continued cries of sea birds from one direction indicate their roosting place on nearby land. Usually more birds are found near land than over the open sea. The direction from which flocks fly at dawn and to which they fly at dusk may indicate the direction of land. During the day, birds are searching for food and the direction of flight has no significance.

In the tropics, mirages may be seen, especially during the middle of the day. Be careful not to mistake a mirage for nearby land. A mirage will disappear or change its appearance and elevation if viewed from slightly different heights.

You may be able to detect land by the pattern of the waves, which are refracted as they approach land. This method was used by Polynesian navigators in the Pacific long before the white man came to the area.

GETTING ASHORE

Swimming. Usually it is safer to swim ashore, using the raft as flotation, than to ride the raft ashore, especially through surf. Wear your shoes, an inflated life belt and at least one thickness of clothing if you plan to swim ashore. Use the side or breast stroke to conserve strength.

If the surf is moderate, ride in on the back of a small wave by swimming forward with it. Shallow-dive to end your ride just before the wave breaks. In a high surf, swim shoreward in the trough between waves. When the seaward wave approaches, face it and submerge. After it passes, work shoreward in the next trough.

If you must land on a rocky shore, look for a place where the waves rush up onto the rocks. Avoid places where the waves explode with a high white spray. Swim slowly in making your approach—you will need your strength to hold on to the rocks.

After selecting your landing point, advance behind a large wave into the breakers. Face shoreward and take a sitting position with your feet in front, two or three feet lower than your head, so that your feet will absorb shocks when you land or strike submerged boulders or reefs. If you don't reach shore behind the wave you have picked, swim with hands only. As the next wave approaches, take sitting position with feet forward. Repeat procedure until you land.

Water is quieter in the lee of a heavy growth of seaweed. Take advantage of such growth. Don't swim through the seaweed; crawl over the top by grasping the vegetation with overhand movements.

Cross a rocky reef just as you would land on a rocky shore. Keep your feet close together and your knees slightly bent in a relaxed sitting posture to cushion blows against coral.

Rafting Ashore.—Going ashore in a strong surf is dangerous. Take your time. Select your landing point carefully. Try not to land when the sun is low and straight in front of you; instead try to land on the lee side of an island or of a point of land. Keep your eyes open for gaps in the surf line, and head for them. Avoid coral reefs and rocky cliffs. Coral reefs don't occur near the mouths of fresh-water streams.

Keep your clothes and shoes on to avoid severe cuts, and adjust and inflate your life vest. Trail the sea anchor over the stern with as much line as you have. Use the oars or paddles and constantly adjust the sea anchor to keep a strain on the anchor line. It will keep your raft pointed toward shore and prevent the sea from throwing the stern around and capsizing you. Use the oars or paddles to help ride in on the seaward side of a large wave.

Against strong wind and heavy surf, the raft must have all possible speed to pass rapidly through the oncoming crest in order to avoid being turned broadside or thrown end over end. If possible, avoid meeting a large wave at the moment it breaks. In medium surf with no wind or offshore wind, keep raft from passing over a wave so rapidly that it drops suddenly after topping the crest. If the raft turns over in the surf, try to grab hold and cling to it.

As the raft nears the beach, ride in on the crest of a large wave. Paddle or row hard and ride in onto the beach as far as you can.

Don't jump out of the raft until it has grounded, then get out quickly and beach it.

If you have a choice, don't land at night. If you have reason to believe that the shore is inhabited, lay away from the beach, then signal and wait for the inhabitants to come out and bring you in.

Landing on Sea Ice.—Land only on large, stable floes. Avoid icebergs (which may capsize), small floes, and those that are obviously disintegrating. Use oars and hands to keep raft from rubbing on ice edge. Take the raft out of the water and store well back from ice edge, but keep it inflated and ready for use—any floe may break up without warning.

15

Seawater: Survival or Suicide*

A currently popular fallacy is that seawater, taken in small doses, can be utilized by the human body in lieu of fresh water, and that therefore the survivor of an aircraft crash or shipwreck will not need to carry fresh water in his survival or lifeboat kit. This theory is discussed in detail in this chapter.

One very hot day in July, 1943, Lt. (j.g.) George H. Smith of the United States Navy was sitting on a small rubber raft somewhere between Munda and Guadalcanal. He was very thirsty, and he was cursing man's inability to drink sea water. To his surprise, he saw a booby bird land on the water, put its long neck under the surface, and apparently take a drink.

In Smith's own words, "It made me mad. I couldn't understand why the bird, which was only flesh and blood like myself, could drink sea water while I couldn't."

Smith's next reaction was the crucial one. Though under all the strain of a life-and-death predicament, he set himself a plan of scientific investigation.

"I shot the bird," he relates, "cut him open, and traced the course of the water through his digestive system. Around the intestines of the bird I found a handful of fat, and I reasoned that if I greased my mouth with this fat, I might be able to swallow sea water without tasting it. For five days then I drank a pint of sea water each day."

Lt. Smith was picked up after 20 days afloat, still in fairly good physical condition.

Smith's story was widely circulated. His procedure for making sea water drinkable, and the fact that he had drunk a pint of it a day, were even incorporated into survival instructions used by some Navy and Army Air Force crews. Soon, however, less optimistic reactions began to be expressed.

* This chapter, by William H. Allen, first appeared in *Natural History*, Vol. LXV, No. 10, December 1956, and is reprinted here with the permission of the publisher, The American Museum of Natural History.

Articles appeared in service publications pointing out that men are not booby birds and that drinking sea water as Smith had done could kill a man. U.S. Navy medical authorities reported that the reason Smith had suffered no ill effects from five continuous days of imbibing sea water was that he was not seriously dehydrated at the beginning of the ordeal and that on the fifth day a rain squall provided him with all the fresh water he could drink. If he had been dehydrated when he started or if the rain squall had not come when it did, he might have lost his life.

Smith himself had noted that the amount of water he lost in urine during the five days was apparently three times the quantity of sea water he drank. Obviously, excretion of the salts in the sea water was taking water from his body, and he would have been dangerously dehydrated if he had continued drinking sea water.

Unfortunately, the medical reports on the incident were not read as widely as the original report, and Smith's experience is still cited by some survival "experts" as proof that man can survive at sea without fresh water.

Recently several newspapers and magazines of large circulation have carried stories purporting to "prove" that it is safe to drink sea water. Most of these stories are based either on the account of Dr. Alain Bombard, who drifted from the Canaries to Barbados in his raft *L'Hérétique* in 1952, or on the experiments carried on by the French Navy, which are essentially a continuation of Bombard's work. The French experimenters now maintain that a man can survive for six days by drinking only sea water. But he must drink it in small quantities—approximately one-tenth of a pint (50 cc) at a time. If sea water is to be drunk beyond the sixth day, the French say that the survivor must drink 1000 cc (1.05 quarts) of fresh water on the sixth day to help get rid of excess salt.

In short, it is claimed that the survivor could live for eleven days on little more than one quart of fresh water, although this claim has not been subjected to experiment. Unfortunately, many of the stories written about the French experiments omit any mention of the restrictions on the use of sea water and leave the reader with the impression that the sea will provide all the water a man needs for an indefinite period.

The U.S. Naval Aero-Medical Safety Journal stated in 1955 that "all physiological knowledge at present indicates that sea water is inimical to the human organism and that its use will shorten rather than prolong survival time." This view has been repeated in other official Navy publications. The *U.S. Air Force Manual 64-5* entitled "Survival," which is carried in all Air Force survival kits and on many commercial airplanes, says: "Do not drink sea water."

Why do the services take this stand? Is it due to the natural reluctance of medical men to accept a theory that has not been thoroughly tested? Or is it because the theory has been tested and found wanting? The fact is that the problem of providing water for the survivors of shipwreck and aircraft ditchings has been thoroughly investigated, and the investigators have found that the use of sea water is not the answer.

During World War II, the armed forces and the merchant marines of all the combatants were faced with the problem of providing seamen and airmen with a supply of water in case of disaster. This problem posed many questions, the first of which was: How much water does a man need in a survival situation?

The standing rule of thumb used prior to World War II on board naval vessels and merchant ships was "a pint a day per man." However, tests on subjects placed in a simulated survival situation soon showed that this was not enough to keep a man in water balance. Different investigators came up with different answers as to the exact amount of water needed to prevent dehydration, but all agreed that the minimum amount was a great deal more than a pint a day. The following table, compiled by Dr. E. F. Adolph and his associates, gives the values generally accepted by the end of the war.

A team of United States scientists directed by Dr. Adolph went even further and estimated the relationship between total water supply and survival time at various temperatures. Dr. Adolph computed that at environmental temperatures under 70 degrees F, a man who starts out in water balance can survive for ten days. These values apply to an inactive man, in the shade, and with a low-calorie intake.

Note that the advocates of drinking sea water claim only that a man can survive for six days by drinking sea water alone and for eleven days if he drinks slightly over one quart of fresh water while drinking sea water. Thus it appears that by drinking no water at all a man would survive for four days longer than he

TABLE 15-1

TOTAL WATER INTAKE REQUIRED TO BALANCE
WATER LOSSES AT VARIOUS TEMPERATURES

Mean Air Temperature, Degrees Fahrenheit	Water Requirements for Bare Maintenance in Pints Per Man	
90	6.2	▽▽▽▽▽▽ᒳ
80	4.0	▽▽▽▽
70	3.3	▽▽▽ᒳ
60	3.0	▽▽▽
50	2.8	▽▽ᒳ
40	2.7	▽▽ᒳ

would on sea water, even if the claims of the advocates of sea water are valid.

Environmental temperatures of 70 degrees F and under were used in the estimate above because all the sea water experiments recorded have been carried out in temperate and cool climates. As is shown in the table below, expected survival time goes down sharply at higher temperatures, even if the subject can remain in the shade.

The accuracy of Adolph's predictions has been borne out

TABLE 15-2

HOW LONG A MAN CAN SURVIVE IN THE SHADE*

Max. Daily Shade Temp., °F.	With no water	With 1 qt.	With 2 qts.	With 4 qts.	With 10 qts.	With 20 qts.
			Days of Expected Survival			
120	2	2	2	2.5	3	4.5
110	3	3	3.5	4	5	7
100	5	5.5	6	7	9.5	13.5
90	7	8	9	10.5	15	23
80	9	10	11	13	19	29
70	10	11	12	14	20.5	32
60	10	11	12	14	21	32
50	10	11	12	14.5	21	32

* From E. F. Adolph's *Physiology of Man in the Desert.*

several times in actual survival incidents. An extensive study of shipwreck survivors during World War II showed that the maximum time without water recorded by any survivor was eleven days—just one day longer than the prediction.

Adolph also demonstrated that, as the body becomes increasingly deficient in water, certain symptoms follow in order. The degree of dehydration was rated by measuring the per cent loss of body weight. At the beginning of dehydration there is thirst and discomfort. Succeeding symptoms, in order, are lassitude, loss of appetite, sleepiness, rise in body temperature and, at about 5 per cent dehydration, nausea. At from 6 to 10 per cent dehydration, the victim will experience dizziness, headache, tingling in the limbs, dry mouth, difficulty in speaking, and inability to walk. At more than 10 per cent dehydration, delirium is common, and the senses fail. Dehydration of 25 per cent is probably fatal at any temperature. At air temperatures above 90 degrees F, 15 per cent dehydration is the theoretical fatal limit.

Yet records of shipwreck survivors show that very few die of dehydration alone. MacDonald Critchley, a British physician who made an extensive study of the factors affecting survival at sea, believes that as dehydration increases, the victim's will to resist the desire to drink sea water weakens until finally he succumbs to the temptation and death is caused by the ingestion of sea water. Critchley says, "Sea water poisoning must be accounted, after cold, the commonest cause of death in shipwrecked sailors."

Critchley tells what happens when a very dehydrated person drinks sea water. There is "immediate slaking, followed quite soon by an exacerbation of the thirst, which will require still more copious draughts. The victim then becomes silent and apathetic, with a peculiar fixed and glassy expression in the eyes. The condition of the lips, mouth, and tongue worsens, and a peculiarly offensive odour has been described in the breath. Within an hour or two, delirium sets in, quiet at first but later violent and unrestrained; consciousness is gradually lost; the color of the face changes and froth appears at the corners of the lips. Death may take place quietly: more often it is a noisy termination, and not infrequently the victim goes over the side in his delirium and is lost."

Those who advocate the drinking of sea water argue that the effects so graphically described by Critchley do not follow when sea water is drunk by a man in water balance. They point out, moreover, that anyone who goes swimming in the sea swallows some sea water and that many castaways swallow substantial amounts of sea water before reaching the safety of a lifeboat or raft. The advocates of sea water maintain that by drinking small quantities of it immediately, a man can both slake his thirst and keep his body in water balance.

The question of whether or not a man can stop or avoid the sensation of thirst by drinking sea water is difficult to prove or disprove. In several experiments on drinking small quantities of sea water, the subjects have reported that they had no feeling of thirst. All these experiments took place in cool climates, and none of them ran for more than six days. In actual survival incidents under similar environmental conditions, survivors who had no water denied any feelings of thirst, and some who drank small amounts of sea water were thirsty.

Actually thirst is only a signal of the body's need for water. Thirst is often satisfied while the body is still slightly dehydrated. This is especially true in cool climates. Tests made by the U.S. Army in cold climates show that if men drink only when they are thirsty, they stay in a continuously dehydrated state.

The sensation of thirst varies a great deal with individuals. A person's description of how he feels changes with his psychological as well as his physiological condition, so the term "thirst" can be regarded as little more than an expression of personal opinion. However, the effect of drinking sea water on the body's water balance can be computed and the computations verified by experiment. It is possible to determine by actual test how much sea water the body can tolerate, though for obvious reasons laboratory experiments cannot carry the study to a point where the subject's life is actually endangered.

A vital function of the water in our bodies is to permit the kidneys to extract waste products from the blood in the form of urine. The chemical and physical processes involved in this function would take us beyond the scope of a general article. So we are centering our attention on the effect of the ingestion of the dissolved salts in sea water, predominately sodium chloride or common salt. And the basic point is that the body uses only a very small amount of salt. Additional salt ingested must be excreted with the urine, using water which could be utilized by the body in other functions.

With the osmotic concentration of sea water only slightly below that of urine, the daily pint of sea water that the body will tolerate will yield only about $\frac{3}{10}$ of a pint (143 cc) of free water for the excretion of other urinary constituents, as Dr. Homer W. Smith points out in his book *From Fish to Philosopher*. The amount of water actually needed for urine formation is about a pint, not to mention upward of 1500 cc more (over 3 pints) for sweat, if the individual is exposed to sun and wind. Yet 500 cc, or about 1 pint, is the greatest amount of sea water that can be swallowed each day without gastrointestinal disturbance from the unabsorbable magnesium and sulphate. Consuming larger amounts, concludes Dr. Smith, would only lead to diarrhea and further dehydration and would hasten the end.

The most favorable report on the use of sea water is that of W. S. S. Ladell, printed in *The Lancet*, October 9, 1943. Ladell ran a series of experiments with a group of seventeen men on a "shipwreck ration" such as was carried in lifeboats. Some of the subjects drank sea water, others fresh water or fresh water plus sea water.

Ladell summarized the effects of drinking up to 400 cc (a little less than a pint) of sea water daily. The subjects were either totally or partially deprived of fresh water and were on the low-calorie and low-salt diet of the "man on the raft." Thus they were getting almost all the salt their bodies used from the sea water they drank. Ladell's conclusions were as follows, both for men drinking only sea water and for those using sea water as an "extender" for an inadequate fresh-water ration:

(a) At first, the subject retains the same amount of chloride that his body had lost before he began to drink sea water. Subsequently he excretes the full amount of chloride taken in. (b) The output of urine is increased, but there is a slight gain in the amount of the water in the body, because the extra water lost in the urine is less than the extra water taken in as sea water. (c) There is a gain in the total urea clearance.

(It should be noted that this experiment was performed in a laboratory where sweating would be at a minimum.)

Ladell's experiment indicated that a *slight advantage* was to be gained when a man on limited fresh water or without any fresh water drank *small quantities* of sea water. However, the agency sponsoring the research did not recommend the drinking of sea water. Evidently it was felt that the small gain to be expected did not warrant the risk involved. Even if the survivor was able to hold his intake of sea water down to the limit recommended by Ladell (400 cc, or less than 1 pint), the small volume of water gained in this way could not support human life indefinitely and would give little if any extension in survival time over that to be expected by a man drinking no water at all.

The sea-water enthusiasts argue that Dr. Alain Bombard drank sea water and survived; therefore, sea water must be beneficial. What was Bombard's experience and how does it compare with that of shipwreck survivors? Bombard departed from Las Palmas, Canary Islands, on October 19, 1952, and landed at St. Lucia, Barbados, on December 23, 1952—a journey of 65 days. But 52 days after setting out, he boarded the S.S. Aroka, stayed an hour and a half, and had a meal. These 52 days represent his longest period of survival without outside help.

Bombard's voyage was a truly remarkable exhibition of fortitude and an impressive demonstration of the capacity of the human body to withstand abuse. However, several shipwreck survivors, less well prepared than Dr. Bombard, have made longer drifts.

The longest drift on record is that of Poon Lim, a native of Hong Kong, who spent 133 days on a raft in the South Atlantic after his ship, the S.S. *Ben Lomond,* was torpedoed in 1942.

Poon Lim spent the first hour after the torpedoing floating in his life jacket. Then he had the good fortune to reach an unoccupied raft. The raft had food and water for 50 days—but the last 83 days of his drift he subsisted on rainwater and fish. Brazilian fishermen picked him up, still in good physical condition after 133 days on his own.

Has the survivor no choice but to rely on rainwater as Poon Lim did, or take a chance on sea-water poisoning as Bombard did? Fortunately, most survivors of ditchings or shipwreck will not be limited to these alternatives. Two devices developed during World War II give today's survivor a margin of safety— the desalting kit and the solar still.

The desalting kit provides a method of converting salt water to fresh in practically any weather, but it can be used only once. The solar still functions only when the sun is shining or under a light cloud cover, but it can be used indefinitely.

The desalting kit precipitates dissolved salts in sea water so that they can be filtered out. Each desalting kit contains a number of briquettes of silver aluminum silicate and a plastic processing bag. Each briquette will desalt about a pint of water. The kit will produce six or seven times as much water as could be carried if the same space were used to carry canned water.

In use, the processing bag is filled with sea water up to a

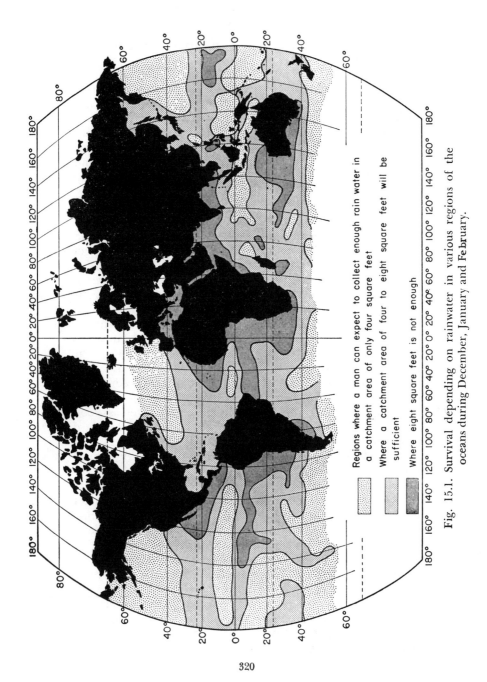

Regions where a man can expect to collect enough rain water in a catchment area of only four square feet

Where a catchment area of four to eight square feet will be sufficient

Where eight square feet is not enough

Fig. 15.1. Survival depending on rainwater in various regions of the oceans during December, January and February.

marked line and the briquette dropped in. The bag is kneaded and agitated gently for an hour, allowing the briquette to break up and the chemical reaction to take place. Desalted water is drawn off through a filter in the bottom of the bag, from which it can be drunk directly or squeezed into a storage bag.

The solar still is a spherical plastic envelope that can be inflated either by mouth or by using the pump carried on most life rafts. Inside the sphere is stretched a black cloth, upon which sea water drips from a reservoir. The sun heats the moist black cloth, and from it the water evaporates—fresh. The evaporated fresh water condenses on the inner surface of the plastic sphere in small drops, which run down to the fresh-water trap at the bottom of the still. The salt stays in the black cloth.

Each solar still can produce about two pints of fresh water a day, and most life rafts on aircraft carry several stills. Each still takes up about the same amount of space as a pint of canned water.

The stills operate most efficiently in direct sunlight but will operate on cloudy days if the overcast is not too thick. They will not operate at night or on very dark days.

The map (Fig. 15-1) shows how much help can be expected from rain in various parts of the world. Rain plus the water from the solar stills usually carried on life rafts will usually yield between 80 and 130 per cent of the requirement for survival in almost all areas commonly traversed by planes and ships.

Desalting kits provide an additional supply to carry castaways through periods of unfavorable weather. The inherent ability of the human body to withstand abuse provides a further safety factor.

In view of the resources now available to the castaway, it seems foolish to recommend that a survivor drink sea water. In most emergencies, he will drink some accidentally, and a certain amount of dried salt is also taken in. This unintentional salt would, in most cases, nullify the meager benefit that might be gained from drinking sea water. The drinking of sea water, then, is just another of the recurrent fables that should be given a quiet burial. Man is no more able to drink sea water than Coleridge's Ancient Mariner.

Appendix 1—Selected Bibliography

Adolph, E. F. and Associates. *Physiology of Man in the Desert.* New York, Interscience Publishers, 1947.

Bagnold, R. A. *Physics of Blown Sand and Desert Dunes.* London, Methuen & Co. Ltd., 1941.

Bates, Marston. *Where Winter Never Comes.* New York, Scribner, 1952.

Benson, Lyman and Darrow, R. A. *Trees and Shrubs of the Southwestern Deserts.* Tucson, University of Arizona Press, 1954.

Burton, A. C. and Edholm, O. G. *Man in a Cold Environment.* London, E. Arnold, 1955.

Chalfant, W. A. *Death Valley, The Facts.* Stanford, California, Stanford University Press, 1945.

Critchley, McDonald. *Shipwreck Survivors, A Medical Study.* London, J. & A. Churchill Ltd., 1943.

Desert Magazine, The. El Centro, California, Desert Publishing Co., monthly issues 1937-58.

Dickson, H. R. P. *The Arab of the Desert.* London, Allen and Uwin, 1949.

Freuchen, P. and Salomonsen, Finn. *The Arctic Year.* New York, Putnam, 1958.

Greathouse, G. A. and Wessel, C. J., editors. *Deterioration of Materials: Causes and Preventive Techniques.* Reinhold Publishing Corporation, 1951.

Jaeger, Edmund C. *California Deserts.* California, Stanford University Press, 1955.

Jaeger, Edmund, C. *Desert Wild Flowers.* California, Stanford University Press, 1947.

Jaeger, Edmund C. *The North American Deserts.* California, Stanford University Press, 1957.

Kimble, G. H. T. and Good, Dorothy. *Geography of the Northlands.* New York, American Geographical Society and J. Wiley, 1955.

Newburgh, L. H., Editor. *The Physiology of Heat Regulation and the Science of Clothing.* Philadelphia, Saunders, 1949.

Philby, H. St. J. B. *Arabian Highlands.* Washington, D. C., The Middle East Institute, 1952.

Richards, P. W. *The Tropical Rain Forest, an Ecological Study.* London, Cambridge University Press, 1952.

Rodahl, Kare. *North.* New York, Harper, 1953.

Schmidt-Nielson, Bodil and others. Osmotic Regulation in Desert Mammals. *Memorandum Report of the USAF Air Materiel Command,* Wright-Patterson AFB, Ohio, 1948.

Stell, C. V. *Death Valley,* Federal Writers Project. Boston, Houghton Mifflin Co., 1939.

UNESCO. *Biology of Deserts.* Proceedings of London Symposium on Hot and Cold Deserts. New York, Hafner, 1954.

United States Air Force: *Air Force Manual 64-3, Survival* (training edition). Washington, D. C. Dept. of the Air Force, 1956.

Air Force Manual 64-4, Handbook for Survival Training and Personal Equipment Officers. Washington, D. C., Dept of the Air Force, 1954.

Air Force Manual 64-5, Survival. Washington, D. C., Dept. of the Air Force, 1952.

Air Force Manual 160-30, Physiology of Flight. Washington, D. C., Dept. of the Air Force, 1953.

ADTIC Publication A-103, Down in the North. Maxwell AFB, Alabama, Air University, Research Studies Institute, 1953.

ADTIC Publication D-100, Afoot in the Desert. Maxwell AFB, Alabama, Air University, Research Studies Institute, 1952.

ADTIC Publication D-102, Sun, Sand and Survival, An analysis of desert survival experiences during World War II. Maxwell AFB, Ala., Air University, Research Studies Institute, 1953.

ADTIC Publication T-100, 999 Survived, An analysis of survival experiences in the Southwest Pacific. Maxwell AFB, Ala., Air University, Research Studies Institute, 1949.

ADTIC Publication G-104, Airmen Against the Sea, An analysis of water survival experiences. Maxwell AFB, Ala., Air University, Research Studies Institute, 1955.

Flying Safety Magazine. California, Deputy Inspector General, Norton Air Force Base, Vol. IX, no. 6, 8, 10, 1953; Vol. X, no. 2, 1954.

United States Navy: *How to Survive on Land and Sea.* Annapolis, Md., U. S. Naval Institute, 1951.

Appendix 2—Survival Kit
Components

There is no magic list of equipment for a survival kit. No one kit can contain all items which a survivor might need. Each kit should be made up for the environment in which it is likely to be used. The items in the kit should be selected so as to provide the maximum protection against survival stresses for the minimum weight. The following listings are intended as a guide for the selection of kit components, not as hard and fast rules. However, this listing does represent the recommendations of more than two thousand Air Force aircrewmen who survived after an aircraft crash or bailout.

In compiling this list it is assumed that the survivor would crash land, not use a parachute.

CONTAINER

The first item to be selected is the container in which the kit will be carried. The logical container for a survival kit is a pack which can be easily carried. Personal preference will determine which type of pack. The mountain rucksack is good though relatively expensive.

CLOTHING

Clothing, except for supplemental protection, is out of place in a survival kit. Most clothing is bulky and takes up too much space in the kit. Also, clothing needs change with environment and season. *Wear* clothing suitable for the area over which you are flying or in which you are traveling. Proper shoes are especially important. Rely on the survival kit only for small items to supplement the protection of the clothes you are wearing.

Cold Climates—Knitted cap to cover head and ears.
Extra socks (at least two pairs, one light and one heavy)
Extra gloves or mittens
Exposure suit *

Hot Climates—Broad brimmed fabric hat
Extra socks—light weight

Wet Climates—Plastic raincoat
Plastic rain hat
Extra socks
Exposure suit *

* The R-1 exposure suit, a light weight, one-piece suit is often available at surplus stores. It is useful as protection against both cold and water.

FOOD

The ideal survival ration, suitable for all men and all environments, has not yet been devised. Take foods of high caloric value which you know *you* can eat cold or cooked. Arctic explorers and mountain climbers recommend pemmican. Some hot weather travellers swear by a mixture of honey for quick energy, and nuts for high protein and high caloric density. Southwestern Indians use pinole, a meal ground from parched corn.

Even experts on nutrition disagree as to the best food. Select your own but remember that a survival ration cannot be bulky and must have a long shelf life. If possible, pack your ration in light weight plastic containers rather than in metal cans.

All climates—Carry two days rations as a minimum. Add more where fast rescue is unlikely.

FORAGING EQUIPMENT

Elaborate fishing gear is out of place in a survival kit, but a few hooks, a length of strong line, leaders, sinkers, and lures should be included in all kits except those for completely dry desert areas. The small pocket-sized kits used in World War II are still available in surplus stores. Use one of these or make up your own kit to suit the needs of the country. But keep it simple. A small gill net (1½ inch or 2 inch mesh) should also be carried.

A rifle is desirable, but difficult to pack in a kit. The survival rifles used by the Air Force are not yet available commercially, and because of their short barrels may be illegal in some states. There is no need for a separate survival rifle if

All climates—Fishing kits
Gill net
Rifle (carried separately)
Ammunition
Snares or wire from which snares can be made.

you have a rifle with you anyway. Carry at least one box of ammunition in the kit.

HEAT AND LIGHT

All survivors down overnight will need a fire if only for signalling. In cold climates a fire is essential.

Stories from survivors of military airplane crashes indicate that the item most often unavailable when needed is a flashlight. Stow a hand-energized flashlight (no batteries needed) in your survival kit and leave it there except for emergencies.

All climates—Hand energized flashlight
Waterproof, strike-anywhere matches
One large candle
Fire starters
Cold climates (barrens or ice-caps) —Liquid fuel stove and fuel in leak-proof container
Temperate climates and Deserts— Solidified alcohol in cans or a liquid fuel stove and fuel in leakproof container

MEDICAL AND HEALTH

A survivor cannot carry medical supplies to meet all possible emergencies but he can carry medication for the more common ailments. The most common health problems faced by survivors are diarrhea, cuts and abrasions, burns, nausea, and fever. Make up your own kit with medications recommended by your physician to treat these conditions.

Prevention of disease is easier than cure. Carry water purification tablets and use them at all times. Do not buy Halazone tablets discarded by the government. These have outlived their usefulness.

Protect yourself from the sun. Sunburn and snowblindness have incapacitated many survivors.

Although snakebite is not a common hazard, play safe and carry a snakebite kit except in the Arctic.

Insect repellent can save you much misery. Use repellent in

All climates—First Aid kit
Water purification tablets
Toilet paper
Insect repellent
Sunny climates—Anti-sunburn cream or oil
Dark glasses
Non-arctic areas—Snakebite kit (Cutter Compak or equivalent)

solid form or packaged in plastic squeeze bottles, not in glass or metal containers.

NAVIGATION

Even if you don't plan to travel, carry a compass. It doesn't weigh much and may save your life.

If you travel in the same area all the time pack duplicate maps in the survival kit. If not, remember to take the maps you have been using with you when you leave the aircraft.

All climates—Compass
  Maps

SHELTER AND SLEEPING

Even the smallest tent is too bulky for a personal survival kit. The best substitute for a tent is half a parachute canopy. With this cloth you can construct shelters suitable for any climate. Parachute canopies can be purchased at salvage sales held periodically at Air Forces bases.

In cold weather areas a sleeping bag is often essential. Down-filled bags provide more warmth for less weight than other types.

In jungle areas a jungle hammock (available at most surplus stores) provides both shelter and bedding.

All climates—Half a parachute canopy (11 to 14 panels)
Cold climates—Down-filled sleeping bag
Hot climates—Jungle hammock

SIGNALING

You can't be rescued if you are not seen, and you may not be seen if you do not use signals. Signals are *essential*.

All climates—Signal mirror
  2 smoke signals
  2 flares
Overwater— (carried on life-vest or in life-raft)
  Sea-marker dye
  Waterproof flashlight

TOOLS

The basic survival tool is the knife, preferably a machete or other large knife with a blade about 12 inches long, and with the point of balance in the blade, not in the handle. Bowie knives and Gurkha knives are satisfactory. A machete type knife can be used in lieu of an axe, as a knife, as a digging tool, or as a weapon.

A Boy Scout knife, or Swiss army knife, is also useful but is no substitute for a machete.

A six-inch file, mill-cut or smooth-cut, should be carried for sharpening the machete.

Many survivors recommend carrying a pair of side-cutter pliers to assist in improvising equipment from metal containers or other available materials.

All climates—Machete
   Boy Scout knife
   Six-inch file
   Pliers

WATER

Water is essential to survival but is difficult to carry in a kit unless canned. Yet canned water is heavy and is bulky. As a compromise, carry two quarts of canned water in the kit and one or more gallons in containers filled just before the flight. (See page 315 for water requirements.)

Also carry an empty canteen, preferably one with a water purification filter, in the kit.

All climates—Two quarts canned water
   Canteen with filter

Hot climates—Additional water

FLOTATION

Life vests and life rafts should be carried whenever flying over water —but should be packed separate from the survival kit and ready for instant use. There are many vests and rafts on the market. Not all are adequate. To make sure that you have reliable equipment, check your flotation gear in a simulated ditching. The vest should keep your head above water without additional effort on your part. The life raft should be easy to inflate while you are in the water. Be especially careful of surplus military equipment. It may have cracks or leaky valves. Find out the faults, if any, in a test, not in an actual emergency. Carry a signal mirror, sea-marker dye, a waterproof flashlight, shark repellent, and a flare attached to the life vest.

Index